THE OLD CHEQUE-BOOK

or

Book of Remembrance

of

The Chapel Royal

Da Capo Press Music Titles

FREDERICK FREEDMAN, General Editor

University of California at Los Angeles

CAMDEN SOCIETY EDITION

THE OLD CHEQUE-BOOK

or

Book of Remembrance

of

The Chapel Royal

From 1561 to 1744

Edited by

Edward F. Rimbault

With an Introduction to the Da Capo Edition by
Elwyn A. Wienandt
Baylor University
Waco, Texas

𝄞

Da Capo Press
New York
1966

A
Da Capo Press
Reprint Edition

Library of Congress Catalog Card No. 65-23407

© *1966 Da Capo Press*
A Division of Consultants Bureau Enterprises, Inc.
227 West 17th Street • New York, N. Y. 10011

Printed in the United States of America

INTRODUCTION TO THE DA CAPO EDITION

Certain areas of music history must remain forever closed to authoritative research unless new sources are found with which to establish disputed or little-known facts regarding chronology, the movement of individuals from place to place, the types of work done during certain periods of time, and other matters that may have some bearing upon the activities of musicians and, more particularly, the musical climate of their times. The written records providing evidence of musical activity in religious establishments of early generations are meager when compared to those surviving from many other fields of study, and those that do exist are often interwoven with general documents, or they appear as subordinate sections in the records of non-musical activities or financial transactions. Even so, such lists and account books are few, and their existence is a matter of importance since documents are essential to our understanding of historical circumstance and continuity. When the reprinting of one of the principal sources for such information is undertaken, and the wider distribution of an important body of facts becomes possible, an important link in the chain of church music history is forged. The link has existed for nearly a century, dating from the appearance of Edward Francis Rimbault's edition of *The Old Cheque-Book*, but copies of that edition are not numerous. With the emergence, in this generation, of a serious approach to the study of religious music, it is appropriate that this important work is again being made available to libraries and to students of church music.

The Old Cheque-Book contains the documents of the Chapel Royal from 1561 to 1744, with a hiatus of two decades. The entries cease in 1640 and are not resumed until 1660, the Chapel personnel being dispersed during the Republican Interregnum. Unfortunately also, the record is not so complete as one might hope, for there are places where one wishes for more thorough explanations of what must have been obvious to the Clerk of the Cheque, and others in which legibility is not sufficient for the complete understanding of the entry. Still, Rimbault has filled in the gaps whenever possible, and he has left brief notes of explanation about the situations and people described in the book.

But what good is such a volume? Does it not simply expose a limited amount of musical activity in a single place? These questions are far from pointless. The Chapel Royal was certainly an inbred organization, showing relatively little inventive skill, and certainly contributing little to the international development of music. But we must not expect momentous things of every musical organization. The understanding of the Chapel Royal provides a fair sample of the prevailing taste to be found in the Anglican Service, and of the cathedral practice, in which a fully staffed resident choir, trained to its duties, was available for daily musical observances. This, naturally, was not representative of parish churches, especially the smaller or rural ones; but it gives a true picture of what the best composers of the period wrote, and of how they lived, for it was they who inhabited the precincts of the Chapel, or, if they were not already there, who bent every effort to become a part of it.

Furthermore, the materials contained in *The Old Cheque-Book* were known and used long before Rimbault produced his edition in 1872. A century earlier both Burney and Hawkins had examined the manuscript entries in the preparation of their histories, and both made repeated references to them. These references have been widely read and quoted, but inasmuch as they were taken from the manuscript in order to support some specific point or other, they lack the breadth that is found in ideas taken as large parts of the whole rather than as smaller segments out of context.

The publication of other material since Rimbault edited *The Old Cheque-Book* has increased the store of knowledge immeasurably because we now have access to information that both precedes and parallels that of the King's Chapel material. One such publication is a critical transcript of the documents of a parish church in London (St. Mary at Hill) between the years 1420 and 1559.[1] While the records are not all of specific interest to the musician, they do more than a simple extract of the musically pertinent entries could. They tell us, among many other matters, of priests and services, decorations and repairs, visitors and parishioners, furniture and fabrics, and in proper proportion to these, of music and musicians. Another volume of considerable interest and importance is made up of a transcript, without much editorial annotation, of the musical items in the Record Office and in the accounts of the Lord Chamberlain during the period 1460–1700,[2] with a hiatus between 1644 and 1660, a period closely approximating that in which records cease in *The Old Cheque-Book*. Added perspective is given in some matters that appear in both books because the entries in *The King's Musick* are not restricted to details of religious musical practice, so that one can sometimes note the activities of the same musicians in secular music as well.

The periods covered by each of the three documents can best be seen in diagram form, as given on page VIII.

It is at once obvious that, even though there is less specific musical information in the volumes concerned with St. Mary at Hill, the entries cover a period of great importance. One can see therein the normal

1. *The Medieval Records of a London City Church (St. Mary at Hill) A.D. 1420–1559.* Early English Text Society Original Series, 125, Henry Littlehales (ed.), 2 vols. (London: Kegan Paul, Trench, Trübner & Co., 1904–1905.)
2. Henry Cart De Lafontaine, *The King's Musick.* (London: Novello and Company, 1909.)

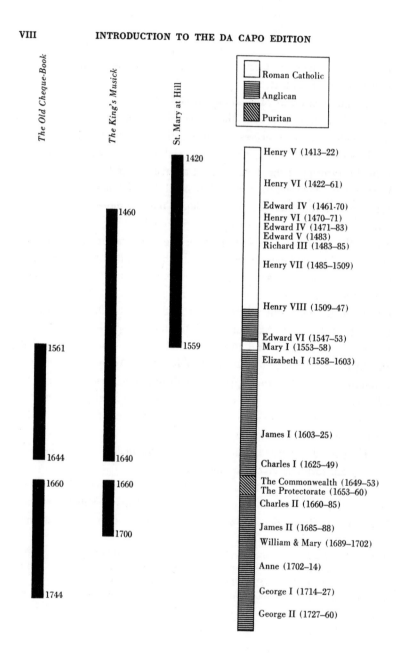

activity of a church prior to the Reformation and, to a certain degree, the changes that took place in its practices and its physical organization at the time of Edward VI, its return to the older system under Mary, and, briefly, the end of the old order with the accession of Elizabeth. Neither of the books covering the years after 1559 reflects the life of a typical church situation, so it is fortunate that the accounts of the Lord Chamberlain, given in *The King's Musick*, overlap for a century with those in the earlier volumes, making possible some degree of comparison with another source.

Both *The King's Musick* and *The Old Cheque-Book* are concerned with the leading musical establishment of London (and consequently, of England), for the musicians supported by the King made up the best and largest musical organization in the country, whether in secular or religious circles, at least until the appearance of Italian opera in England. The two sets of records carry some fortunate duplications of names and occasions during the years when they overlap. While *The King's Musick* is concerned with the fiscal matters touching upon the entire musical activity connected with the royal household, *The Old Cheque-Book* deals only with matters on the religious scene, more often in connection with procedures and events. That the combination of general and specific can be extremely useful is readily seen in a number of instances, of which one will serve as sufficient example.

The Old Cheque-Book contains a specific account of the funeral of James I and the coronation of Charles I in 1625. It is detailed in its description of the religious services, including even the texts of the several anthems sung in the course of the ceremonies. The mention of particular musicians who were present at the funeral is limited almost entirely to those who received allowances for black apparel (usually nine yards of material), and the list includes Nathan Giles, Master of the Children; John Hewlett, Clark of the Check; John Steephens, Recorder of Songes; and Orlando Gibbons, senior Organist. Their importance is further shown in the authorization of two yards of material for their servants. *The King's Musick,* on the other hand, is not concerned with the formal aspects of these matters; rather, the attention is centered on people and what they were paid. The lists, therefore, are quite complete, running to "Trumpettors," "players of Drums and Phife," "Musitions for Violins," "Musicians for windy Instruments," "The Consorte," "The Chappell," "Gentlemen of the Chappell," "Singing men of Westminster," "Choristers of Westminster," and, finally, "Bell-ringers." Coupling the specific and sometimes lengthy lists with the descriptions of events as given in *The Old Cheque-Book* adds the flesh of reality to the skeletal information that is available from either of these sources by itself.

The use of Rimbault's volume is by no means restricted to those who have access to the other two works mentioned here. It is a fascinating document in many respects, and can be read by itself, but it gains in usefulness to the student of church music since it can be compared with other works of the same type.

Edward Francis Rimbault (1816–1876) is best known in our time as a music editor, although his generation in England knew him as an accomplished organist and teacher. He was a pupil of Samuel Wesley and Dr. William Crotch, took his first appointment as an organist at age sixteen, and at twenty-two began to lecture on music history. He was active in the Musical Antiquarian Society, the Motet Society, and the Handel Society, editing a significant amount of English church music, and serving these organizations in important capacities. More important, however, since his editions are somewhat dated and of little use to present-day performers, are his studies on organ building.

The Old Cheque-Book came late in Rimbault's life and, while it is not among his best-known publications, it remains significant because it has not been superseded by stylistic change or modernized editorial practice. Rimbault's compositions have not survived the period for which they were intended; his musical editions are no longer authoritative; and the memory of his organ performances has long since become dim. *The Old Cheque-Book* stands, with his edition of Arnold's *Cathe-dral Music* and his work, with E. J. Hopkins, *The Organ, Its History and Construction*, as one of his most important contributions to musical knowledge. His commonplace book of 1848,[3] on the other hand, shows him to be an equally avid collector of trivia related to music and musicians.

The Old Cheque-Book is not going to excite the general reader, but its appearance in the Da Capo edition will render it accessible to another generation of students who have known it only by hearsay, or not at all.

Elwyn A. Wienandt

Baylor University
Waco, Texas
October 1, 1965

---

3. Now part of the Drexel Collection in the Music Division of The New York Public Library (presently housed in the Library-Museum at Lincoln Center). It is of particular interest that Joseph Drexel, the Philadelphia philanthropist, acquired a portion of Rimbault's private library when it was sold at auction in 1877. Through a series of unusual circumstances, the Drexel Collection, extremely rich in English materials and containing more than 6000 items, including dozens of manuscripts and hundreds of early prints, became part of The New York Public Library.

THE OLD CHEQUE-BOOK

or

Book of Remembrance

of

The Chapel Royal

FACSIMILES OF AUTOGRAPH SIGNATURES IN THE CHEQUE-BOOK.

THE OLD CHEQUE-BOOK,

OR

BOOK OF REMEMBRANCE,

OF

THE CHAPEL ROYAL,

FROM 1561 TO 1744.

EDITED, FROM THE ORIGINAL MS. PRESERVED AMONG THE MUNIMENTS OF
THE CHAPEL ROYAL, ST. JAMES'S PALACE,

BY

EDWARD F. RIMBAULT, LL.D.,
ETC., ETC.

PRINTED FOR THE CAMDEN SOCIETY.

M.DCCC.LXXII.

[NEW SERIES, III.]

INTRODUCTION.

The Chapels attached to the Palaces of Sovereigns form a remarkable feature of Christian Europe, and, from the earliest time on record, they seem to have been served on the same grand scale as the Cathedrals.

In England the Chapel Royal is the most ancient choir concerning which we have any authentic account. In olden times it was the fullest, best appointed, and the most remarkable for its excellence in the performance of the choral service.

As regards the constitution of this establishment, Dr. Jebb, in his valuable work on " The Choral Service of the United Church of England and Ireland " (1843, 8vo. p. 147), gives us the following particulars:—

" The Chapel Establishment of the English Sovereign is not a corporate body. It has subsisted, however, according to its present constitution for a long time antecedent to the Reformation. Over the Chapel presides a Dean; next to him a Sub-Dean; then forty-eight Chaplains, with ten Priests in ordinary, and a numerous lay Choir, styled Gentlemen of the Chapel. The Chaplains' duty is confined to preaching on Sundays; they take no part in the performance of Divine Service: The liturgical offices are performed by the Dean, Sub-Dean, and Priests in ordinary. They have been often, but not uniformly, appointed from the Minor Canons of Westminster and St. Paul's, and it would appear as if they were originally considered as forming part of the Choir.   *   *   *   From ancient lists, it appears that formerly the officiating members of the Chapel Royal were more numerous than now. In Queen Elizabeth's time, thirty were in attendance at a time, at least occasionally.

" In strictness, this establishment belongs to no fixed place, but is bound to attend the Sovereign wherever he may be resident. Of this ambulatory service there are proofs in records of King Henry VIII.'s reign; and in later times, King George IV. used to command the attendance of his Choir at Brighton. But in general their services have been confined to the King's Palace in London; formerly to the magnificent Chapel at Whitehall, which was destroyed by fire after the Restoration; and since that time to the small oratory in St. James's Palace, a place altogether too mean for its high destination." *

The earliest facts on record relating to the " King's Chapel " are contained in the *Liber Niger Domus Regis*, a MS. of the time of Edward IV. in which an account is given of this establishment in the reign of that monarch.†

First we have a " DEANE OF THE CHAPPELLE " who was " served, after a barrone service," with a daily allowance of

" iij. loaves, ij. messe of great meate, a picher of wyne, two gallones of ale; and for wintere seasone one torche, one picher, ij. candles waxe, iij. candles piche, iij. talsheids,‡ lyttere and rushes all the yeare of the serjante usher of the hall and chambere."

He had also " lodginge suffytyente for his horse and his servants " in town or country. We are told that the Dean was also " curate of confession of household," in other words, " Confessor to the Royal Household," a title which is still kept up in the patent granted to the Sub-Dean.

---

* The old Chapel Royal, Whitehall, was consumed by fire Jan. 5, 1698; and the new Chapel opened Dec. 9, in the same year. Dr. Blow composed an anthem, " Lord remember David," for the occasion. The Chapel Royal St. James's was occasionally used in the sixteenth and seventeenth centuries, but the service was not regularly instituted there until the beginning of the eighteenth century. The celebrated Henry Purcell (according to Wheatley's Piccadilly, p. 294,) once lived in " a suite of apartments in St. James's Palace, access to which was obtained by a winding staircase in the clock-tower." Dryden when in debt used to stay with him for weeks together in these apartments, where he was secure from his creditors.

† Harl. MSS. 293 and 642. See also Ordinances for the Government of the Royal Household, &c. 1790, 4to.

‡ Firewood cleft and cut into billets of a certain length; each talsheid (or talwood) being sixteen inches in compass.—COWELL.

There were also " CHAPLENES AND CLERKES OF THE CHAP-PELLE," twenty-four in number,

" endowed with virtues morolle and specikatyve, as of the musicke, shewinge in descante, eloquent in readinge, suffytyente in organes playinge, syttynge at the deane's boarde."

The daily wages of each was sevenpence. They had clothing allowed, and furniture for their chambers; with two loaves of bread, one " picher " of wine, and six gallons of ale; and from All-hallow-tide to Easter, two wax candles, twelve of " pich," and eight " talsheids," amongst them all, daily. Those who were priests had one servant each, and the others one to every two; besides stabling and keep for their horses.

" And if any of thes be let bloode in courte, he taketh daily ij. loaves, one messe of great meate, one messe of roste, one galone of ale; and when the chappelle synge mattenes over nighte, called 'Blacke Mattynes,' then they have allowed spice and wine."

Of " YEOMEN OF THE CHAPPELLE," called " Pisteleres,"* there were two, who were chosen from amongst those children of the chapel whose voices had recently changed; and this seems to have been an intermediate step between the latter and the " Clerkes" just mentioned. They had three-pence a day with clothing and other allowances.

The " CHILDREN OF THE CHAPPELLE " were eight in number, with a " Master of Songe " to teach them. They were boarded and lodged in the royal palace, and had daily amongst them

" two loaves, one messe of greate meate, ij. galones of ale; and for wintere seasone iiij. candles piche, iij. talsheids, and lyttere for their pallets. * * And

---

* Epistellers, i. e. readers of the Epistles; they are frequently mentioned in the pages of the Cheque-Book. Gospellers, also of frequent occurrence, were the readers of the Gospels.

amongeste them all to have one servante to trusse and beare their harnesse and lyverey in Courte. And that day the King's Chappelle removeth, every of thes children then present receaveth iiij d. at the Greene Clothe, for horsehire daily, as long as they be jurneinge. And when any of these children comene to be xviij. years of age, and their voices change, ne cannot be preferred in this chappelle, the nombere being full, then yf they will assente, the Kyng assynethe them to a College of Oxeford or Cambridge of his foundatione, there to be at fynding and studye both suffytyently, tylle the King may otherwise advaunse them."

There was likewise provided a " MASTER OF THE GRAMERE SCHOLE " for the choristers and other persons of the Court, so that the former were not only instructed in music, but also received what in that day was termed a learned education ; a practice which continued down to the period of the Commonwealth.

The first Master of the Children (or " Master of the Song," as he is called,) of the Royal Chapel, whose name has descended to our times, was Henry Abingdon, who, according to an Act of Resumption 13 Edward IV. (1473-4) was protected in the enjoyment of 40 marks per annum, which had been granted him in May, 5 Edward IV. (1465), " for the fyndyng, instruction, and governaunce of the children of the chapelle of our Housholde."* No particulars of this worthy are known, if we except a slight notice contained in an epitaph printed in " The first foure Bookes of Virgil's Æneis, translated into English Heroick Verse by Richard Stanyhurst. Lond. Imprinted by Henry Bynneman. 1583." 8vo.† Even these doggrel rhymes only inform us that he was a good organist and a " loud "

---

* Rot. Parl. v. 594; vi. 86.

† " An Epitaph written by Sir Thomas More upon the death of Henrie Abyngdon, one of the Gentlemen of the Chappell. Wich devise the author was fayne to put in meeter, by reason the partie that requested his travel did not like of a very proper epitaph, that was first framed, because it ran not in rythme, as may appeare at ful in his Latin epigramms. Whereupon Syr Thomas More shapt these verses ensuing, with which the suppliant was exceedingly satisfyed, as if the author had hit the nayle on head:—

singer ; and that he had been a Clerk of Wells Cathedral before entering the royal establishment.

He was succeeded by Gilbert Banestre or Banister, who according to the Act of Resumption of the 22 Edward IV. (1482-3) was protected in the enjoyment of the same salary as his predecessor, for " the exhibition, instruction, and governaunce of the children of the chapelle." Banister was a poet of some note in his day, and among other things wrote " The Miracle of St. Thomas," MS. in Bennet College Library, of which an account is given in Warton.

His successor in office was William Cornyshe, or Cornish, a musician of considerable skill, and who appears to have been esteemed by his brethren in the craft. We first read of him in 1493, when, in Henry the Seventh's Privy Purse Expenses, a payment was made on the 12th of November " to one Cornyshe for a prophecy, in rewarde, 13 s. 4 d.;" and on Christmas day, 1502, a similar sum for a Christmas Carol. Under him the Gentlemen of the Chapel were accustomed to act plays before the King and his Court, and received rewards as the " Players of the Chapel," as distinguishing them from the King's and Prince's Companies of " Players of Interludes." When the children took part in a dramatic performance under Cornish, they received a gratuity of 6l. 13s. 4d. This " Master of the Song " was a great favourite with Henry VIII., and on one occasion received as a reward the large sum of 200l. The entry, thus

> " Here lyeth old Henry, no freend to mischievous envy,
> Surnam'd Abyngdon, to all men most hartily welcom :
> Clerck he was in Wellis, where tingle a great many bellis ;
> Also in the chappell he was not counted a moungrel ;
> And such a loud Singer, in a thousand not such a ringer :
> And with a concordance, a'most skilful in organce.
> Now God I crave duly, sence this man serv'd the so truly,
> Henry place in kingdoom, that is also named Abyngdon."

worded—"8 Henry VIII. Nov., To Master Cornishe, gentylman of the King's Chapell, upon a warraunt, in rewarde, 200*l*."—may have included gratuities to his fellows. Cornish, like most of his musical brethren, was a poet, and wrote some rhymes entitled " A Treatise between Trouth and Informacion." This was written in the Fleet Prison in 1504, when the author was confined in consequence, as he himself asserts, of false information given by an enemy. " As one of the King's servants, and dating from the Fleet prison, we may suppose that he had fallen under the displeasure of the Star Chamber, perhaps for some ' prophecy ' or ballad, not so agreeable to the King as the former. The semi-disguise of his name, (William Cornishe otherwise called Nyshewhete,) changing ' corn ' into ' wheat ' and transposing the syllables, seems to show that he had written some things that he did not wish to avow. However this may be, he was eventually restored to the favour of the King, for in the last year of his reign, viz. in December 1508, we again find ' To Mr. Kyte, Cornishe, and other of the Chapell that played affore the King at Richmonte, 6 li. 13 s. 4 d.' "*

William Crane, who was a Gentleman of the Chapel in 1510, succeeded Cornish as Master of the Children, but at what date is uncertain. He was certainly Master in 1526, for in the Household Book of Henry VIII. we find under that date this entry :—" For borde wages of the children of the Chapel, to Maister Crane, xxvj s. viij d. ;" and in 1529, " Item, to Maister Crane, for playing before the King with the children of the Chapell, in rewarde, vj li. xiij s. iiij d." A Book of Receipts and Payments of the Exchequer, 18 Henry VIII. (1526-7,) shows that his annuity was 40*l*.:—" Will⁰ Crane,

---

* See " Some Account of an unpublished Collection of Songs and Ballads by King Henry VIII. and his Contemporaries, communicated to the Society of Antiquaries by W. Chappell, Esq. F.S.A." *Archæologia*, vol. xli. p. 380.

Magistro Puerorum Capellæ Dom. Regis de annuitate sua ad xl li. per ann. sibi debit. pro termino Michaelis Anno xviij^{mo} Regis nunc Henrici VIII. rec. den. Will^o Gonson, x li."[*]

This brings us down to the period of the commencement of the MS. printed in the following pages, where the various Masters of the Children who succeeded Crane are duly recorded ; while such biographical particulars as I have been able to glean concerning them are given in the notes at the end of the volume.

An ancient custom existed in the Chapel Royal, perhaps coeval with its establishment, of pressing men and boys with good voices for the service of the choir. This practice may be traced as far back as the time of Richard III.,[†] in the second year of whose reign a warrant was issued to John Melyonek, one of the Gentlemen of the Chapel, in the following terms :

" Ric. &c. To all and every our subjects, as well spirituell as temporell, these letters hering or seeing, greeting. We let you wite, that for the confidence and trust we have in our trusty welbeloved servaunt, John Melyonek, one of the Gentilmen of our Chapell, and knowing also his expert habilitie and connyng in the science of

---

[*] Lysons, Environs of London, iv. 467, speaking of the old church at Greenwich, says it contained memorials " of Clement Adams, Master of the Children of the Chapel, 1516, and his wife, who is said to have survived him 72 years, dying in 1588." He quotes Strype's Circuit Walk, annexed to Stowe's Survey, p. 91, as his authority. Lysons is altogether wrong in stating that Adams was Master of the Children of the Chapel. The fact is that he was appointed, May 1552, " Schoolmaster to the King's henchmen at Greenwich," with a salary of 10*l.* per annum, but was in no way connected with the Chapel establishment. The true date of his death is Jan. 9, 1586-7. See Cooper's Athenæ Cantabrigienses, ii. 6. I take this opportnuity of mentioning that *John* Hunnis, spoken of in Malone's Shakspeare (edit. 1821, iii. 423) as Master of the Children of the Chapel in 1572-3, is a mistake for *William* Hunnis, who was Master at the time. The extract from the Council Registers must have been wrongly transcribed by Malone.

[†] Probably earlier. Henry VI. authorized the pressing of minstrels (a word of large signification), and his precept, dated 1456, may be seen in Rymer's Fœdera, xl. 375.

musique, have licenced him, and by these presents licence and give him auctoritie, that within all places in this our realme, as well Cathedral-churches, colleges, chappells, houses of religion, and all other franchised and exempt places, as elliswhere, our Colege Roil at Wyndesor reserved and except, may take and sease for us and in our name all such singing men and children, being expart in the said science of musique, as he can finde, and thinke sufficient and able to do us service. Wherfore, &c. Yeven, &c. at Nottingham, the xvj day September, A° Secundo." (1484-5).*

Subsequent monarchs were not reluctant to follow the example set them by this proceeding. Accordingly we find a similar warrant was granted in 1550 to Philip Van Wilder, Gentleman of the Privy Chamber, " in anie churches or chappells within England to take to the King's use, such and as many singing children and choristers, as he or his deputy should think good ;" and, two years later, Richard Bower, then Master of the Children, had a warrant authorizing him to take up children from time to time " to supply vacancies as they might occur " among the choristers of the Chapel Royal.

Commissions " to take up well-singing boys for furnishing the Royal Chapels," are frequent among the Patent Rolls of the sixteenth and early part of the seventeenth centuries. One of the latest of these, granted to Dr. Nathaniel Giles, Master of the Children of the Chapel Royal, Aug. 26, 1626, is remarkable for a clause showing the growth of puritanical opinions at this period, by which the boys, who from a very early date had been accustomed occasionally to act plays for the amusement of the Court, were prevented from doing so, in consequence of its being for the first time thought inconsistent with their religious duties. It is in these words :

" Provided always, and we straightly charge and command, that none of the said Choristers or Children of the Chappell, soe to be taken by force of this Commission, shalbe used or imployed as Comedians, or Stage Players, or to exercise or acte any Stage plaies, Interludes, Comedies or Tragedies ; for that it is not fitt or desent that

---

* Harl. MS. 433.   See also Collier's Annals of the Stage, i. 34.

such as should sing the praises of God Almighty should be trained or imployed in such lascivious and prophane exercises."*

In the early part of the reign of Henry VIII. we get a glimpse at the Chapel Royal through the Lansdowne MS. No. 171, where the following is given as the establishment of the King's Chapel, with the charge for it :—

	£	s.	d.
Master of the Chapel, fee	40	0	0
Largess to the Children at high feasts . .	9	13	4
Allowance for their breakfast . . .	10	0	0
Thirty-two Gentlemen of the Chapel, fee to every of them 7½d. per diem, i. e.	365	0	0
Making the total expence of the Chapel	£424	13	4

This charge is independent of the cost of apparel, which, as Mr. Collier remarks, must have been considerable. "In the Wardrobe Accounts, in the 3d and 4th Henry VIII., formerly in the possession of Mr. Craven Ord, is a warrant for furnishing Thomas Sexton, one of the Gentlemen of the Chapel, with a gown which was to cost 11l. 18s. Another warrant directs that William Crane shall be furnished with a gown costing 9l. 12s. The gowns of three others were to cost 26l. 13s. 3d."†

As regards the internal management of the Chapel Royal, and the duties of its various members at this period, we are without records, but, in the absence of direct evidence, we may safely take the rules and regulations for the chapel of Algernon Percy, fifth Earl of Northumberland, from his Household Books, (published by Bishop Percy, and afterwards reprinted,) as a guide to what was being done in the Royal establishment in the early part of the sixteenth century.

* Collier's Annals of the Stage, ii. 16.
† Ibid. i. 69.

With respect to the Chapel establishment of Edward VI. we are fortunate in possessing a curious account of its yearly expenditure, with the names of the various gentlemen.* This record is especially valuable as being the earliest list of the kind that has descended to our times. It is as follows :—

OFFICERS OF THE CHAPPELL.

		£	s.	d.	
Master of the Children, Richard Bowyer.	Fee	40	0	0	
	Largesse to the children at high feasts	9	13	4	65 13 4
	Allowance for breakfast for the children	16	0	0	

Gentlemen of the Chappell, 32, every of them 7d. ob. a day.	Emery Tuckfield. John Kye. Nich. Archibald. John Angel. William Walker. William Huchins. R. Chamberleyn. Robert Phelipps. W. Gravesend. Thomas Birde. Richard Bowyer. Robert Perry. William Barber. Thomas Wayte. R. Richmounte. Thomas Tallis. Nicholas Mellowe. Thomas Wright. John Bendebow. Robert Stone William Mawpley. J. Shepharde. George Edwards. Wil. Hynnes or Hunnis. Robert Morecock. Thomas Manne. R. Ayleworth. Roger Kenton. T. Palfreman. Lucas Caustell. Richard Farrant. Edward Addams.		365 0 0

2 at 4d. ob. a day either of them,	13	13	9
5 at 4d. ob. a day every of them,	30	8	4

46 2 1

Summa totalis   £476 15 5

* Printed by Hawkins and Burney, but without any reference to the particular MS. from which it has been taken. It is probably from one of the Cottonian MSS. although I have not succeeded in tracing it.

The " Old Cheque-Book of the Chapel Royal" (the MS. printed in the following pages) commences in the 3rd year of Elizabeth, and carries on the history of this establishment, from that period, in a more perfect manner than has yet been done. The MS. abounds with information of various kinds (much entirely new), and I feel convinced the volume will be welcomed by the Members of the Camden Society as a valuable addition to the mass of curious matter the Society has already put forth to the world.

The MS. is written on large folio paper, measuring 16 and ½ inches by 11. It is in the original binding, much dilapidated, with an ornamental device on each side of the covers, and the letters " E. R." stamped in gold. On the fly-leaf is written " Old Cheque-Book of the Chapels Royal." It consists of 87 leaves folioed, the last leaf being pasted down on the cover. Out of these folios, 30 are entirely blank, one leaf has been torn out (probably blank), and many of the pages are only partly written upon. It has also 4 preliminary pages (not folioed), three of which are written over.

The writing of the MS. is of various periods, from the last quarter of the sixteenth century to the beginning of the second half of the eighteenth. The earliest entries are written subsequently to the period to which they refer, probably copied from some older record now lost. The utmost irregularity is displayed with regard to the various entries, chronology, and subject-matter being equally set at defiance. For instance, " the names of the Sub-Dean, Gentlemen, and others of their Majestyes Chappell Royall, at the time of the Coronation of King William and Queen Mary, Aprill the 11th, 1689," occur at folio 54 *b* (about the middle of the book), whilst a similar list of the officers of the chapel at the " Coronation of King James the First " occurs on the *last* folio of the MS. pasted down on the binding.

This is only one example out of the many similar ones that occur.

From the miscellaneous character of the MS. rendering it something like a common-place book, and the manner in which the entries were made from time to time, the clerk evidently sometimes opening the book at random, and only seeking for a vacant space to make his note, it seemed undesirable to print it page for page. Believing that a certain classification or arrangement of the materials would make the work more generally useful and interesting, I have entirely recast the matter, placing it under the various heads in which it seemed naturally to arrange itself. The reader thus has the advantage of getting at one glance a glimpse of all that the MS. contains upon a certain subject, whilst those who at any time might desire to refer to the original MS. will find no difficulty in tracing any particular passage by the references to the folios after each entry.

In thus recasting the materials of the "Cheque-Book" I have not thought it desirable to disturb two portions of the original MS. *i. e.* the "Appointments and Obituary Notices of the Gentlemen, &c." and the "Notices appertaining to the Serjeants, Yeomen, &c." As these lists were kept with some degree of regularity for a long series of years I have preserved them intact, supplementing them by two additional lists made up from other parts of the MS.

The writer of the MS. was in most cases the "Clerk of the Cheque" for the time being.* The duties of this officer, as far as I can ascertain, were to keep an account of the attendance, and to note the absence of the priests and gentlemen in order to lay the same before the Dean or Sub-dean at certain times, probably every month.

---

* An officer established in conformity with a similar one in other departments of the Royal Household.

Likewise to attend all admissions into the Chapel appointments, and to *keep a record of the same as well as of all rules and regulations issued by the Dean and Chapter for the government of the Chapel.* To this office no salary was attached, but there were certain fees paid upon the admission of Members and upon other occasions.*

The dates in the MS. range between 1561 and 1744. The entries cease in 1640, and are not resumed again till 1660, leaving a gap of twenty years, during which time the choral service was entirely discontinued in the Chapel, and its members scattered abroad to get their living as best they could. At the Restoration things were speedily set in order again, and such of the Members of the Chapel as were living were restored to their places, as may be seen by the subsequent entries.

In pointing out a few of the important features of the MS. I must first allude to the biographical entries, many of which contain valuable notices of eminent poets and musicians, often supplying new and reliable dates. For instance, Richard Edwards, so well known in connection with " The Paradise of Dainty Devices," is recorded on p. 1 to have died " on the last day of October, 1566," a date that was wanting to complete our biography of the poet.† We also read of William Hunnis the equally well-known author of " The Hive full of Honey," and many other quaint productions of the sixteenth century. Thomas Palfreyman, a name remembered in connection with Baldwin's " Treatise of Morall Philosophie," also comes in for

---

* The office of " Clerk of the Cheque " is now virtually abolished. The duties are performed by the Sub-dean.

† " The precise year of his death is nowhere recorded." Collier's Bibliographical Account of Early English Literature, i. 242. It is to this valuable work that I have been indebted for the poetical extracts given in my note about Edwards at the end of the volume.

his share of notice; and many other of the poet-musicians of the sixteenth and beginning of the following century receive mention of some kind in the pages of the Cheque-Book.

Among Church Musicians we find much new and valuable material for the biographies of Tallis, Byrd, Bull, Gibbons, Humphries, Blow, Purcell, and indeed all the famous men of the sixteenth and seventeenth centuries. The later entries must not be overlooked as they contribute equally curious and minute details for the historian and biographer. Take as an instance the notices relating to Luke Flintoft, the author of one of the earliest of our double chants. Nothing whatever was known of his biography until, some years since, I published the information given in the Cheque-Book. Indeed the importance of this portion of the MS. cannot be overrated.

Among the " Suits for Additional Pay " we have a circumstantial account of King James the First's " royal bounty to the officers of the Royal Chapel in the second year of his reign," an event which has received the notice of Howes in his edition of Stowe's Chronicle. This record in the pages of the Cheque-Book was considered of so much importance that an anathema, " Cursed be the partie that taketh this leafe out of this booke," was written in the margin.

The " Orders, Decrees, and Reprimands," contain some valuable material for the history of the government of the Chapel, and afford an insight into the private life of several well-known musicians. I may call especial attention to the " Acts done in Chapter, March 29, 1630," and to a curious notice contained in it concerning Thomas Warwick, the father of the statesman Sir Philip Warwick.

Among the " Royal Warrants " are some of great interest to the ecclesiologist, particularly those which relate to vestments, furniture, incense, &c. in the Royal Chapel shortly after the Restoration.

The " Chapel Feast " forms a feature in the Cheque-Book. This was an annual dinner of the Priests, Organists, and Gentlemen of the Chapel, each having privilege to bring a friend. The King or Queen supplied venison, wine, and a sum of money; and the extra expenses were defrayed by two stewards chosen every year out of the body at large. This social meeting, which had been held almost from time immemorial, was discontinued some fifty years since, when instead of the contributions from the royal parks, larder, and cellar, a pecuniary compensation was accepted. Much information concerning this old custom is given in these pages, adding materially to the notices contained in the Privy-Expense Books of Henry VIII. and Elizabeth of York.

It is remarkable that neither the *Liber Niger Domus Regis* nor the Northumberland Household Book notice the existence of a distinct officer under the title of Organist. The duties were subordinate in early times, and appear to have been performed by the monks or clerks according to arrangement. The understanding in the Earl of Northumberland's Chapel was this :—

' The ORDURYNGE for Keapynge Weikly of the ORGAYNS oon after an outher as the NAMYS of them hereafter followethe WEIKELY:

The Maister of the Childer yf he be a Player, The Fyrst Weke.
A Countertenor that is a Player, the ij^de^ Weke.
A Tenor that is a Player, the thirde Weike.
A Basse that is a Player, the iiij^th^ Weike.
Ande every Man that is a Player to kepe his cours WEIKELY."

In Cathedrals of the old foundation the Organist is not a statutable officer, except as holding a lay-clerkship.

Much curious information respecting the office of Organist may be gleaned from the pages of the Cheque-Book, which possess the advantage of never having been seen by writers on the subject.*

The notices of " Serjeants, Yeomen, &c." are not devoid of interest. The particulars concerning George Whicher, the founder of certain alms-houses in Westminster, and of John Patten, father-in-law of the celebrated Orlando Gibbons, are new and valuable additions to the scanty biography we possess of these old worthies.

Perhaps the most generally interesting portions of the Cheque-Book are the curious and minute particulars it gives us of Royal ceremonies, Funerals, Coronations, Churchings, Baptisms, Christenings, Royal and Noble Marriages, &c. Many of these entries are of historical value.

Among the first we have a curious account of " The Princely coming of her Majesty [Queen Elizabeth] to the Holy Communion at Estre [Easter] in 1593;" the meetings of King James I. and the Spanish Ambassador " for the maintenance and continuance of the Spanish League ;" the " Order of the Funeralls of King James I.;" the " Order of the Chapells Service at the Coronation of Charles I." &c.

The " Marriages in the Royal Chapel at Whitehall" contain the names of many distinguished in history, besides a minute account of the ceremonies attending " the Marriage of the two great Princes, Frederick Elector Counte Palatine of Rheine, and the Ladie Elizabeth, the only daughter of the right highe and mightie Prince the Kinge of Great Brittaine."

As regards these marriage entries I would here point out that some

---

* See Warton's Life of Sir Thomas Pope (*Appendix*, p. 425), and the Rev. M. E. C. Walcott's article on " Choral Matters, " in the Musical Times, April 1, 1871, for notices of Organists in early times.

of the dates must be accepted with caution. The object of the Clerk of the Cheque was to record the fees paid upon these occasions, rather than to register any particular event. Hence the carelessness with regard to dates. Nevertheless in the absence of authentic documents we are glad to accept these entries asth ey are.

Colonel Chester, who has taken much interest in the following pages, informs me that the Marriage Registers of Whitehall (in Somerset House) date only as far back as 1704. According to the same authority there is an earlier book going back to 1675, but it is merely the Note-book of Marmaduke Alford, Serjeant of the Vestry, copied from the original register, which in all probability no longer exists. This being the case, I have not been able to correct the dates by any authentic register of the marriages here recorded.

The entries of Baptisms, Christenings, Churchings, &c. are full of historic interest, and some of them supply information long sought for from other sources. In proof of this assertion I need only refer to Colonel Chester's valuable paper on " An Official Inaccuracy respecting the Death and Burial of the Princess Mary, daughter of King James 1." (read at a Meeting of the Historical Society of Great Britain, on Monday, June 12, 1871,) where several notices of the Princess, extracted from the present MS., are of considerable use in strengthening the learned writer's argument.

With regard to the Notes at the end of the volume, great care has been taken to bring together from authentic sources a variety of biographical particulars, some of which are entirely new, and others not generally known to the reader. It has not been thought necessary to include notices of the Deans, or to repeat any information that could be found in easily accessible works. Possibly more might have been done towards identifying many members of the Chapel who have received no notice in the following pages, but it would have been impossible to have done this throughout, and I have succeeded, perhaps, as far as the most important names are concerned.

The thanks of the Council of the Camden Society are due to the Lord Bishop of London, Dean of the Chapel Royal, and to the Lord Chamberlain of the Household, for permission to publish the MS. now presented to the Members of the Society ; and I may add my especial thanks for the accommodation afforded me in having the MS. in my own possession during the process of transcription and collation.

Before concluding this Introduction it remains to acknowledge the kind assistance which I have received in carrying these sheets through the press.

My thanks are due in the first place to my old friend, W. CHAPPELL, Esq. F.S.A., whose advice has been of the greatest use upon many points, and who kindly revised for me the Latin document relating to the resignation of Dr. Pearce.

To SIR JOHN MACLEAN, F.S.A., for the information relative to the *Inquisitio post mortem* on the Earl of Northampton.

To the Rev. CANON ROBERTSON, for his obliging collation of Dart's copy of the Latin inscription on the monument of Orlando Gibbons with the original at Canterbury.

To JOHN GOUGH NICHOLS, Esq. F.S.A., for numerous acts of kindness while passing the work through the press, and for the notes upon the Whitehall marriages bearing his initials.

But above all my thanks are rendered to COLONEL JOSEPH LEMUEL CHESTER, who not only freely gave me access to his extraordinary collections (the result of years of research and industry) in illustration of the Registers of Westminster Abbey, but assisted me in every possible manner by the copies of registers, wills, &c. For whatever original value the notes to the present work may possess, the Members of the Camden Society are largely indebted to COLONEL CHESTER, without whose assistance they could not have been so prepared. It is a source of great gratification to me to have been brought into communication with a gentleman who has taken such interest in the success of this undertaking.

EDWARD F. RIMBAULT.

29, *St. Mark's Crescent,*
   Regent's Park.

CONTENTS.

THE OLD CHEQUE BOOK

CHAPEL ROYAL.

I.—APPOINTMENTS AND OBITUARY NOTICES OF THE SUB-
DEANS, PRIESTS, ORGANISTS, AND GENTLEMEN.—*LIST I.**

The Subdeanes and Gentlemen succeedinge since the third yeare
of the raigne of Queene Elizabeth, Mr. Angell then Subdeane:—

1561. Mr. Paternoster was sworne gent the 24th of Marche, and
Jones, Gospeller, and Thos. Rawlins, Yeoman, A° 3°.

1563. Thomas Wiles sworne gent the 8th of Marche, from Poules,
A° 5to.

1563. Merton died the 22d of September, and Roberte Parsons
sworne in his place the 17th of October, A° 5to.

1563. Mr. Walker was slaine the 27th of November, and Wm.
Munday was sworne in his place the 21st of February, from
Poules, A° 6to.

1564. Tho. Sampson was sworne gent in Ric. Farrants roome the
24th of Aprill, from Lincolne, A° 6to.

1561. Tho. Bird died in Februarie, Clarke of the Checke, and
Morcocke made Clarke [of the] Checke, A° 3°.

1563. Rich. Bower died, Mr of the children, A° 5to.

1566. Rich. Edwards died, Mr of the children, the last [day of] October

---

* This List extends from f. 5 to f. 14 of the original MS. The entries respecting
serjeants, yeomen, and grooms of the vestry have been removed to Section xiv. of
the present volume.

and Wm. Hunnis was made M^r of the children the 15th of November, A° 8°.

1566. Hechins died the 9th daie of November Anno 9°, and Nicholas Morgan was sworne in his place the 9th of December, A° 10°.

1566. Mr. Alsworthe died the 22d of Januarie, and Robert Greene of Poules sworne in his place the last of the same, A° 10°.

1567. Jo. Denman died the 28th of Maie, and Jo. Addie priest of Lichfield was sworne in his roome the 27th of June, Anno 10°.

1567. Subdeane Angell died the 17th of August, and Mr. Norrice was sworne Subdeane the last of the same, A° x°.

1567. Jo. Hottost priest of Poules was sworne the 4th of December in Mr. Angell's place, A° 11°.

1568. Mr. Norrice, Subdeane, died the 6th of Maie, and Mr. Gravesend was sworne Subdeane in his place the 15th of Maie Anno 10°, and Mr. Hottost substitute at Greenwich.

1568. Wm. Ivett of West Chester was sworne the 18th of June in Mr. Norrice['s] place, A° 11°.

1569. Subdeane Grevesend died the 8th of Aprill, and Rich. Tirwitt sworne Subdeane in his place the 13th of October Anno 12°.

1569. Roberte Goodale was sworne the 13th of October, in Mr. Hughe Sullyes place, A° 12°.

1569. Mr. Causton died the 28th of October, and Rich. Farrant was sworne in his place the 5 of November A° 12°, from Winsore.

1569. Roger Centon died the 16th of Februarie, and Nich. Beighton was sworne in his place the 25th of the same A° 13°, from Lichfield.

1569. Robt. Parsons was drowned at Newwark uppon Trent the 25th of Januarie, and Wm. Bird sworne gentleman in his place at the first the 22d of Februarie followinge, A° 14°, [from] Lincolne.

1571. Henry Alred died the 30th of Marche, and Rich. Granwall sworne gentleman in his place at the first the 8th of Aprill following, A° 14°, from Cambridge.

1571. Robt. Goodale died the 19th of September, and Giles Carott sworne in his place the 13th of October A° 14°.

1569. Mr. Ednye bought James Causters roome and entred into his place the first of October A° 12°.

1573. Dominus Giles Carott pisteler died the 20th of June, and Barth. Mason from Lichfield (minister) was sworne in his place the 10th of October following A° 16°.

1575. Jo. Ridley died the 11th of Januarie, and Wm. Bodinghurst of Lichfeeld sworne in his place the 28th of Februarie followinge A° 18°.

1578. John Addie, preist, died the 9th of Febr. and Jo. Savill, priest, was sworne in his place the 28th of Marche A° 20°, from Westminster.

1579. Jo. Russell died the 30th of Marche, and Rich. Morrice sworne in his place the first of Aprill followinge A° 21°, from Glocester.

1580. Tho. Raulins died the 22d of August, and Ellis Stempe was sworne genͭ in his place the 9th of November A° 22°.

1580. Jo. Savill, Priest, was slaine, and buried the 25th of August, and Crue Sharpe was sworne in his place the 9th of November A° 22°.

1580. Rich. Farrant died the 30th of Novr., and Anth. Todd sworne in his place the 26th of Febr., havinge allowed Decr. and Januarie before at the Greenclothe, and wages from the deathe of Farrant A° 23°.

1580. Wm. Jones, priest, gospeller, was buried the last of Februarie, and Leonard Davies from Lichfield sworne gospeller in his place the 15th of Maie, and received paie from the 10th of Marche before, A° 23°.

1581. Roberte Moorcock, clark of the Checke, died the 15th of June, and Edmund Browne sworne in his place the 25th of December A° 24°.

1581. Jo. Moore, clarke of the Check, died the second of October, and Robt. Tallentier sworne in his place the 25th of December A° 24°.

1581. Wm. Edney died of the Plague the 13th of November, and Thos. Woodson of Poules sworne in his place the 25th of Decr. A° 24°.

> Note, that these three persons had bothe wages and bord wages from the daie of the others deathes untill the daie of the swearinge by my Lord Chamberlaines warrant to the Greenclothe.

1581. Salomon Compton was sworne pysteler the 15th of Maie A° 24°, from Cambridge.

1583. Anthony Harrison sworne the   of October in Mr. Morrice['s] roome, who fledd beyond the seaes A° 25°, from Winsore.

1583. Wm. Maperley died the last of Maie, and Wm. Barnes sworne gospeller at the first in his place the 11th of October A° 25°, from Exeter.

1584. Robert Greene sworne Subdeane the 14th of Februarie in Mr. Tirwitts roome.

1584. Wm. Randoll sworne pisteler the 15th of Februarie in Mr. Tirwitt's roome, from Exōn.

1585. Tho. Tallis died the 23rd of November, and Henry Eveseed sworne in his place the last of the same. Childe there.

1585. Jo. Bull sworne the   of Januarie in Mr. Bodinghurst['s] place. Childe there.

1586. Isaak Burgis sworne in Januarie in Mr. Richmondes roome.

1587. Tymothie Greene sworne the 12th of June in Mr. Gooches roome.

1588. George Waterhouse sworne genℸ at the first in Salamon Comptons [place] in July, who was displaced, from Lincolne.

1588. Edward Pearce sworne the 16th of Marche in Ellis Stempes place.

1589. Roberte Allisone sworne the 12th of December in Mr. Palfriman's place.

1590. Jo. Steevens sworne the 11th of August in Mr. Wiles his place.

1591. Jo. Hewlett sworne the 23rd of Maye in Mr. Blithman's place, of Welles.

1591. Richard Plumley sworne the   of August in Mr. Ivettes roome.

1591. Anthony Anderson sworne the 12th of October in Mr. Mundaies roome.

1591. Tho. Goolde sworne the 14th of November in Mr. Beightones roome.

1592. Tho. Morley sworne the 24th of July in Mr. Greene's roome.

1592. Anthony Anderson sworne Subdeane the 26th of July in Subdeane Greenes roome.

1592. Peeter Wrighte from Westminster was sworne the 23rd of November in Mr. Benbowes place.

1592. Tho. Madoxe was sworne the 10th of Januarie in Mr. Hottost's place, from Heryford.

1593. Anthony Anderson, Subdeane, died the 10th of October and Leonard Davies sworne Subdeane in his place the 15th of the same.

1593. Mr. Laurence from Poules was sworne the 17th of Octr. in Mr. Anderson's place.

1593. James Davies from Canterburie was sworne the 29th of Januarie in Timothie Greenes place.

1595. Jo. Amery from Norwiche was sworne the 4th of Dec. in Mr. Madoxe['s] place.

1596. Robert Paternoster died the last of July, and Roberte Stuckey sworne in his place the 20th of Aug. from Exōn.

1597. William Hunnis died the 6th of June, Master of the Children, and Nathaniell Giles sworne genť and Master of the Children in his place the 9th of the same, from Winsore.

1598. Roberte Tallentire died the 15th of August, and Jo. Baldwin sworne in his place the 20th of the same, from Winsore.

1598-1599. Nath. Todd died the   of Marche, and Francis Wiborow sworne in his roome the 26th of the same.

1600. Edward Pearce yealded up his place for the Mastership of the children of Poules, and John Heathman was sworne in his place the 15th of August, from Westminster.

1601. George Waterhouse died the 18th of Februarie, and Arthur Cock from Exön was sworne the 8th of Marche followinge.

1602. Isaack Burgis was drowned in cominge out of the Lowe Countries, and Stephan Boughton (minister from Herifford) was sworne in his place the 25th of Aprill.

1602. George Woodson (from Winsore) was sworne the 7th of October in Thos. Morleyes roome.

1602. Wm. Lawes (from Chichester) was sworne the first of Januarie in Tho. Sharpes place.

1602. Anthony Kirkby (from Canterbury) was sworne the   of Marche in John Heathman's place.

1603. Jo. Wooddeson (from Winsore) was sworne the second of July in Mr. Buckes roome.

1603. Edmund Shergold sworne the first of Januarie in Mr. Barnes['s] roome.

1603. Edmund Hooper of Westminster was sworne the first of Marche in Mr. Randoll's roome.

1604. Arthur Cock died the 26th of Januarie, and Orlando Gibbons sworne in his roome the 21st of Marche followinge.

1605. Barth. Mason, Priest, died the last of October, and Rich. Coton, Minister, from Winsore was sworne in his place the 12th of November.

1605. Tho. Woodson solde his place to Wm. West of Canterbury, who was sworne in his place the 20th of Marche.

1606. Edmund Browne died the 27th of Aprill, and Randoll Tinker of Poules was sworne in his place the same daie.

1606. Randoll Tinker died of the Plague the 20th of Sept., and Luke Jones of Poules was sworne in his place the last of the same.

1606. Wm. Laurence died of the Plague the 10th of Novr., and David Henly of Winchester was sworne in his place the third of Decr.

1606-7. Mr. Granwall died the second of Marche, and Tho. Paine was sworne in his place the 27th of the same.

1607. Edmund Shergold died the 19th of Januarie, and George Cooke was sworne in his place the 21st of the same, from Winsore.

1608. Tho. Goolde died the 28th of July, and John Clarke was sworne in his place the 24th of August followinge. Childe of the Chappell.

1609. Tho. Paine died the 4th of Januarie, and George Sheffield of Durham was sworne in his place the 6th of Feb. followinge.

1609. Roberte Allison solde his place the 8th daie of Februarie unto Humfrie Bache who was sworne into the same the selfe same daie.

1609. Robert Stuckey died the last of Febr., and Tho. Pearce of Westminster sworne in his place the 24th of Marche.

1611. Wm. Lawes resigned his place the 5th of Maye unto Ezechiell Waad who was sworne into the same that very daie, from Westminster.

1611. Richard Plumley died the third of October, and Jo. Frost of Westminster sworne in his place the 5th of November.

1613. Roberte Stone of the age of iiij^{xx}xvij [97] yeares died the second day of July, and Mathew White, Minister, and a Basse (from Welles), was elected and admitted gospeller in his place at the first the second of November followinge and was sworne the 27th daie of December then next ensuinge: the wages of Mr. Stone from his death to Mr. White's admission was disposed of by the Deane of his Majestes Chappell.

1613. John Bull, doctor of Musicke, went beyond the seas without licence and was admitted into the Archduke's service, and entered into paie there about Michaelmas, and Peter Hopkins a Basse from Poules was sworne in his place the 27th of December followinge: his wages from Michaelmas unto the daie of the swearinge of the said Peter Hopkins was disposed of by the Deane of His Majestes sayd Chappell.

1614. Mathew White resigned his place unto my Lord Bishopp of Bathe and Welles Deane of his Majestes Chappell the 25th of September, and Wm. Crosse servant unto our sayd Deane was sworne in his place the 27th day followinge.

1614-15. Henry Eveseed died the 18th of November, and Wm. Heather from Westminster was sworne in his place the 27th of Marche followinge ; the wages in the meane tyme was disposed of by the Deane.

1615. John Miners genł was sworne genł in ordinarie the 28th of Marche for the next place in the Chappell, of what parte soever.

1615. John Amyon of Westchester was sworne genł extraordinarie the 13th daie of Aprill.

1615. Thomas Sampson, Clark of the Check, was drowned the 24th of Aprill and John Myners was sworne in his place the 4th daye of June followinge; and John Hewlett havinge executed the place of Clark of the Check for Mr. Sampson above eight yeares, was allowed to be Clarke of the Check by our Lord Deane and consent of the Company.

1615. John Miners died the second daye of July, and Thomas Daye was sworne in his place the last of September followinge, the wages disposed by the Deane for that quarter.

1615. John Baldwin died the 28th of August, and Martin Otto was sworne in his place the last of September followinge, by the procurement of our gracious Ladie Queene Ann.

1616. David Henly died the 12th daie of August, and John Greene a secondary of the churche of Exon was preferred to the place by order of our Lord Deane the 28th of December next following, for a yeare of probacōn of his manners and good behavior, and he to receave the payé of the pisteler, but not sworne his Majestes servaunt in ordinarie, but to the supremacie, and so to stand for one whole yeare.

1616. Walter Porter, by warraunt from the reverend Father in God James Lord Bishopp of Winton and Deane of his Majestes

Chappell, was sworne genĩ of his Majestes said chappell in
ordinarie, without paye, for the next place that shall happen
to be and shall fall voyd by the deathe of any tenor that now
is in ordinarie in the said chappell, and tooke and receaved
his oathe to that effect the 5th daie of Januarie the yeare
abovesaid, and paid for his oathe five poundes and other
duties.

1617. John Greene beinge allowed to receave the wages of the pisteler by the Lord Deane of his Majestes chappells order, and
standinge uppon probation of his manners and good behaviour
for one yeare, did so misdemeane himselfe and also marryed a
second wiffe (the first beinge livinge) was therfore dismissed
from his Majestes service the 28th of September, and Edmund
Nellam (Deacon), a basse of the churche of Westminster, was
sworne in his roome the 6th of November followinge.

1617. Peter Wright died the 27th daye of Januarie, and Walter
Porter was sworne in his place the first daie of Februarie followinge.

1619. Roger Ni[gh]tingall was sworne the 29th day of June in
ordinary for the next place of a base that shall fall voyd in
his Majestes Chappell.

1620. Memorandum, that of late ther[e] was a question proposed that
Jo. Hewlett was not lawfully elected to be clark of the check
uppon the death of Mr. Sampson, who died five yeares past,
wheruppon ther was a vestery called by Mr. Davies, Subdeane, on the 20th of June 1620, and ther[e] by a scruteny
he was ellected and allowed to be clerk of the check by the
major part of the genĩ, being then 25 in number.

1620 June 29. Thomas Peirse, servant to the Right Reverend Father
in God Lancellott Bishop of Winton and Deane of his
Majestes Chappell, was sworne a genĩ of his Majestes Chappell
in Ordinary, to enter into pay uppon the deathe of Mr. James
Davies, if he chance to live so longe.

1620. Martin Otto died the 2 of July, and Roger Ni[gh]tingall, clerk, a base from Poules, was sworne in his place the 20th day followinge.

1621. John Frost, Clerk, a base from Salisbury, was sworne the 26th day of Aprill in Ordinarie for the next place of a base that shall fall voyd in his Ma^{tes} Chappell.

1621. Edmund Hooper, Organist, died the 14th daye of July, and Thomas Tompkins, Organist of Worcester, was sworne in his place the second daye of August followinge.

1621. Anthony Harrison, Clark, died the 20th of Februarie, and John Frost, a base and chauntor of Westminster, was sworne in his place the 14th of Aprill 1623; the wages in the meane tyme was disposed of by the Deane for pricking of songes and for a new sett of bookes for the Chappell, and other disposinges and allowances by his said Lordship.

1623. Wm. Bird, a Father of Musick, died the 4th of July, and John Croker, a conter tenor of Westminster, was admitted the 24th of December following for a yeare of probacõn of his good behaviour and civill carriage, or else to resigne and yeald up the promise graunted to him at the yeares end, and so to receave the wages of the pisteler in the meane tyme.

1623. John Amery died the 18th daye of July, and Ralphe Amner, Clark, a basse from Winsore, was sworne in his place the 16th of December following : the wages in the meane tyme was disposed of by our Lord Deane, &c.

1623. Leonard Davies, Subdeane, died the 9th of November, and John Cooke, a basse from Litchfield, was sworne pisteler in his place the 16th of December following, with this proviso, that the whole wages to the end of the quarter should be given unto Mr. Subdeane Davies['s] wiffe by our Lord Deane his order.

1623. Stephan Boughton sworne Subdeane the 14th of Decr. in Subdeane Davies['s] place by my Lord Deane himselfe.

1623. James Davies died the 24th of Marche, and Thomas Peirs was sworne in his place the 26th of the same, in the presence of Rich. Coton, substitute, John Stephens, John Hewlett, Frauncis Wiborow, Wm. West, Roger Nightingale, Tho. Tomkins, Luke Jones and Ralph Amner.

1625. Mr. Orlando Gibbons, Organist, died the 5th of June, being then Whitsonday, at Canterbury, wher the Kinge was then to receave Queene Mary who was then to com[e] out of Fraunce, and Thomas Warwick was sworne in his place organist the first daie of July followinge and to receave the pay of the pistoler.

1625. John Croker died the 25th of August, and George Wooddeson the younger was sworne in his place the 20th of November followinge, pisteler and gospeller, by the death of Mr. John Cooke, and lastly genť uppon the death of Mr. Hopkins; the wages in the meane tyme was imployed in pricking of songes by my Lord our Deanes order.

1625. John Cooke died the 12th of September, and Henry Lawes was sworne in his place the first of Januarie followinge, pistoler, and Mr. Warrick genť, and George Wooddeson, the younger, gospeller, as above said; the wages in the meane tyme was disposed of by our Lord Deane.

1625. Peter Hopkins died the 25th of November, and Mr. Richard Boughton, a base from Winsore, was admitted by warrant into his place the 29th of Aprill 1626; the wages in the meane tyme was disposed of by my Lord of Winchester our Deane.

1625. Memorandum, that Mr. John Tomkins, Organist of St. Paule London, was sworne extraordinarie gentleman of his Majestes Chappell for the next place of an organist there, or the place of Anthony Kirkby, which of them shall first fall voyde.

1626. Frauncis Wiborowe died at Ely the 28th of October, and John Tomkins, Organist of St. Paule, was sworne in his place the third of November following, pisteler, and Richard Boughton gospeler, and Henry Lawes gentleman.

1626. Memorandum, that Crue Sharpe died the 21st of December, and Thomas Rayment, a basse from Salisbury, was sworne pisteler in his place the 30th daie of Januarie followinge, and Jo. Tomkins gospeller, and Richard Boughton genͭ.

1627. Mr. Luke Jones, Clerk, genͭ of his Majestes Chappell and Subdeane of St. Paules London, died the 18th daie of July, and Richard Sandy, a contra tenor of St. Paules, was sworne pisteler in his place the 19th daie following, and Thomas Raiment gospeller, and Jo. Tomkins genͭ.

1627. William Heather, Doctor in Musick, dyed the   of July, and Thomas Laughton was sworne in his place the   of October followinge pisteler, and Master Rayment genͭ, and Richard Sandie gospeller; the wagis in the meane tyme was disposed of by our Lord Deane beeing then Lord Bishopp of Bath and Wells.

1627. John Hewlet, Clarke of the Check, dyed the 11th of Februarie and Nathaniell Pownall was sworne in his place the 12th of the sayd moneth pisteler, and Master Sandy genͭ, and Thomas Laughton gospeller, and John Stephens, by the generall consent of the genͭ, was elected Clarke of the Check.

1630. Humphry Bache died the 31st of Marche, and George Nutbrowne was sworne in his place the same daye pistler, Thomas Laughton genͭ, and Nathaniell Pownall gospeller.

1633. Upon the resignation of Thomas Peerce, Doͬ of Divinity, Thomas Holmes was sworne in his place, according to the Custome and order of the Chappell, the 17th September.

1638. Thomas Holmes dyed at Salsburye at our Lady Day, and John Hardinge was sworne in his place.

1638. John Clarke dyed the   July, and John Cobb was sworne in his place.

1638. John Tompkins dyed the 27th September, and Richard Portman was sworne in his place.

1660. George Cooke dyed in August 1660, and 'tis suppos'd Edwd. Braddock was sworn in his place.

1661. Roger Nightingale, one of the Gentlemen of His Majesties Chappell and Confessor to his Majesties household, died

November 25, 1661, into whose place as gentleman was admitted Roger Hill, as Confessor Philip Tucker, one of the Gentlemen of his Maties Chappell.

1662. George Yardly, a base from Worcester, was sworne gent of his Majesties Chappell, in the place of George Low, June 7, after a resignation made by the sayd Geo. Low, Vicar Chorall of Salisbury.

1662. Mr. Henry Lawes, one of the Gentlemen of his Majesties Chappell Royal and Clerke of the Check, died Oct. 21, and in his place was sworne as Gentleman Dr. John Wilson, Dr. of Musick, Oct. 22, and about the same time Mr. Thomas Blagrave was chosen Clerk of the Check.

1663. Mr. John Cave, one of the Gentlemen of his Majesties Chappell Royall, goeing home to his lodgeing upon the 30th of January about 7 or 8 of ye clock in the evening, about the new Exchange, was by one James Elliott, a Scott, run through the body, of which wound he departed this life the 16th day of February following 1663; into whose place was sworne Charles Husbands, a counter tenor from Windsor, a probacōner, &c. the 14th day of March 1663.

1663. Mr. William Jackson, Clarke, one of the Gent of his Majesties Chappell Royall, departed this life the 27th day of February 1663; into whose place was re-admitted George Lowe of Salisbury the 12th of March 1663.

1663. Mr. Ralph Amner, Clarke, one of the Gentlemen of his Maties Chappell Royall, dyed at Windsor the third day of March 1663; into whose place was sworne Mr. Blaze White, a base, Master of Art[s], the 14th day of March 1663.

1664. Mr. George Lowe, Clarke, one of the Gentlemen of his Maj^ties Chappel Royall, dyed at Westminster the 16th day of May 1664.

1664. Mr. Henry Purcell, one his Majesties Gentlemen of the Chappell, dyed the eleventh day of August 1664, in whose place came Mr. Thomas Richardson.

1664. Mr. William Hopwood was admitted (a basse from Exeter) in Mr. George Lowes place the 25th day of October 1664, his pay to commence the first of Nov. following: the dead pay was disposed of by our Lord Deane, &c.

1664. Mr. Andrew Carter, a Priest of Salesbury, was sworn Genͭ of his Majesties Chappell Royall the 16th day of January 1664, and to come into pay when [a] the next tenor or counter tenor's place shalbe voyde.

1666. Mr. Thos. Peers, one of the Genͭ of his Majesties Chappell Royall, departed this life the tenth of August 1666, in whose place Mr. Carter was sworne the first day of Sept. 1666.

1666. Mr. Henry Smith, a Priest of St. Paul's London, was sworne Genͭ of his Majesties Chappell Royall the 4th day of October 1666, and to come into pay when [b] the next place shalbe voyde.

1666. Mr. Matthew Peniall departed this life the 12th day of January 1666; in whose place came Mr. Henry Smith as above written 1666.

1666. Mr. Thomas Hazard, one of the Genͭ of his Majesties Chappell Royall, departed this life the 23 of January 1666, in whose place was admitted Mr. Pelham Humphrey the next day following, and sworne the 26th of Octr. 1667.

1669. Mr. Edward Colman, Genͭ of his Maᵗⁱᵉˢ Chappell Royall, departed this life at Greenwich on Sunday the 29th of August 1669, in whose place was sworne Mr. Wm. Turner, a counter tenor from Lincolne, the eleventh day of October 1669.

1669. Mr. Edmund Slauter, a base from Windsor, was sworne Genͭ of his Maᵗⁱᵉˢ Chappell Royall the 13th day of October 1669, and to come into pay the next vacancy.

1669. Mr. Andrew Carter, Genͭ of his Maᵗⁱᵉˢ Chappell Royall, departed this life at Salesbury the 18th day of October 1669, in whos[e] place came Mr. Edmund Slauter, a base from Windsor.

1670. Mr. Edmund Slater, Genͭ of his Maᵗⁱᵉˢ Chappell Royall, de-

[a] " in " in MS.   [b] " in " in MS.

parted this life the 10th day of Sept. 1670, in whos[e] place was sworne Mr. James Hart the 7th day of November, 1670, a base from Yorke.

1670. Mr. Gregory Thorndale, Gent of his Maties Chappell, departed this life the 17th day of January 1670, in whos place was sworne Mr. Rich. Hart the 26th day of Aprill 1671.

1671. Mr. Durant Hunt, Gent of his Maties Chappell, departed this life at Salesbury the 23 of Aprill, being Easter day, 1671, in whos place was sworne Mr. Andrew Trebeck, a basse from Worster, the 5th day October 1671.

1672. Dr. Walter Jones, Sub Deane of his Maties Chappell Royall, departed this life at Westminster the 12th day of July 1672.

1672. Capt. Henry Cooke, Gent of his Maties Chappell Royall and Master of the children, departed this life the 13th day of July 1672, in whos place as Master of the children came Mr. Pelham Humfrey, and in his place as Gent of the Chappell was sworne Mr. Burges Howes, a base from Windsor, the 11th day of September 1672.

1672. Dr. Richard Colebrand was sworne Subdeane of his Maties Chappell Royall the 7th day of Sept. 1672.

1673. Mr. Philip Tynchare, Gent of his Maties Chappell Royall and Confessor, departed this life the ninth of May 1673, into whos place as Gent of the Chappell was sworne Mr. Stephen Crispin, a student of Christ Church in Oxon, the 13th day of May 1673. And upon the first day of November 1675 the said Mr. Stephen Crespion was sworne Confessor to his Maties Houshold.

1673. Dr. John Wilson departed this life the 22nd day of Feb. 1673, in whos place was sworne Mr. Rich. Gadbury, a counter tenor from Windsor, the 16th day of March 1673.

1673. Mr. Roger Hill, Clearke, one of the Gent of his Maj^ties Chappell, departed this life the 2 day of March 1673, in whos place was sworne Mr. John Blow the 16th day of March.

1674. Mr. Pelham Humfrey, one of the Gent of his Maj^ties Chappell

Royall and Master of the children, departed this life at Windsor the 14th day of July 1674, in whose place as Master of the children came Mr. John Blow, and as Genᵗ of the Chappell was sworne Mr. William Powell, a tennor from Salesbury, the 21 of July 1674.

1674. Dr. Richard Colebrand, Sub Deane of his Maᵗⁱᵉˢ Chappell Royall, departed this life the 28th day of August 1674.

1674. Dr. William Holder was sworne Subdeane of his Majesties Chappell Royall the second day of Septr. 1674. Be it remembred that Dr. William Holder was sworne Subdeane by the Lord Chamberlane, at the speciall request of the Deane who was then absent at the Bath.

1675. Mr. Raphell Courteville, Genᵗ of his Maᵗⁱᵉˢ Chappell Royall, departed this life the 28 day of December 1675, in whos place was sworne Mr. Michaell Wise, a counter tenor from Salisbury, the 6th of January 1675.

1676. Mr. William Howes, Genᵗ of his Maᵗⁱᵉˢ Chappell Royall, departed this life the 21st of Aprill 1676, in whos place was sworne Mr. Alphonso Marsh, junr. the 25 of the same month, being S. Markes Day, 1676.

1676. Dr. Christopher Gibbons, Organist of his Maᵗⁱᵉˢ Chappell Royall, departed this life the 20th day of October 1676, in whos place was sworne Mr. John Chrissostome Dusharroll the 26 day of the same month 1676.

1678. Mr. Charles Husbands, one of the Genᵗ of his Maᵗⁱᵉˢ Chappel Royall, departed this life at Windsor the 26 day of March 1678, in whos place was sworne Mr. Thomas Hawood the 29 day of March 1678.

1678. Mr. John Dowsing sworn Genᵗ of his Maᵗⁱᵉˢ Chappel extraordinary the 4th of December 1678.

1678. Mr. John Gostling sworn Genᵗ of his Maᵗⁱᵉˢ Chappell extraordinary the 25th of February 1678.

1678. Mr. William Tucker, Genᵗ of his Maᵗⁱᵉˢ Chappell Royall, departed this life the 28 day of February 1678, in whos place was admitted in ordinary Mr. John Gostling, a base from Canterbury, Master of Arts.

1679. Mr. John Abell sworn Gent of his Maties Chappell extraordinary the first of May 1679.

1679. Mr. Burges Howes, one of the Gent of his Maties Chappell Royall, departed this life at Windsor the 10th day of January 1679, in whos place was admitted Mr. John Abell in ordinary.

1679. Mr. Rich. Gadbury, one of the Gent of his Maties Chappell Royall, departed this life at Windsor the 18th day of January 1679, in whos place was sworn Mr. Morgan Harris the 20 of Feby. following 1679.

1681. Mr. Alphonso Marsh, Senior, Gent of his Maties Chappel Royall, departed this life the 9th day of Aprill 1681, in whos place was sworne Mr. Leonard Wooddeson the 15th day of August 1681, to enter into pay the first day after Michaelmas following.

1682. Mr. Edw. Lowe, Organist of his Maties Chappel Royall, departed this life at Oxford the 11th day of July 1682, in whose place was sworne Mr. Henry Purcell the 16th of Sept. 1682, but to take place according to the date of his warrant which was the 14th of July 1682.

1682. Mr. Thomas Purcell, one of the Gent of his Maties Chappel Royall, departed this life the last day of July 1682, in whose place was sworne Mr. Josiah Boucher the sixt day of August 1682, at Windsor.

1683. Mr. Nathaniel Vestment sworne Gent of his Maties Chappell Royall the 28th of June 1683, at Windsor.

1683. Mr. William Hopwood, Gent of his Maties Chappell Royall, departed this life the 13th day of July 1683, in whose place was admitted in ordinary Mr. Nathaniell Vestment the 23rd day of July 1683.

1683. Mr. Samuell Bentham sworne Gent of his Maties Chappell Royall the 24th day of July 1683, extraordinary.

1683. Mr. Thomas Browne sworne Gent of his Maties Chappell

Royall extraordinary, by virtue of an Order from the Right Reverend Father in God Henry Lord Bishop of London and Dean of his Maties Chappel Royall, &c.

1684. Mr. John Harding, Gent of his Maties Chappell Royall, departed this life the 7th day of November 1684, in whose place was admitted in ordinary Mr. Samuell Bentham the 10th day of November 1684.

1685. Edward Morton sworne Gent of his Maties Chappel Royall extraordinary Aprill the 12th 1685.

1685. William Davis sworne Gent of his Maties Chappel Royall extraordinary May the 23d 1685.

1685. John Lenton sworne Gent of his Maties Chappel Royall extraordinary November the 10th 1685.

1687. Mr. John Sharole, one of the Gent of His M^ties Chappell Royall, departed this life the 5 day of August 1687.

1688. Mr. John James Gaches sworn Gentleman of his Maties Chappell Royal ordinary November 8, 1688.

1688. Mr. Henry Smith, one of ye Gentlemen of the Chappell Royall, departed this life May the 23, 1688.

1689-90. Mr. Richard Hart, one of the Gentlemen of the Chappell Royall, departed this life Feb. the 8th 1689-90.

1689. Mr. Thomas Heywood, one of the Gentleman of the Chappell, resigned his place at Michaelmas 1688.

King William and Queen Mary.

1689. Mr. Moses Snow was sworne Gentleman of there Majesties Chappell Royall exterordinary [*sic*] into the first vacancy that shall fall, Dec. the 17, 1689.

1689. Mr. Thos. Linacre sworne Gentleman of there Majesties Chappell extordinary [*sic*], December the 27, into the second vacancy.

1688. Thomas Blagrave, Clerke of the Checke, departed this life the 21 day of November 1688, and Edward Braddocke, one of the Gentlemen of there Majesties Chappell Royall, was chosen Clerk of the Cheque in his place.

1686. Dr. Holder, Subdeane of there Majesties Chappell Royall, resigned his place before Christmas in the yeare of our Lord
1689 unto Dr. Battle, who was accordingly sworne Subdeane
of the saide Chappell Royall, 1689.

1690. Mr. Alixander Damascene was sworn Gentleman of their
Majesties Chappel Royall extraordinary the 6th day of
December 1690, by mee R. Battell, S.D.

1691. Mr. John Howell was sworne Gentleman of there Majesties
Chappell Royall exterordinary the 30th day of August 1691,
by R. Battell, S.D.

1691. Mr. David La Count was sworne Gentleman of there Majesties Chappell Royall exterordinary the 31 day of August
1691, by mee R. Battell, S.D.

1691. Mr. William Battle was sworne Gentleman of there Majesties
Chappell Royall exterordinary the 10 day of December 1691,
by me R. Battell, S.D.

1691. Mr. Symon Corbitt sworne Gentleman of there Maties Chappell Royall exterordinary the 11 day of December 1691, by
mee R. Battell, S.D.

1692. Mr. Snow was sworne Gentleman of there Majesties Chappell
Royall the 8 day of Aprill, and admitted in ordinary in the
place of Mr. Allphonso Marsh in the year 1692, by mee R.
Battell, S.D.

1692. Mr. Allphonso Marsh departed this life the 5 day of Aprill
1692.

1692. Mr. Daniell Williams sworne Gent of there Majesties Chappell Royall exterordinary the 16 day of December 1692, by
mee R. Battell, S.D.

1692-3. Mr. Charles Greene sworn Gent^{n} of there Majesties Chappell Royall exterordinary the 2 day of Jan. 1692-3, by mee
R. Battell, S.D.

1693. Mr. John Sayr, a Gentleman of the Chappell Royal, dyed in
January 1693, and in succession to him (according to a
former president) were sworne Mr. Linacre and Mr. John

Howell into the place of Gospeller, by warrant from the Right Reverend the Lord Bishop of London, Dean of the Chappell Royall, by mee R. Battell, Sub Dean, Witnes Edw. Braddock, Clerk of the Check.

1693. Also soon after, viz. Feb. 24, 1693, Mr. Moses Snow was by order and warrant from the Dean of the Chappell advanced to the place of Epistler, and sworn also unto that place by mee R. Battell, Sub Dean, Witnes Edward Braddock, Clerk of the Check.

1693. The same day, viz. Feb. the 24th, Mr. Samuel Bentham, by a warrant from the Right Reverend Dean, was advanced to the place of a Gentleman of the Chappell in ordinary, and sworn accordingly by mee R. Battell, Sub Dean, Witness Edw. Braddock, Clerk of the Check.

1694. Sept. the 22, 1694, Mr. Moses Snow was sworn into the ful place of a Gentleman of the Chappell Royal, by virtue of a warrant from the Right Reverend Dean of the Chappel, by mee R. Battell, Sub Dean, Wittnes Edw. Braddock, Clerk of the Check.

1695. Mr. George Bettenham, one of the Gentlemen of their Majesties Chappell Royall, departed this life the 19 day of September 1694.

1694. Mr. George Hart and Mr. Barnes were both sworn Gentlemen of there Maties Chappell Royall exterordinary the 10 day of Sept. 1694, by R. Battle, Sub Dean, Wittnes Edw. Braddock, Clerk of the Cheque.

1694. Mr. John Howell was sworne in the place of Epistler in there Maties Chappell Royall by warrant from the Right Reverend Lord Bishop of London, Deane of the Chappell, the first day of October 1694, by Ralph Battle, Subdean, Witnes Edward Braddock, Clerk of the Cheque.

1694. Mr. Thos. Linacre was alsoe sworne Gospeller in their Majesties Chappell Royall by warrant from the Right Reverend Lord Bishop of London, Dean of their Majesties Chappell, the 1st day of October 1694, by Ralph Battle, Subdean, Wittnes Edward Braddock, Clerk of the Cheque.

1695. Mr. Henry Purcell, Organist in his Majesties Chappell Royall, departed this life the 21 day of Novem. 1695.

1695. Mr. Josias Boucher, one of the Genͭ of his Majesties Chappell Royall, departed this life the 16 day of Decͬ 1695.

1695. By virtue of four warrants from the Dean of the Chappel Mr. John Howel was sworn Gent. of the Chappell in a ful place in the room of Mr. Bowchēr, Dec. 10, 1695, by mee Rʰ Battell, Wittnes Edw. Braddock.

1695. Mr. Damascene was sworn in a full place of Gentleman upon the death of Mr. Henry Purcell, Dec. 10, 1695, by mee Rʰ Battell, S.D., Wittnes Edw. Braddock.

1695. Mr. Charles Barns was sworn into the place of Epistler upon the advance of Mr. Howell, Dec. 10, 1695, by mee Rʰ Battell, S.D., Witt. Edw. Braddock.

1695. Mr. Francis Piggot was sworn Organist extraordinary Dec. 11, 1695, by mee Rʰ Battell, S.D., Witt. Edw. Braddock.

1696. Mr. Frost dyed upon the first day of June, upon whose decease Mr. Charles Barns was by a warrant from the Right Reverend the Dean sworn into a ful place of Gentleman of the Chappell, and Mr. George Hart was also sworn Gent. into the pay of Epistler, by mee Rʰ Battell, S.D., Witnes Edw. Braddock.

1696. Mr. John Church was sworn Gentleman extraordinary of his Majᵗⁱᵉˢ Chappell Royall on the 31 day of January 1696-7, by vertue of a warrant from my Lord of London our Right Reverend Dean to mee Rʰ Battell, S.D., Witnes Edw. Braddock, Clerk of the Check.

1697. Mr. Francis Piggott was sworn Organist in ordinary upon the death of Dr. Child, March the 24, 1696-7 (by vertue of a warrant from our Right Reverend Dean Henry Lord Bishop of London), by mee Rʰ Battell, S.D., Wittˢ Edw. Braddock.

1697. April 1st, Mr. Daniell Williams was sworn Gentleman of the Chappell Royall in ordinary and admitted into the ful pay of 73^{li} per annum in the place of Mr. Stephen Chrispion, whose place became vacant upon his refusal to sign the association (his pay is to begin from Lady Day last past, by order of the Right Reverend Dean Henry Lord Bishop of London) by mee R^h Battell, S.D., Wittnes Edw. Braddock, Clerk of the Check.

1697. Mr. James Cob dyed on the 20th of July 1697, and by a warrant from the Right Reverend the Lord Bishop of London, Dean of the Chappell, Mr. John Church was sworn into his place in ful pay of Gentleman the first day of August, by mee R^h Battell, S.D., Wittnes Edw. Braddock, Clerk of Cheque.

1697. Mr. Morgan Harris dyed the 2d of November 1697, and by vertue of a warrant from the Right Reverend Dean, Mr. Thomas Jennings was sworn Gospeller on the 8th of November, by mee R^h Battell, S.D., Wittnes Edw. Braddock, Clerk of the Cheque.

1697. Nov. 9, Mr. George Hart was sworn into a ful place by vertue of a warrant from the Right Reverend Dean by mee R^h Battell, S.D., Wittnes Edw. Braddock, Clerk of Cheque.

1699. By vertue of a warrant from the Right Reverend Dean of the Chapel, dated June 20, 1699, I have sworn Mr. William Washbourn a Gentleman extraordinary of the Chapel Royal, R^h Battell, S.D.

1699. On Feby. 25th Mr. Blaze White, one of the Priests and Gentlemen of the Chapell, dyed, and upon Feb. the 29th Mr. George Hart, another of the Gentleman of the Chapel Royal, dyed. R^h Battell, S.D.

It was then ordered that these removes following should bee made, by five warrants from the Right Reverend Dean, granted March the 2d, 1699.

To Mr. Thos. Lynacre to advance to a ful place of Gentleman.

To Mr. Thos. Jennings to advance to a ful place of Gentleman.

To Mr. Thos. Edwards to succeed Mr. White and to bee admitted to the place of Epistler.

To Mr. William Washbourn and Mr. John Ratcliffe jointly to succeed to and share the Gospeller's place; these were all sworn in by mee R^h Battell, S.D., Wittnes Edw. Braddock, Clerk of the Check.

1699. Upon a new establishment of a composer's place for the Chapell Royal Dr. John Blow was admitted into it by a warrant from the Right Reverend Dean, and sworn in by mee Ralph Battell, S.D., Wittness Edw. Braddock, Clerk of the Checke.

1699. April 2. By vertue of a warrant from the Lord Bishop of London, Dean of the Chapell, Mr. Humphry Griffith was sworn Gentleman extraordinary of the Chapell, by me R^h Battell, S.D., Wittnes Edw. Braddock, Clerk of the Checke.

1700. July 7. By vertue of a warrant from the Right Reverend the Dean of the Chapell Royal Mr. Jeremiah Clerk and Mr. William Crofts were both sworn Gentlemen extraordinary of the King's Chapell (and to succeed as Organists according to merit, when any such place shal fall voyd) by mee R^h Battell, S.D., Wittnes Edw. Braddock, Clerk of the Cheke.

1700. Dec. 6. Mr. John Freeman was sworn Gentleman extraordinary of the Chapell Royall by the Right Reverend the Dean's order, by mee R^h Battell, S.D., Wittnes Edw. Braddock, Clerk of the Cheque.

1701. June the 6th. By vertue of a warrant from the Right Reverend the Lord Bishop of London, Dean of the Chapell

Royall, I have sworn Mr. John Welden Gentleman extraordinary of the said Chapell. R^h Battell, S.D., Wittnes Edw.
Braddock, Clerk of the Cheque.

1702. May 8th.   Upon the death of Mr. Watkins, a Gentleman of
the Chapell, Mr. Stephen Crispion was sworn into a ful place
by a verbal order of the Right Reverend the Lord Bishop of
London, Dean, by mee R^h Battell, S.D., Witness Edw.
Braddock, Clerk of the Cheque.

1702. Mr. R^d Elfford was sworn Gentleman of the Chapel the 2d of
Aug. 1702, in an additional place to be added to the establishment, by me R^h Battell, S.D.

1702. Mr. Watkins, one of the Gentlemen of the Chappell Royall,
departed this life the 8th day of May 1702.

1702. Mr. Vestment, one of the Gentlemen of the Chappell Royall,
departed this life the 23rd of August 1702.

1702. Sept. 5.   By vertue of a warrant from the Right Reverend
the Lord Bishop of London, I have sworn and admitted
Mr. John Freeman and Mr. Humphry Griffith Gentlemen
of the Chappell Royal, joyntly into the place of Mr. Vestment, lately deceased, to be divided equally between
them.   R^h Battell, Wittness Edw. Braddock, Clerk of the
Cheque.

1702. Mr. Moses Snow, one of the Gentlemen of the Queen's
Chapell, departed this life the 20th of December 1702.

1702. Dec. 23d.   By vertue of two warrants from the Lord Bishop
of London I have sworn in Mr. John Freeman and Mr.
Humphry Griffith into (each of them) a ful place in the
Chapel Royall, upon the death of Mr. Moses Snow. Ralph
Battell, S.D., Wittnes, Edw. Braddock, Clerk of the
Cheque.

1703. Aprill 14th.   Mr.   Harper and Mr.   Palmer
were sworn in Chaplains of St. James, Mr.   Richardson
also and Mr. Nicholas Phipps, Closet Keeper at Whitehal, by

order from the Lord Bishop of London, Dean, by mee
Ralph Battell, S.D., Witnes Edw. Braddock, Clerk of the
Cheque.

1704. May 15. Mr. Peggott, organist of her Majesties Chappell
Royall, departed this life May the 15th, 1704.

1704. Mr. Goodgroome, one of the Gentlemen of her Majesties
Chappell Royall, departed this life June the 27th, 1704.

1704. May 25th. By vertue of a warrant from the Right Reverend
the Lord Bishop of London I have sworn and admitted Mr.
Jeremiah Clark and Mr. William Crofts joyntly into an organist's place vacant by the death of Mr. Francis Pigott. R^h
Battell, S.D., Witnes Edw. Braddock, Clerk of the Cheque.

1707. November the 5th. By vertue of a warrant from the Lord
Bishop of London, Dean of the Chapell, I have sworn and
admitted Mr. William Croft into an organist's place now
become ful (*sic*) by the death of Mr. Jeremiah Clerk. R^h
Battell, S.D.

1708. June the 12th. Mr. Edward Braddock, Clark of the Cheque,
departed this life the 12th of June 1708, and Daniell Williams, one of the Gentlemen of her Majesties Chappell Royall,
was chosen Clerke of the Cheque in his place.

1708. Mr. Jo. Howell, Gentleman of her Majesties Chappell Royall,
dyed the 15th of July 1708, and Mr. Barnard Gates was
sworn Gentleman in his place.

1708. Mr. Humphry Griffith, Gentleman of her Majesties Chappell
Royall, dyed the 14th of Septr. 1708.

1708. Dr. John Blow, Organist, Composer, and Master of the
Children, dyed the 1st of October 1708, and had his full pay
for both places to Christmas.

1708. Mr. Edward Braddock, Gentleman of her Majesties Chappell
Royall and Clarke of the Cheque, departed this life the 12th
of June 1708, and by vertue of a warrant from the Right
Reverend the Lord Bishop of London I have sworne and admitted Mr. John Mason Gentleman of her Majesties Chappell

Royall in the said Mr. Braddock's roome. R^h Battell, S.D., Wittness Dan. Williams, Clark of the Cheque.

1708. Mr. John Howell, Genᵗ of her Maj. Chappell Royall, dyed the 15th of July 1708, and by vertue of a warrant from the Right Reverend the Lord Bishop of London, Dean of her Majesties Chappell, Mr. Bernard Gates was sworn Gentleman in his place, by me R^h Battell, S.D., Wittness Daniel Williams, Clerk of the Cheque.

1708. Mr. Humphry Griffith, Gentleman of her Maj. Chappell Royall, dyed the 14 of Sept. 1708, and by vertue of a warrant from the Right Reverend the Lord Bishop of London, Dean of Her Majesties Chappell Royall, Mr. Frances Hughes was sworn Gentleman in his place, by me R^h Battell, S.D., Wittness Daniel Williams, Clerk of the Cheque.

1708. Dr. John Blow, Organist, and Master of the Children of her Majesties Chapell Royall and Composer in ordinary to her Majesty, dyed the first of October 1708, and by vertue of a warrant from the Right Reverend the Lord Bishop of London, Dean of her Maj. Chappell Royall, I have sworne Mr. William Croft Master of the Children and Composer; and likewise by vertue of a warrant bearing date the same day Mr. John Weldon was sworn Organist in the sayd Dr. Blow's place, by me R^h Battell, S.D., Wittness Daniell Williams, Clerk of the Cheque.

1710. Mr. Charles Barnes dyed on the 2d day of January 1710, and by vertue of a warrant from the Right Reverend the Lord Bishop of London, Dean of her Maj. Chappell, Mr. William Battell, Chanter of Westminster, was sworne Gentleman in his place, by me R^h. Battell, S.D., Wittness D. Williams, C. Cheque.

1711. Mr. Ste. Crespion dyed the 25th Novr. 1711, and by vertue of a warrant from the Right Reverend the Lord Bishop of London, Dean of Her Majesty's Chappell, Mr. Edward Aspinwall was sworne Gentleman in his place the first day of January 1711-12, by me R^h Battell, S.D., Wittness Daniell Williams, Clerk of the Cheque.

1712. Mr. Thomas Richardson, Gentleman of her Majesties Chapel Royall, dyed on the 23d of July 1712, and by vertue of a warrant from the Right Reverend the Lord Bishop of London, Dean of her Majesties Chapel, Mr. George Laye, a countra tenor from Windsor, was sworne Gentleman in his place, by me Rh. Battell, S.D., Wittness Daniel Williams, Clerk of the Cheque.

1714. Mr. Richard Elford, Gentleman of his Maj. Chapel Royal, departed this life the 29th of October, 1714, and by vertue of a warrant from the Right Reverend John Lord Bishop of London, Dean of his Majesties Chapel Royal, Mr. Samuel Weely, a base from St. Paul's, was sworne in his place, by me Dolben, Subdean, Wittness Daniel Williams, Clerk of the Cheque.

1715. His Majesty having been graciously pleas'd to add four Gentlemen of the Chappell to the old establishment, viz. Mr. Wm. Morley, Mr. Geo. Carleton, Mr. Tho. Baker, and Mr. Samuel Chittle, and by vertue of four several warrants from the Right Reverend Father in God John Lord Bishop of London, Dean of his Maties Chappell Royall, I have sworne and admitted the aforesayd gentlemen Gentlemen in ordinary of his Maties Chappell Royall, to enjoy the same, together with all priviledges and advantages thereunto belonging. Wittness my hand this 8th day of August 1715, Dolben, Subdean. Dan. Williams, Clerk of the Cheque.

1715. The Revd. Mr. Andrew Trebeck, Gentleman of his Maties Chappel, dyed the 19th day of November 1715, and by vertue of a warrant bearing date December the 4th following, from the Right Reverend the Lord Bishop of London, Dean of His Majesties Chappell Royall, the Revd. Mr. Flintoft from Worcester was sworne Gentleman in ordinary in his place, by me Dolben, Subdean. Witness Dan. Williams, Clerk of the Cheque.

1716. The Revd. Mr. John Radcliffe, Confeser and Gentilman in ordinary of his Majesties Chappell Royall, dyed the 29th of October 1716, and on the 9th day of November following the Rev. Mr. Samuel Bentham succeeded the said Mr. Radcliffe as Confeser, and Mr. John Gethin as Gent in ordinary of the Chappell, and wear accordingly sworne in the same day, being the 9th of Novr. by the Right Revd. the Lord Bishop of London, Dean of his Maj. Royall Chappell, Dolben, Subdean. Wittness Dan. Williams, Clerk of the Cheque.

1717. Mr. Leonard Woodeson, Gentleman of his Majesties Chappell, dyed the 14th day of March 1716-17, and by vertue of a warrant bearing date the 27th day of June, 1717, from the Rt. Revd. the Lord Bishop of London, Dean of his Majesties Royall Chapels, Mr. Peter Randall was sworne Gentleman in ordinary by me Dolben, Subdean. Wittnes Daniell Williams, Clerk of the Cheque.

N.B. Aug. 8. 1715. That besides the four additional Gentlemen of the Chappell abovementioned, there were added in King George's establishment, as follows: viz. a second Composer in Ordinary which place Mr. John Welldon was sworn and admitted into.

A Lutanist, which place Mr. John Shore was sworn and admitted into.

A Violist, which place Mr. Francisco Goodsens was sworn and admitted into.

All these three were sworn and admitted into their respective places by me Dolben, Subdean. Wittness Daniell Williams.

There was likewise inserted in the aforesaid establishment an allowance to Dr. William Croft (as Master of the Children) of eighty pounds per annum, for teaching the children to write and accompts, and for teaching them to play on [the organ], and to compose musick. Dolben, Subdean.

1718. Mr. James Hart, Gentleman of his Majesties Chappell, dyed the 8th day of May, 1718, and by vertue of a warrant bearing date the 12th day of June following, from the Right Reverend the Lord Bishop of Salisbury, Dean of his Maj. Royall Chappells, Mr. James Chelsum was sworne Gentleman in Ordinary in his place, by me Edw. Aspinwall, Subdean. Witness Dan. Williams, Clerk of the Cheque.

1717-18. The Reverend Mr. Edw. Aspinwall, A.M., was sworne Subdean of his Majesties Royall Chappells, in the room of Dr. Dolben, the 20th day of March 1717-18.

1719. Mr. Luke Flintoft, by vertue of a warrant from the Rt. Revd. the Lord Bishopp of Sarum, Dean of his Majesty's Royal Chappels, was sworn Reader in the Chapel of Whitehall, in the room of Dr. Mangey, this 9th day of July 1719, by me Edw. Aspinwall, Subdean.

1719. Mr. Alexander Damassene, Gentleman of his Majesty's Chapel, dyed the 14th day of July, 1719, and by vertue of a warrant from the Rt. Revd. the Lord Bishopp of Sarum, Dean of his Majesty's Royal Chapels, Mr. Talbot Young was sworn Gentleman in Ordinary in his place, this eight day of August 1719, by me Edw. Aspinwall, Subdean.

1719. The Revd. Mr. Thomas Linacre, Gentleman of his Majesties Chapel, dyed the   day of   1719, and by vertue of a warrant from the Rt. Revd. the Lord Bishopp of Sarum, Dean of his Majesty's Royal Chappels, the Revd. Mr. Thomas Blennerhaysett was sworn Gentleman in ordinary in his place this twenty-first day of September 1719, by me Edw. Aspinwall, Subdean.

1719-20. The Revd. John Henry Winckelhausen, by vertue of a warrant from the Rt. Revd. the Lord Bishop of Sarum, Dean of his Majesty's Royal Chapels, was sworn Reader of the Dutch Chapel at St. James's, vacant by the surrender of the

Revd. Mr. Sebastian Vander Eyken, this first day of January 1719-20, by me Edw. Aspinwall, Subdean.

1719-20. Mr. Daniel Williams, Gentleman of his Maj^{tys} Chapel, dyed the 12th day of March, 1719-20; and by vertue of a warrant from the Rt. Revd. the Lord Bishopp of Sarum, Dean of his Majesty's Royal Chapels, Mr. Thos. Bell was sworn Gentleman in Ordinary in his place, this 14th day of March 1719-20, by me Edw. Aspinwall, Subdean.

1720. Mr. Daniell Williams, Clark of the Cheque, dyed the 12th day of March, 1719-20, and by vertue of a warrant from the Rt. Revd. the Lord Bishopp of Sarum, Dean of his Majesty's Royal Chapels, Jonathan Smith, Esqre, Serjeant of his Majesty's Chappells and Vestryes, was sworn Clark of the Cheque of the said Chappels in his place, this 4th day of Aprill, 1720, by me Edw. Aspinwall, Subdean.

1721. The Revd. Mr. John Henry Winckelhausen, Reader of the Dutch Chappell at St. James's, dyed 21 day of October 1721, and by vertue of a warrant from the Rt. Revd. the Lord Bishopp of Sarum, Dean of his Majesties Royal Chappells, the Revd. Mr. Sebastian Vander Eyken was sworn Reader of the said Dutch Chappell at St. James's in his place, this thirtieth day of October 1721, by me Edw. Aspinwall, Subdean.

1721. Mr. William Morley, Gentleman of his Majesty's Chappell, dyed Oct. the 29th, 1721, and by vertue of a warrant from the Rt. Revd. the Lord Bishopp of Sarum, Dean of his Majesties Royal Chappells, Mr. William Perry was sworn Gentleman in ordinary in his place, this first day of November 1721, by me Edw. Aspinwall, Subdean.

1732. Dr. Edward Aspinwall, Subdean of his Majesty's Chapels, departed this life Aug. the 3d, 1732, and the Revd. Mr. George Carleton, A.M., was sworn Subdean of the said Royal Chapels by the Rt. Revd. Edmund Lord Bishop of London, and Dean of his Majesty's Chapels Royal, on the 16th day of the same month.

1732. By vertue of a warrant from the Rt. Revd. the Lord Bishop of London, Dean of his Majesty's Royal Chapels, the Revd. Mr. Richard Howe was sworn into the place of one of the Priests in Ordinary of his Majesty's Chapels Royal (vacant by the death of the Revd. Dr. Edward Aspinwall) the 3rd day of September 1732, by me Geo. Carleton, Subdean.

1732. By vertue of a warrant from the Rt. Revd. Edmund Lord Bishop of London, Dean of his Majesty's Chapels Royal, the Revd. Mr. Henry Alard Butjealer was sworn into the place or office of one of the ministers of his Majesty's German Chapel at St. James's (void by the death of the Revd. Mr. Ruperti), Oct. 22, 1732, by me George Carleton, Subdean.

1732. By vertue of a warrant from the Rt. Revd. Edmund Lord Bishop of London, Dean of his Majesty's Chapels Royal, the Revd. Mr. James Richardson was sworn into the place or office of Reading Chaplain at the Chapel of Whitehall (void by my own resignation) the 30th day of December in the year of our Lord 1732, by me George Carleton, Subdean.

II.—APPOINTMENTS AND OBITUARY NOTICES OF THE SUB-DEANS, PRIESTS, ORGANISTS, AND GENTLEMEN.—*List II.*

The names and sirenames of all soche as are sworne extra-ordynarye into the Feloship of her Majestes Royall Chappell, sence the 29 of Maye 1592. Eliz. Dominæ Nostræ Reginæ 34.

William Phelps of Tewksburye, in the Countye of Glocester, trayned up in the noble science of musick, for his care [and] kindnes to Mr. Bull, Organiste in her said Majestes Chappell, was as in gratification therof admitted by our generall consent (*quantum in* 1592, Maye 29. Phelps.

nobis est) by corporall othe, the said William, an extraordynarye man into our companye, with this proviso, that he shall not at any tyme herafter, he shall not by any means whatsoever, private or publick, secrett or open, make suite or obteyn to be ordinarye or to receive waiges with us without the special consent in Chapter of the Subdeane, or Substitute in his absence, and the consente of soche, or the moste parte of soche, the ordynarye gentlemen as then shalbe present for that cawse or other in chapter then assembled. In which sorte the sayd William hathe so taken his oathe, promised his faythe, and subscribed his name, with his owne hand, as aperethe in the laste leaffe and page of this booke, the 29 of Maye 1592. Eliz 34. [f. 17.]

At the Courte at Greenwiche, May 29, 1592. Mr. William Phelps of the Towne of Tewksbury, in the countie of Glocester, beinge trayned up in the noble science of Musicke, and also for that he dyd show a moste rare kyndnes to Mr. Doctor Bull in his great distresse, beinge robbed in those parts, is at his humble suicte admitted by me the Substitute for the present, and, with the common consent of all the companye which then were presente at the Chapter then holden, an extraordinarye gentleman of her Majestes moste honorable Chappell, and sworne thereto accordinglye the 29 daye of Maye 1592, Eliz. 34, with this specyal proviso in his oathe, that he shall not at any tyme herafter by any means, privatly or openly, make suicte, ob-teyne, use or holde our societye as an ordinarye man therin, to receive wages with us in any sorte, by any favor whatsoever, excepte by the Subdeane, or his Substitute for the tyme, and the reste of our Companye, he be therunto called and admitted, on which condicion the sayd William is admitted into our feloship as extra-ordynarye and not otherwyse, the daye and yere abovesayd.

Anth. Anderson, Substitute.
Wylliam Phellpes. [f. 86 b.]

1592, June 18. Davies. The 18 daye of June 1592 dyd James Davies of Canterburie receyve the like oathe as the sayd William abovenamed, and undre the same condicions and not otherwise in any sorte, and therupon only and not otherwise was (ás before is sayd) by our generall consentes by Anthony Anderson the Substitute, and the chapter assembled in the vestrye at Greenwich, admitted extraordynarye. J. Davies. [f. 17.]

The same daye, at the ernest request of Mr. Greene our Subdeane, Westerne. and for the good qualitie in the man, was, in the same sorte, and under the same condicions, with his and the other above named special promes and consent, Humphreye Westerne of the Cittie of London sworne and admitted into our feloship extraordynarye as beffore is sayd and no otherwise. Humfrey Westerne. [f. 17.]

Mr. Robert Greene, late Subdeane of Her Majestes Royall 1592. Chappell, departed this liffe the tenthe daye of Julye 1592, at Àbdye his benefice in Norffolk. [f. 20.]

Anthonye Anderson, Preacher sence the first yere of her Majestes July 26, 1592. moste happie raigne, vicare of Stebinhythe (Stepneye nere London) Midd., Gospeller in her Majestes Royall Chappell, was by common consente and election of the gentlemen of the sayd chappell, in a Chapter holden in Greenwich, by petition to the Right Honorable the Lord Chamberlain to her Majestie, under all their hands then present, presented to his honor with desire to her sacred Majestie to electe and admitt the sayd Anthonye the Subdeane of her Majestes sayd Chappell; the sayd Noble Lorde, by her Majestes speciall grace bestowing the same, gave command to Mr. Leonarde Davies, one of her Majestes Chaplens in the sayd Chappell, to sweare the sayd Anthonye Subdeane as beffore, and was so sworne Subdeane by him upon Wedensday the 26. of Julye in the vestrye at Greenwich upon the Gospell of St. Mathewe, and in the presence of

Mr Tho. Sampson, Clerke of the Checke in the Chappell.

Mr. Randall, Organiste.

Mr. Hewlett, and sondrye others.

Laus Deo in Christo Jesu. Amen. [f. 20.]

Oct. 23, 1592.   Peter Wright was sworne in ordinary (namelye the Epistoler) in her Majestes moste honorable Chappell, the 23. of October 1592, at her Majestes Manor of Greenwich, in the presence of us undernamed, the othe geven by the Subdeane,   Anth. Anderson.[a]

           Anthony Todd.
            Robert Tallentyer.   John Hottoste.
                 Robert Allison.   [f. 20.]

Nov. 18, 1592.   The 18th daye of November 1592 was Thomas Goolde sworne Gentleman from the Gospeler's place, and from hence to have the place and waiges of a gentleman as other gentlemen of the same societie.

    The same daye also was sworne (and bothe by me the Subdeane) Thomas Morleye from the Epistler's place to the Gospeller's place and waiges, and bothe thes sworne in the vestry at Hampton Courte in the presence of

Anth. Anderson,⎫ Subdeane. ⎭	Bartholomew Mason.	Leonard Davies.
Ricardo Granwall.	Crue[?] Sharpe.	Anthony Harrison.
William Randall.		Robert Tallentyer.
George Waterhouse.		
John Stephines. [f. 20.]		

1593.   William Asplend, gentleman, dwellinge at hie Ester in the countie of Essex, was in a chapter holden for that purpose sworne by Mr. Anderson, Subdean, the whole chapter thereto gevinge their consent, a gentleman extraordynarye in and of her Majestes Chapple Royall, and in and under soche condicion, pointe, and points in all points, as William Phelps aperethe to be sworne before him above in this paige. Sworne forther that he shall not make any kynde of sewte to her Majeste but shall first acquainte the

---

[a] A signature follows this which it is impossible to decipher.

Subdean therwith, and his substitute, with the consent of the sayd
Subdean and other of the societie. Marche 26, 1593. Eliz. 35.

Anth. Anderson, Subdean.	William Asplænd.	Henry Eveseede.
Leonarde Davies.	Anthony Todd.	
Antho. Harrison.	Thomas Woodsonn.	
	William Randall.	
℞ 5ˡⁱ for his entrance,	Tymothe Greene.	
and delyvered to Mr.	Edw. Pyers.	
Hewlett to the use of	Jo. Hewlett.	
the Companye.	Peter Wryght. [f. 17.]	

The Right Honorable Lord Chamberlen dyd, the 14th daye of 1593,Aprill 14.
Aprill 1593, commaunde me to admitt John Marchant (now an
extraordynarye man) into ordinarye, that is to say, to have the third
place and waiges accordinglye, after that Mr. Laurence and James
Davies be placed into ordinary waiges; the sayd John Marchant
presented him selfe into our chapter, submitted himselfe unto this
order, and dothe promise to contente himselfe with this favor, and
not to use any mediation or favor to prevent the forsayd tyme by
any meanes, and therto and in witnes therof hathe subscribed his
name.   John Marchand.

In the presence of

Anth. Anderson, Subdean.	Anthony Todd.
John Bull.	Robert Allison.
Richarde Granwall.	John Stevens.
Thomas Madockes.	[f. 22.]

The Right Honorable the Lord Chamberlayne, uppon the thirde 3 Feby. 1593-4.
day of February Anno Domini 1593, did commaunde me Leonard
Davies, Subdean at Hampton Courte, to recorde in this our Booke
of Remembrance, that his Honor's pleasure is that John Bauldwyne
of the College of Wynsor shoulde be placed next in ordynarye in
Her Majesties Chapple, all former promyses made to any other not-

withstandinge, and the same dyd my Lord graunte at and throughe the election and requeste of the whole companye then waytinge.

Leonard Davies, Subdean. [f. 22 b.]

Feb. 19, 1594-5.

The Right Honorable the Lord Chamberlaine, by his speciall warrant directed to me, which was dated the 19th of Febr. in the yeare of our Lord 1594, did commaund me to sweare George Woodson, of the quire of Wynsor, gentleman extraordinarye in her Majesties Chappell, commaundinge further by the same warrant that the saide Woodson should be sworne gentleman in ordinarie in the place of a counter tenor, whensoever any shall fall voyde, and that before anie other; the firste parte of which warrante I did fulfill one the 18th day of Marche, in the yeare above written, then being present those whose names are inserted in this bye paper.[a] By me,

Leonard Davies, Subdean. [f. 22b.]

1594-5, March 23.

The 23d of March, in the yeare of our Lord God 1594, the Right Honorable the Lord Chamberlaine gave me order to swere John Bauldwin (named before in this page) gentleman in ordinarie (without pay) in her Majesties Chappell, and until a tenor's place be voyde, and then he to have and be sworne into wages for the firste and nexte tenor that shalbe admitted and placed in her Highnes Chappell, noe man whatsoever to prevent him, and thereto all the gentlemen whose names are written in this loose paper[a] gevinge ther full consentes. By me,   Leonard Davies, Subdean. [f. 22<i>b</i>.]

The 6th day of June, Anno Domini 1596.

1596, June 6.

The Right Honorable the Lord Chamberlaine gave order to sweare Mr. Roger Godbalde extraordinarie in her Majestes Chappell, which thinge was done the day and yeare above written, with this condicōn, that the same Mr. Godbalde shall not sue by anye meanes directe or indirecte, as by frendes or otherwyse, to come to be sworne into ordynarye into her Highnes saide chappell, untill he be firste called and proved fytt for the same by the Subdeane and the major

<hr>

[a] The " loose paper " and " bye paper " are not preserved with the MS.

parte of her Majestes Chappell, whereto he hathe taken his othe as
appeerethe by the subscripcōn hereto under his owne hand.

Roger Godbald.   [f. 23].

The twentieth daye of Februarie 1596, at the specyall request of
Mr. Wm. Randall, was sworne Rychard Martyn extraordynarie in
her Majestes Chappell, by the consent of the gentlemen then present,
with this condicon, that the same Richard Martyn shall not sue by
any meanes, dyrect or indyrect, as by friends or otherwise, to come
to be sworne into ordinarie into her Highnes sayd chappell without
the consent of the Subdeane and the major parte of her Majestes
Chappell, wherto he hathe taken his othe, as appearethe by the subscription heerto under his owne hande.

1596-7,
Feb. 20.

T. Sampson.   Richard Martyn.   [f. 23.]

The Right Honorable the Lord Chamberlaine, upon the 9th day of
June, commaunded me, Bartholomew Mason, Substitute at Greenwich,
to sweare Nathaniell Gyles Gentleman of her Majestes Chappell
(being before extraordinary), whoe accordingly receaved his oth as
other gentlemen before him hath done, in the presence of us whose
names are subscribed.

1597, June.

Bar. Mason.

Thomas Sampson.   Robt. Tallentyer.   Thomas Woodson.
Crew Sharpe.   William Randall.   Peter Wryght.   [f. 24.]

The Right Honorable the Lord Chamberlaine uppon the thirde
day of Marche, Anno Domini 1600, at Whitehall, did geve order
unto Mr. Mason, then Substitute in Her Majestes Chapple, to sweare
Arter Cocke gentleman in ordinary and organiste (without pay) in
her Majestes saide chapple, untill an organiste place shalbe come
voyde, and the saide Arter Cocke (by his Honor's appointment) to
geve his attendaunce, and to supplye the wantes of organistes which
may be throughe sicknes or other urgent causes, and that at the

1600-1, Mar. 3.

commaundement of the Subdeane or Substitute of her Majestes
Chappell for the tyme being, and at his owne proper costes and
charges. The which othe was ministred accordinglie in the presence
of those gentlemen whose names are hereunder subscribed.

S. Davies.   John Heathman.   Bar. Mason, Substitute.
Nathaniell Giles.   Francis Wiborowe.   William
Lawrence.   Richarde Granwall.   Isaac Burges.
Tho. Goolde.   John Baldwine.   [f. 24b.]

1601, Nov. 23.   The Right Honorable the Lord Chamberlaine, uppon the 23th
daye of November, Anno Domini 1601, at his house in Blacke-
fryers, did geve order unto Mr. Harrison (then Substitute in her
Majestes Chapple) to sweare George Greene gentleman extraordinarye (without pay) in her Majestes Chappell.   And that the
saide George Greene should be ready at all tymes (being called by
the Subdeane or his Substitute) to gyve his attendaunce for her
Majestes better service, which was accordingely donne the 24th of
the same monethe, in the presence of those gentlemen whose names
are hereunder subscribed.

Anthony Harrison, Substitute.   Francis Wiborowe.
Thomas Sampson.   Peter Wryght.   Richard Plumley.
Thomas Woodson.   Jo. Hewlett.   S. Davies.
Isaac Burges.   John Amery.   Robert Stuckey.
Robt. Allyson.   John Baldwine.   Richarde Granwall.

[f. 24b.]

1602, June 16.   The Right Honorable Sir John Stanhop, Knight, Vice Chamberlaine to her Majestie, uppon the 16th daye of June, Anno Domini
1602, at her Majestes Court at Greenewich, gave commaundement
unto Mr. William Barnes, then Substitute in her Majestes Chappell,
to sweere Anthony Kirckbie Clarke, gentleman exterordinary
(without paye) in her Majestes Chappell, and that the said Anthonye Kirckbie shalbe redy at all tymes (beinge caulled by the
Subdeane or his Substitute) to geve his attendance for her Majestes

better service; which was accordingly done the daye and yeare above wretten, in the presence of those gentlemen whose names are hereunder wrytten.

Willm̃ Barns, Substitute.	Robert Stuckey.	John Stevens.
Thomas Sampson.	John Baldwine.	Peter Wrighte.
Richarde Granwall.	Francis Wiborowe.	Willm. Lawrence.
Henry Eveseed.	John Heathman.	S. Davies.
Robt. Allyson.		John Amery. [f. 25]

Mem. that the 22d of December, Anno 1603, uppon the com-1603, Dec. 22. mandment of the Right Honorable the Earle of Suffolke, Lorde Chamberlayne to his Majestie, directed unto the Subdeane of the Chapple, videlicet, That he should swere into the service of the Kinges Majestie Edmund Sheregowlde extraordinary in the Chapple for the next place that shall fall voyde there, the which accordinglie was donne, in the presence of these gentlemen of the Chapple whose names are here under written, without their appro-bacõn, or allowance of the sufficiency of the saide Edmund for that place, their opinions for the same beinge neyther required nor com-maunded.   Leonard Davies, Subdean.

Stephan Boughton.	Francis Wiborowe.	Nathanaell Giles.
Jo. Stevens.	Georg. Wooddeson.	Thomas Sampson.
John Amery.	John Wooddeson.	Richarde Granwall.
John Baldwine.	Anthony Harrison.	Henry Eveseed.
	Peter Wryght.	
	Thomas Woodson. [f. 25b:]	

Be it remembered that uppon the 25. day of December, Aº 1603, 1603, Dec. 25. and in firste yeare of the raigne of our Soveraigne Lorde Kinge Doctor Mount-James, the Right Worshippfull Mr. Doctor Mountague was by order ague sworne Deane of the of the Kinges Majestie sworne Deane of his honorable Chappell, in Chappell. the vestry at Hampton Courte, at which tyme Leonard Davies, beinge Subdeane, did minister the othe unto him, in the presence of the Gentlemen of the Chappell-there assembled for that cause, the day and yeare above wrytten. [f. 28.]

Mem. that the 20. of Auguste 1604, William Weste, at the especiall request of dyveres of the Gentlemen of the Chappell whose names are under written, was sworne extraordinarye in his Majesties Chappell, and the rather for that he did attend by the space of eighte dayes at the greate solemnitye of the leage of Spayne to his greate charge, yet uppon this condition followinge, namely, that the sayde William Weste shall not suie by any meanes, directly or indirectlye, as by freindes ore otherwise, to com to be sworne into ordinarye in his Highnes sayde Chappell untill he be firste called and approved fitt for the same by the Deane, Subdeane, and the majore parte of his Majesties Chappell; whereunto he hathe voluntarrye taken his oathe, as appeareth by the subscription herunto under his hande.   William West.

  Leonard Davies, Subdeane. Willm. Lawes. Frances Wiborowe. S. Davies. Anthonie Kirckby. Nathanaell Gyles. Richard Granwall. Peeter Wryghte. Georg. Wooddeson. Anthony Harrison. John Baldwine. Richard Plumley. John Amery. Thomas Sampson. Thomas Woodson. John Wooddeson. Arthur Cocke. [f. 25*b*.]

Mem. that the 24th daye of October, Anno 1604, uppon the comandment of the Right Worshipfull Mr. Deane of his Majestes Chappell, Michaell Vasco was sworne a Gentleman of his Majestes Chappell extraordinarie, and to have the next minister's place, beinge a base in his Majestes Chappell, when ther shall any be voyde ther. At ministringe of which sayd othe, the above sayd Mychaell Vasco hathe subscribed his name in the presence of the gentlemen hereunder named.   Micheall Vasco.

  Anthony Harrison, Substitute. Nathanaell Giles. Willm̃ Lawes. Stephan Boughton. Thomas Sampson. Anthonie Kirckby. Jo. Stevens. Thomas Woodson. Richard Plumley. John Amery. John Baldwine. Francis Wiborowe. Arthur Cocke. Georg. Wooddeson. Willm. Lawrence. John Wooddeson. Edmond Sheregold. [f. 26.]

Mem. that the 24th daye of Aprill in the yeare of our Lord 1605, George Tucker, of the Church of Exeter, by the consent of the Right Worshipfull Doctor Mountague, Deane of the Chappell, the Subdeane, and 26 Gentlemen therin then attendinge, was sworne Gentleman of his Majestes Chappell, who, at the takinge of his oth, bound hym selfe therby to com and to attend when he shall be commaunded by the Deane or Subdeane to waite. And allso not to sue by any meanes direct or indirecte to be admitted into the ordinarye paye of the Chappell, untill he shall be lawfully called therto by the Deane, Subdeane, and the major parte of the Gentlemen thereof then beinge, as appeareth by his certificatt to hym made, and the same here testified under his owne hand writinge, the daye and yeare first above specified. George Tucker. [f. 26b.]

Mem. that the 12th daye of Maye in the yeare of our Lord 1605, Thomas Payne of the Isle of Wight, by the consent of the Right Worshipfull Doctor Mountague, Deane of the Chappell, the Subdeane, and [a] Gentlemen therin then attendinge, was sworne of his Majestes Chappell, who, at the takinge of his oth, bound hym selfe therby not to sue by any meanes direct or indirect to be admitted in to the ordinarye paye of the Chappell, untill he shall be lawfullye called therunto by the Deane, Subdeane, and the major parte of the gentlemen thereof then beinge ; and for true testimony of the same, the said Thomas Payne hath here unto subscribed his name, the daye and yeare first above specified.

Thomas Payne. [f. 26b.]

Mem. that the 23d day of May, Anno 1605, Richard Gyles, by the consent and order of the Right Worshipfull Doctor Mountague, Deane of the Chappell, the Subdeane, and Gentlemen then attendinge, was sworne Gentleman of his Highness Chappell extraordinary, who, at the takinge of his oth, did voluntaryly binde himselfe therby not to sue by anie meanes dyrect or indirect, as by frendes or otherwaise, to be admitted into an ordynary place and pay in his Highnes

[a] Blank in MS.

saide Chappell, untyll he shalbe called and approved fytt for the same by the Deane, the Subdeane, and the major parte of the Gent then beinge; and for testimonie therof the saide Richard Gyles hath hereunto subscribed his name, the day and yeare above written, in the presence of manie of the Gentlemen then assembled.

Richard Giles.   [f. 27.]

1605, June 3.   Memorandum that the third day of June, Anno 1605, Elway Bevan, by the consent and order of the Right Worshipfull Doctor Mountague, Deane of the Chappell, the Subdeane, and Gentlemen then attendinge, was sworne Gentleman of his Majestes Chappell extraordinary, who, at the takinge of his oth, did voluntarily binde himself thereby not to sue by any means direct or indirect, as by frendes or otherwise, to be admitted into an ordinary place and pay in his Highnes sayd Chappell, untill he shallbe called and approved fitt for the same by the Deane, the Subdeane, and the major part of the Gentlemen then beinge.   And for testimony thereof the sayd Elway Bevan hath hereunto subscribed his name the day and yeare above written in the presence of many of the Gentlemen then assembled.   Elway Bevin.   [f. 27.]

1605, Dec. 15.   Memorandum that the 15 day of December, Anno 1605, Nicholas Rogers, by the consent and order of the Right Worshipfull Doctor Mountague, Deane of the Chappell, the Subdeane, and the Gentlemen then attendinge, was sworne Gentleman of his Majesties Chappell extraordinary, who, at the takinge of his oth, did voluntarily binde himself thereby not to sue by any meanes direct or indirect, as by frendes or otherwise, to be admitted into an ordinary place and pay in his Highnes sayd Chappell, untill he shall be called and approved fitt for the same by the Deane, the Subdeane, and major part of the Gentlemen then beinge.   And for testimony thereof the said Nicholas Rogers hath hereunto subscribed his name, the day and yeare above written, in the presence of many of the Gentlemen then assembled.   Nicholas Rogers.   [f. 27.]

Mem. that upon the laste daye of Maye, Anno 1606, John Lilliat, 1606, May 31. by the consent and order of the Right Worshipfull Doctor Mountague, Deane of the Chappell, the Subdeane, and Gentlemen then attendinge, was sworne Gentleman of his Majestes Chappell (éxterordinary), who, at the takinge of his othe, did vollentaryly bynd hym selfe therby not to sue by any meanes directe or indirect, as by frendes or otherwise, to be admitted in to an ordinary place of paye in his Highnes said Chappell, untill he shall be caulled and approoved fitt for the same by the Deane, the Subdeane, and major part of the Gentlemen then beinge. And for testimony ther of the said John Lilliat have here unto subscribed his name, the daye and yeare above wretten, in the presence of the Gentlemen then attendinge.

John Lilliat. [f. 27b.]

Be yt remembred that upon the 20th day of Julie, Anno Domini 1606, July 20. 1606, and in the fourth yeare of the Kinges Majesties raigne that Edw. Doughnowe is, Edward Doughtie, Clarke, Bachiler in Divinitie, (by the tie, Confessor. favour and free guift of the Right Worshipfull Mr. Doctor Mountague, Deane of the Kinges Majestes Honorable Chappell,) was sworne Confessor of his Majestes housholde at Greenwich, the day and yeare above written, whose othe was ministred unto him publiquely in the chappell ther by Leonard Davies, Subdeane, who, in testimonie therof, subscribeth his name, the daye and yeare before written. Leonard Davies, Subdean. [f. 29b.]

Mem. that uppon the firste daie of December, Anno Domini 1606, 1606, Dec. 1. John Shepperd, by the consent and order of the Right Worshipfull Doctor Mountague, Deane of the Chappell, the Subdeane and Gentlemen then attendinge, was sworne Gentleman of his Majestes Chappell (extraordinarie), who, at the takinge of his othe, did voluntarilie binde him selfe therby not to sue by any meanes direct or indirect, as by friendes or otherwise, to be admitted into an ordinarie place of paye in his Highnes sayd Chappell, untill he shalbe called and approved fitt for the same by the Deane, the Subdeane, and the major part of the Gentlemen then beynge. And for testimonie ther of the said John Shepperd have heere unto subscribed his name, the daye and yeare above written, in the presence of the Gentlemen then attendinge. John Shepperd. [f. 27*b*.]

1607, Nov. 12.
Wm. Beckett
sworne Confessor.

Be it remembred that uppon the 12th daye of November, Anno 1607, and in the fyfthe yeare of the Kinges Majestes raigne that nowe is, William Beckett, Clarke, Master of Artes, was (by the favoure and free guift of the Right Worshipfull Doctor Mountague, Deane of the Kinges Majestes Hon. Chappell,) sworne Confessor of his Majestes Housholde at Whitehall, the daye and yeare above written, whose othe was ministred unto him publicklye in the chappell ther by Anthony Harrison, Substitute; who, in testimony therof, subscribeth his name the daye and yeare before written.

Anthony Harrison. [f. 29*b*.]

1609-10,
March 24.

Thomas Pearse sworne Pisteler the 24th of Marche, 1609, with this addicŏn:

You shall also sweare that if you lyve unto the full age of 21 yeares, that then accordinge to your faithfull promise now made you shall take uppon you the holy order of a Deacon in Godes church, or to procure a dispensacŏn therby to doe his Majestie the office and dutie of a Deacon in his Royall Chappell, so longe as you shalbe a member of this place. In testimony heerof he subscribed his name the daye and yeare above sayd,

per me, Thomam Pearce. [f. 30*b*.]

1611, May 5.

Ezechiell Wade sworne Pisteler the 5th of May, 1611, with this addicŏn:

You shall also sweare that if you shall live untyll Christmas next, that then or by that tyme, accordinge to your faithfull promise now made, you shall take uppon you the holy orders of a Deacon in Godes churche, therby to doe his Majestie the office and dutie of a Deacon in his Royall Chappell so longe as you shall be a member of this place. In testimony heer of he subscribed his name the daie and yeare above sayd. Ezech. Waad. [f. 30*b*.]

Mem. that uppon the 16th daie of June, Anno Domini 1611, Thomas Brasfield, by the order of the Reverend Father in God, James Mountague, Bishoppe of Bathe and Welles, and Deane of his Majestes Chappell, was sworne Gentleman of the Chappell extraordinarie, who at the takinge of his othe did voluntarily binde him selfe thereby not to sue by any meanes direct or indirect, as by friendes or otherwise, to be admitted into an ordinary place of paie in his highnes sayd Chappell, untill he shalbe called and approved fitt for the same by the Deane, Subdeane, and major part of the gentlemen then beinge. And for testemony therof the sayd Thomas Brasfield hathe hereunto putte and subscribed his name, the daie and yeare above written, in the presence of the gentlemen then attendinge. Thomas Brasfield. [f. 28.]

Mem^d that uppon the first daie of October, 1611, Wm. Lawes, by the order of the Reverend Father in God, James Mountague, Bishopp of Bathe and Welles, and Deane of his Majestes Chappell, without paie, a parte of whose othe was not to sue to be in ordinarie paye, unlesse he be first lawfully called therunto by the Deane, Subdeane, and major parte of the Company. In wittnes heerof he hathe subscribed his name the daie and yeare above written,

p me, William Lawes. [f. 25.]

Mem. that uppon the 28th of Marche, 1615, John Miners, gentleman, by order of the Reverend Father in God the Lord Bishopp of Bathe and Welles, and Deane of his Majestes Chappell, together with the consent of the gentlemen, was sworne Gentleman in Ordinarie of his Majestes said Chappel for the next place that shall fall voyd there whatsoever, with addicōn unto his othe in this manner, viz. You shall also sweare that if you shall live one quarter of a yeare after you shall enter into paye in his Majesties Chappell,

1611, June 16.

1611, Oct. 1.

1615, March 28. Jo. Myners, Gent' sworne in Ordinary for the next place.

you shall then, or by that time, accordinge to your faithfull promise now made, take uppon you the holy orders of a Deacon in Godes churche, therby to doe his Majestie the office and dutie of a Deacon in his Royall Chappell, so longe as you shalbe a member of this place. Mem. these wordes followinge weare delivered in the former part of his othe, viz. which is a gentleman of his Majestes Chappell in Ordinarie, for the next place there that shalbe voyd of what parte soever. In testimonie heerof we have heerunto subscribed our names the daie and yeare above written.

Leonard Davies, Subdean.	Jo. Hewlett.	George Sheyffeilde.
Antho. Harrison.	S. Davies.	John Wooddeson.
Ezech. Waad.	John Amery.	Willm. Crosse.
	David Hinle.	[f. 31*b*.]

1615, Apl. 13.   Mem. that uppon the 13th daie of Aprill, 1615, by order of the Reverend Father Lord Bishop of Bathe and Welles, Deane of his Majestes Chappell, John Amyon, of the cittie of West Chester, was

Jo. Amyon sworne Gentle man Extraordinary.

sworne Gentleman of his Majestes Chappell Extraordinarie. In testimony wherof I have subscribed my name the daie and yeare above written.

Stephan Boughton.   [f. 32.]

1618, June 29.

Memorandum, that uppon the 29th daie of June 1618, Francis Sennock, by order of the Right Reverend Father in God the Lord Bishopp of Winton, Deane of his Majestes Chappell, and consent of the Subdeane and Gentlemen then attendinge, was sworne Gentleman in Ordinary without paye, who, at the takinge of his othe, did voluntarylie bynd himselfe therby not to sue by any meanes direct or indirect, as by friendes or otherwise, to be admitted into an ordinary place of paie in his Highnes sayd Chappell, untill he shalbe called and approved fitt for the same by the Deane, Subdeane, and major parte of the Gentlemen then attendinge. And for testemony therof the said Frauncis Sennock hath heerunto subscribed his name the daie and yeare above said in the presence of the gentlemen then attendinge.   1618.

Fra. Sennocke. [f. 35*b*.]

Be it remembred that uppon the 29th daie of June 1619, by order 1619, June 29. of the Right Reverend Father in God Lancellott, Lord Bishop of Winchester, Deane of his Majestes Chappell, Roger Nitingegale, Clark, was sworne Gentleman of his Maj^tes Chappell in Ordinary, to succead in the place and paye of the next basse that shall happen to die within his Majestes said Chappell, which sayd othe was given by the approbacōn of the Subdeane and gentlemen then attendinge. In testimony wherof we have heereunto subscribed our names the daie and yeare above written.

Leonard Davies, Subdeane.	Nathanaell Gyles.
Antho. Harrison.	George Cooke.	Richard Coton.
John Amery.	George Sheffeilde.	George Wooddeson.
Jo. Hewlett.	Peter Hopkins.	[f. 36*b*.]

Be it remembred that uppon the 29th daie of June 1620, by order 1620, June 29. of the Reverend Father in God Lancellott, Lord Bishop of Winton, Deane of his Majestes Chappell, Thomas Peirs was sworne Gentleman of his Majestes Chappell in Ordinarie to succeede in the place and paye of James Davies, when it shall please God to make his place voyd by his death, which sayd othe was given by the approbacōn and good likinge of the Subdeane and gentlemen then attendinge, beinge 24 in number. In testemony wherof we have heerunto subscribed our names the daie and yeare above written.

Leonard Davies, Subdeane.

Antho. Harrison.	Orlando Gibbons.	Tho. Day.
Richard Coton.	Tho. Tomkins.	Edm. Nelham.
Jo. Stephens.	Witt West.	Walter Porter.
Jo. Hewlett.	George Cooke.	Roger Nightingal.
John Amery.	John Clarke.	John Frost.
Geo. Wooddeson.	Peter Hopkins.	
John Wooddeson.	Wittm Crosse.	[f. 37.]

Be it remembred that uppon the 26th day of Aprill 1621, by
warrant from the Reverend Father in God Lancellott, Lord Bishop
of Winton, Deane of his Majestes Chappell, John Frost, Clark, a
base from Salisbury, was sworne Gentleman of his Majestes Chappell
in Ordinarie, for the next place of a base that shall fall voyd in the
sayd Chappell. And this was don by the approbacion and good
likinge of all the Gentlemen then attendinge. In testimony heerof
we have heerunto subscribed our names the day and yeare above
written.   Antho. Harrison, Substitute.
                                            John Hewlett.
                                            John Amery.   [f. 35.]

Be yt remembred that uppon the 29th daye of March, Anno
Domini 1629, and in the fifte yeare of the Kinges Majesties Raigne
that nowe is, Exechiell Waad, Clarke, one of the gentlemen of his
Majestes Chappell (by the favor and free guift of the Right Reverend
Father in God William Laud, Lord Bishop of London and Deane
of his Majesties Chappell, by virtue of his warrant,) was sworne Confessor of his Majestes housholde att Whitehall, the daye and yeare
above written, whose othe was ministred unto him publickly in the
chappell there, by Richard Coton, Substitute, whoe in testimony
therof subscribeth his name the daye and yeare above written.
                                            Richard Coton.   [f 38b.]

Mr. John Stephens, Clearke of the Check to the gentlemen of his
Maj^tes Chappell, died the 13th of May, and Thomas Day, beeing
then Master of the Children, was chosen and sworne Cleark of the
Check in his place on Whitson Even following, and Richard
Jennings, a base, was sworne in Mr. Steven's place, the twenteth of
Aprill following. [f. 1b.]

Be it remembred that upon the   day of June, Anno Domini
1660, and in the 12th yeare of the reigne of our gracious Soveraigne King Charles the Second, Roger Nightingale, Clerke, one of
the gentlemen of His Majesties Chappell, was sworne Confessor of
His Majesties Household. [f. 38b.]

Be it remembred that upon the 29th day of November, Anno 1661, Nov. 29.
Domini 1661, and in the 13th yeare of the reigne of our gracious Philip Tinker
Soveraigne Lord King Charles 2., Philip Tinker, Clerke, Master of sworne Con-
Arts, and one of the gentlemen of his Majesties Chappell, was fessor.
sworne Confessor of His Majesties houshold by the Right Worship-
full Dr. Walter Jones, Subdeane of his Majesties Chappell Royall,
upon the warrant and free gift of the Right Reverend Father in
God Gilbert Sheldon, Lord Bishop of London and Deane of his
Maj^{ties} sayd Chappell Royall. [f. 38b.]

June 7, 1662. At Hampton Courte. Be it remembred that 1662, June 7.
Mr. George Yardly was this day admitted and sworne Gentleman
of his Majesties Chappell Royall by our Reverend Subdeane Dr.
Walter Jones, in the presence of us whose names are hereunto subscribed.   Philip Tinker, Confessor to his Maties household.
     John Sayer, Gentleman of his Maties Chappell Royall.
     Tho. Raynes, Seargent of the Vestery.   [f. 44b.]

1662, Nov. 8.
Tho. Blagrave,
These are to will and require you that, upon sight hereof, you Clerke of the
sweare Thomas Blagrave, Gentleman of his Majesties Chappell Check, 1662.
Royall, into the office of Clerke of the Check, voyd by the death of
Mr. Henry Lawes lately deceased, and this shall be your warrant.
Given at Whitehall this eighth day of November 1662.
To Dr. Walter Jones, Subdeane of   Gilt London, Dean of his
his Majesties Chappell Royall.   Maties Chappell. [f. 38b.]
1663, Aug. 8.

This day was Mr. William Wake admitted and sworne Gentleman of his Majesties Chappell Royall into the next place that falls,
by our Reverend Subdeane Dr. Walter Jones, in the presence of
Capt. Henry Cooke, Master of the Children, &c.
     The Coppy of my Lord's Warrant:—
Mr. Subdeane. I desire you to sweare William Wake one of
the Gentlemen of the King's Chappell into the next place that falls,

and this shall be your sufficient warrant.   Given under my hand this seventh day of August 1663.

Giłł London. Dean of his Maties Chappell.   [f. 44b.]

1672, Sept. 11.   Mr. Subdeane. I desire you to sweare Burges Howe one of the Gentlemen of his Majesties Chappell into the place of Capt. Cooke lately deceased, and this shall be your warrant.   Given under my hand this 11th day of Sept. 1672.

Walt. Wigorn. Deane of his Maties Chappell.   [f. 45.]

1674, July 21.   July 21, 1674. On which day   Powell, Clerk, Bachelor of Arts, was sworne and admitted Gentleman of his Maties Chappell Royall, into the place of Pelham Humfrey lately deceased, by the Right Reverend Father in God Walter Lord Bishop of Worcester and Deane of his Majesties said chappell.   In the presence of

J. Price, Pub. Notary.   [f. 45.]

1675-6, Feby. 19.   These are to certifie that John Billon La marre is sworne and admitted in the place and quallity of one of the Gentlemen of his Majesty's Chappell Royall in ordinary, by vertue of which place he is to enjoy all rights and priveledges thereto belonging. Given under my hand and seale the 19th of February 1675-6, and in the 28th yeare of his Majesties Reigne.

H. London. Dean of his Majesties Chappell.   [f. 45.]

1712-13.   Doctor Ralph Battell, Subdean of Her Majesty's Chappells, departed this life March the 20th, 1712-13, and the Rev. Mr. John Dolben, A.M. of Christ Church, Oxon, the only son of Sir Gilbert Dolben, Bart. was sworn Subdean of the said Royal Chapells, by the Right Revd Father in God Henry Lord Bishop of London and Dean of Her Majesties Chapells Royal.   [f. 15]

1727, Nov. 22.   This is to remember, that on account of the great age and infirmities of the Rev^d Mr. John Gostling, Priest in ordinary of his

Maj. Royal Chappell, living at Canterbury (being a Minor Canon of that Metropolitan Church), whereby he was altogether unable to perform a journey up to London in order to be sworn and admitted into the Chappell Royal as newly confirm'd by his Maj. King George the Second, I did, with the approbation of the Rt. Revd Edmund Lord Bishop of London, Dean of the said Chappel Royal, commission the Rev^d Dr. Elias Sydall, Prebendary of the Church of Canterbury, in residence there, to administer the oath of admission into the Chappel to the said Mr. John Gostling, by virtue of a warrant directed to me by the abovesaid Lord Bishop of London, to swear to admit the said Mr. Gostling into the chappel. N.B. The commission by me sent to the Rev^d Dr. Sydall was written on paper stamped with sixpenny stamps. Given under my hand this 22^d day of November, Annoque Domini 1727.

Edw. Aspinwall, Subdean. [f. 55b.]

Mr. John Weldon died May the 7th, 1736, and by virtue of a warrant from the Right Reverend Edmund Lord Bishop of London, Dean of his Maj. Chapels Royal, I have sworn and admitted Mr. William Boyce into his place of Composer, June 21st, 1736. 1736.

Geo. Carleton, Subdean.

By virtue of a warrant bearing date the same day Mr. Jonathan Martin was sworn and admitted Organist in the said Mr. Weldon's place by me Geo. Carleton, Subdean. [f. 57b.]

Whereas the Right Reverend the Lord Bishop of London, Dean 1736, June 21. of his Majesty's Chapels Royal, has appointed William Boyce to be Composer, and Jonathan Martin to be organist of the said chapels; and whereas the place of Organist has much more duty and attendance belonging to it than the place of Composer (both which were enjoyed by Mr. Weldon lately deceas'd, during whose long indisposition the two places were joyntly supply'd by the two persons aforesaid), I the said William Boyce do promise and agree that so long as I shall continue in the place of Composer, I will perform one third part of the duty and attendance belonging to the Organist, provided that I am allow'd one third part of the travelling charges belonging to the place. And I Jonathan Martin promise to compose Anthems or services for the use of his Majesty's Chapel whenever required by the Subdean for the time being. In witness whereunto We have set our hands this twenty-first day of June 1736. William Boyce.

Jona. Martin. [f. 58.]

1736, Dec. 8.   December 8, 1736. By virtue of two warrants from the Lord Bishop of London, Dean of his Maj. Chapels Royal, I have sworne and admitted the Reverend John Higgate, Master of Arts, into the places and offices of Confessor of His Majesty's Houshold, and Priest in Ordinary of his Maj. Chapel Royal, vacant by the death of the Reverend Mr Abraham Sharp.

Geo. Carleton, Subdean. [f. 58b.]

1736, Dec. 15.   By virtue of a warrant from the Lord Bishop of London, Dean of his Maj. Chapels Royal, I have sworn and admitted Mr. Francis Rowe into the place of Gentleman of his Maj. Chapels Royal, now vacant by the death of Mr. John Freeman.

Geo. Carleton, Subdean. [f. 58b.]

1737, May 10.   May the 10th, 1737. By virtue of a warrant from the Rt. Revd Edmund Lord Bishop of London, Dean of his Maj. Chapels Royal, I have sworn and admitted Mr. John Travers Organist of the said chapels in the room of Mr. Jonathan Martin deceas'd.

Geo. Carleton, Subdean. [f. 57b.]

1737, May 27.   By virtue of a warrant from the Rt. Rev. Edmund the Lord Bishop of London, Dean of his Maj. Chapels Royal, I have sworne and admitted the Revd Mr. James Serces into the place of Minister of the French Chapel in St. James' Palace, vacant by the death of the Rev^d Mr. Philip Menard.

Geo. Carleton, Sub-Dean. [f. 58b.]

By virtue of a warrant from the Rt. Revd Edmund Lord Bishop 1737, Sept. 21. of London, Dean of his Maj. Chapels Royal, I have sworne and admitted the Rev^d Mr. Francis Flahault into the place of Reader of the French Chapel, vacant by the death of the Rev^d Mr. Declaris. [f. 58b.]

By virtue of a warrant from the Right Revd Edmund Lord 1739. Bishop of London, Dean of His Majesty's Chapels Royal, the Rev^d Mr. John Smith was sworn into the place of one of the Priests in ordinary of his Majesty's Chapel Royal (vacant by the death of the Rev^d Mr. Richard Powell), the 30th day of March 1739, by me,

Geo. Carleton, Subdean. [f. 15.]

By virtue of a warrant from the Rt. Rev. Edmund Lord Bishop 1740, April 4. of London, Dean of his Maj. Chapels Royal, I have sworn and admitted Mr. Prince Gregory into the place of Gentleman of his Maj. Chapel Royal, vacant by the death of Dr. William Turner.

Geo. Carleton, Sub-Dean. [f. 59.]

By virtue of a warrant from the Rt. Rev. Edmund Lord 1740-1, Jan.29. Bishop of London, Dean of his Maj. Chapels Royal, I have sworn and admitted Mr. Anselm Baily into the place of Gentleman of his Maj. Chapel Royal, vacant by the death of Mr. John Church.

Geo. Carleton, Sub-Dean. [f. 59.]

By virtue of a warrant from the Rt. Rev. Edmund Lord 1741-2, Jan.18. Bishop of London, Dean of his Maj. Chapels Royal, I have sworn and admitted Mr. Peter Gillier into the place of Violist of his Maj. Chapels Royal, vacant by the death of Francisco Goodsens.

Geo. Carleton, Sub-Dean. [f. 59.]

1742, May 21.   By virtue of a warrant from the Rt. Rev. Edmund Lord Bishop of London, Dean of his Maj. Chapels Royal, I have sworn and admitted the Rev^d Mr. Bernard Diemel into the place or office of Preacher of the Dutch Chapel, within the Palace of St. James's, vacant by the death of the Rev^d Mr. Phineas Philibert Pielat.

Geo. Carleton, Sub-Dean.   [f. 59.]

1743, May 10.   By virtue of a warrant from the Rt. Rev. Edmund Lord Bishop of London, Dean of his Maj. Chapels Royel, I have sworn and admitted Mr. William Richardson into the place of Gentleman of his Maj. Chapels Royal, vacant by the death of Mr. Thomas Bell.

Thos. Baker.   [f. 59b.]

1743, Aug. 15.   By virtue of a warrant from the Rt. Rev. Edmund Lord Bishop of London, Dean of his Maj. Chapels Royal, I have sworn and admitted Mr. Nicholas Ladd into the place of Gentleman of his Maj. Chapels Royal, vacant by the death of Mr. James Chelsum.

Thos. Baker.   [f. 59b.]

1743, Nov. 12.   By virtue of a warrant from the Rt. Rev. Edmund Lord Bishop of London, Dean of his Maj. Chapels Royal, I have sworn and admitted Mr. Thomas Vandernan into the place of Gentleman of his Maj. Chapels Royal, vacant by the death of Mr. Samuel Weeley.

Thos. Baker.   [f. 59b.]

1743-4, Mar. 13.   By virtue of a warrant from the Rt. Rev. Edmund Lord Bishop of London, Dean of his Maj. Chapels Royal, I have sworn and admitted the Rev. Mr. Anselm Baily into the place of Priest in Ordinary of his Maj. Chapels Royal, vacant by the death of the Reverend Mr. John Abbot.   Thos. Baker.   [f. 59b.]

1743-4, Mar. 13.   By virtue of a warrant from the Rt. Rev. Edmund Lord Bishop of London, Dean of his Maj. Chapels Royal, I have sworn and admitted the Rev^d Mr. Henry Evans into the place of Priest in

Ordinary of his Maj. Chapels Royal, vacant by the death of the
Reverend Mr. John Abbot.   Thos. Baker. [f. 59b.]

By virtue of a warrant from the Rt. Rev. Edmund Lord Bishop   1743-4,
of London, Dean of his Maj. Chapels Royal, I have sworn and   Mar. 13.
admitted Mr. Robert Wass into the place of Gentleman of his Maj.
Chapels Royal, vacant by the resignation of Mr. Anselm Bayly.
      Thos. Baker. [f. 59b.]

By virtue of a warrant from the Rt. Rev. Edmund Lord Bishop 1744, Apl. 14.
of London, Dean of his Maj. Chapels Royal, I have sworne and
admitted Mr. Ben. Mence into the place of Gentleman of his Maj.
Chapels Royal, vacant by the death of Mr. Francis Hughes.
      Thos. Baker. [f. 60.]

By virtue of a warrant from the Rt. Rev. Edmund Lord Bishop 1744, Apl. 14.
of London, Dean of his Maj. Chapels Royal, I have sworne and
admitted Mr. William Savage into the place of Gentleman of his
Maj. Chapels Royal, vacant by the death of Mr. Francis Hughes.
      Thos. Baker. [f. 60.]

By virtue of a warrant from the Rt. Rev. Edmund Lord Bishop 1744, Dec. 11.
of London, Dean of his Maj. Chapels Royal, I have sworn and
admitted the Rev. Mr. Michael Nollet into the place of Reader of
the French Chapel in St. James' Palace, vacant by the death of the
Revd Mr. Francis Flahault.   Thos. Baker. [f. 60.]

III.—The Disposal of Payments due to Deceased Gentlemen.*

How the dead paies have bin allowed and disposed of after the
deathes of the Gentlemen of the Chappell.

1568. Wm. Ivett from West Chester was sworne gentleman the

* This List occupies f. 1 and the reverse in the original MS.

xviijth of June, in Mr. Norrice['s] place, being allowed all June bord wages by the Green cloth for his paines and charges, and xviij daies for quarter's wages.

1581. Richard Farrant died the xxxth of November, and Anthony Todd was sworn yeoman in his place the xxvjth of Februarie, being allowed the bord wages for December and Januarie before by the Green cloth, and the wages from the death of Farrant.

1581. Crue Sharp sworne gentleman ye xxvjth of Februarie, and received wages for Januarie.

1581. Mr. Leonard Davies, minister from Lichfield, was sworne Gospeller in Mr. Jones['s] roome the xvth of Maye, and received paye from the xth of March before, by warrant from the Lord Chamberlaine.

1582. Edmund Browne, Tho. Woodson, and Robt. Tallentire were sworne gentlemen the xxvth of December, in Mr. Morcock's roome, in Mr. Ednie's roome, and in Mr. Moore's roome. And these three persons had both wages and bord wages from the day of the others' deathes, untill the day of the swearing by warrant from the Lord Chamberlaine unto the Green cloth, out of the which the Clark of the Check had of each of them xx^s.

1613. Robert Stone died the second of July, and Matthew White was admitted Gospeller by his death the 2^d of November following; the wages in the meane time was disposed of by the Right Reverend Father in God James Lord Bishop of Bathe and Welles, Deane of his Majesty's Chappell.

1613. Jo. Bull, Doctor of Musick, went beyond the seaes and served the Archduke at Michaelmas, and Peter Hopkins was sworne in his place the xxviijth of December following; the wagis in the mean time was disposed of by the aforesaid Deane in this sort, viz. to Mr. Cotton xx^s. To Mr. Gibbons iij^{li} vj^s viij^d. To Mr. Hooper iij^{li} vj^s viij^d. To the co[mmon] servant ij^s vj^d; and to the Clark of the Check the rest, which was xlj^s i^d.

9 17 0

1615. Tho. Sampson, Clark of the Check, was drowned the 24th of Aprill, and Jo. Miners was sworne in his place the iiij[th] of June following, the wages was disposed of by the Deane from Mr. Sampson's death unto the end of June following unto Mr. Sampson's wife.

1615. Jo. Myners died the second of July, and Tho. Daye was sworne in his place the last of September following. The wages in y[e] meane tyme was disposed of by our Lord Deane in this sorte, viz. to Mr. Daye v[li]. To Mrs. Sampson, to make my Lord's guift to her x[li], the some of xxx[s], and to the Clerk of the Check xxxij[s] vj[d]. $8^{li}\ 2^s\ 6^d.$

1616. David Henly died the xij[th] of August and Jo. Greene was preferred to y[e] place by order of our Lord Deane the xxviij[th] of December followinge: the wages was disposed of in the meane tyme by the Deane in this sort, viz. to Jo. Greene iij[li], to Mr. Coton xx[s], to Mr. Henlies father and mother xl[s], to the Clark of the Check xvij[s] vj[d]. $8^{li}\ 2^s\ 6^d.$

1617. Jo. Greene was dismissed from his Maj[tes] service the xxviij[th] of September for his ill behaviour, and for marrying of two wives, and Edmund Nelham was sworne in his place the vth of November followinge: the wages in the meane tyme was disposed of by the Deane in this sort, viz. given to Mr. Coton xx[s]. Item, to Greene hostis [sic] by my Lordes order xxx[s]. Item, to Mr. Nelham vij[s] ix[d]. Item, to Mr. Subdean iij[s] iiij[d]. Item, to the Comon servant for wages xviij. Item, to y[e] Clark of the Check the rest xxvij[s] xj[d]. S[umma] v[li] vj[s]. $4^{li}\ 10^s\ 6^d.$

1621. Anthony Harrison, Clark, died the 20th of Febr. and Jo. Frost was sworne in his place the xiiij[th] of Aprill 1623: the wages in the meane time was disposed of by the Right Reverend Laurence Bishop of Winton, and Deane of the Chappell, in this sort, viz. to Mr. Amn[er] for attending in the vacacõn xx[s]. To Mr. Frost, who succeaded in the place iij[li]. To the Clerk of the Check iiij[li], and the rest $34^{li}\ 13^s.$

for bookes and prick[ing] of songes for the Chappell as apperes which is xxvj^{li} xiij^s.

1623. Wm. Bird died the iiijth of July, and Jo. Cr[oker] was admitted into his place the 24th of . . . . . * followinge ; the wages in the meane ty[me were] disposed of by the foresayd Bishop our [Deane in] this manner, viz.: to Mr. Richard

14^{li} 11^s.

Bough[ton ?] sent for to be herd uppon the death of [Mr.] Davies xx^s. To the Clark of the Ch[eck] . . . . To Mr. Steephens the xxixth of May . . . parte for pricking of a sett of bookes for the . . . . iij^{li} iij^s. To him the third of December . . . . for pricking in the bookes iij^{li} xij^s. Item, for ij quire of ruled [paper]. Item, paid for a reame of ordinary paper v^s. Item, Mr. Stephens the third of May 1627 for paper, pricking 20 smale bookes for the Chappell iij^{li} ij^s.

1623. John Amery died the 18th of July and Ralph Amn[er], a base from Winsor, was sworne in his place the xvjth of December following: the wages in the meane tyme was disposed of by

13^{li} 10^s 6^d.

our Lord Deane, viz.: allowed by his Lordship for the charge of the gentlemen and children for iij choches [coaches ?] and boat hire from Westminster to Harmonsworth to the funerall of Subdean Davies, as by bill, v^{li} x^d. To the Clerk of the Check xl^s. To Mr. Stephens for pricking as in the next before iij^{li}.

1623. Mr. Leonard Davies, Subdeane, died the ixth of November, and John Cooke was sworne in his place the xvjth of December followinge, with this proviso, that the wages to the end of the quarter should be given to Mr. Subdeanes wiffe by my Lord our Deanes order.

1625. John Croker died the 25th of August and George Wooddeson the yonger was sworne in this place the 20th of November following ; the wages in the meane time was disposed of in

6^{lr} 15^s 6^d.

this sort, viz.: given to Jo. Croker's wyddow xlvj^s. To Mr. Tomkins xl^s for composing of many songes against the coro-

* This leaf of the MS. is, unfortunately, much dilapidated, and in parts torn away.

nacõn of Kinge Charles. To Mr. Stephens for pricking those songes xxx^s. To the Clerk of the Check the rest, which is xix^s vj^d.

1625. John Cooke died the xijth of September, and Henry Lawes was sworne in his place the first of Januarie followinge. The wages in the meane tyme was disposed of by my Lord Deanes order in this sorte, viz.: given to Jo. Cookes widdowe xlvij^s. To Mr. Stephens towards the pricking of songes in the sett of bookes iiij^{li} x^s. To the Clark of the Check the rest, xxvj^s.

[1625?]. Peter Hopkins died the xxvth of November, and Richard Boughton was sworne in his place the 29th of Aprill 1626; the wages in the meane tyme was disposed thus: To Mr. Stephens, in full paiment of xxxvj^{li} ix^s, for pricking the said sett of bookes xj^{li} xix^s, and to the Clark of the Checke the rest, which is xxj^s ix^d.

IV.—RECORDS OF SUITS FOR ADDITIONAL PAY.

Wheras it is intended that we, Leonard Davies, Subdeane, and all the Gentlemen of the Chappell now beinge, will become suters to her Majestie for the obtayninge of some gifte or graunte which may be for the yearly increase of our livynges. And wheras it is thought inconvenient that all the body of the company should take paines and follow the saide suite: We, therfore, whose names are subscribed, doe by this our acte aucthorise and allowe our saide Subdeane and sixe of the auntientes of our companie (moste commonly waytinge) firste to graunte and geve to one Mr. Hills, of London, gentleman (at whose handes we doe receive the suite that we hope to obtayne of her Majestie), suche consideracõn or yearlye parte or pencõn issuinge out of the proffittes of the same sute (when it shalbe obtayned) as he our Subdeane and those sixe of our felowshipp

1595-6.
Jany 20.

(joyned with him) shall thinke convenient: And further, we hereby aucthorise and allow our Subdeane and those sixe his assistantes or associates to doe any acte or thinge whatsoever wherby our suite may be by them the rather obtayned, and also to geve in rewarde to suche persons whom they shall fynde readie and willinge to helpe and further the same our suite suche some and somes of money as shall seeme good in their discretions: Provided alwaies, that those consideracōns and rewardes shall not be demaunded nor taken out of the wages of the Gentlemen of the Chappell, but shalbe paide of the firste proffittes which should come to our companye by meanes of the suite which shalbe delivered us by Mr. Hills, and geven and graunted to us by her Majestie: And, further, also, we doe ordayne that whosoever of our felowship of the Chapple shall refuce to agree and to subscribe to this order and acte (beinge therto required) shall not be partaker with us of the benefite which shall arise to us by the suite, when it is obtayned. In witnes that we, whose names are under written, have agreed to confirme every parte of this our acte we have subscribed therto this 20th day of Januarie Anno Domini 1595, et Anno Tricesimo octavo Regni Reginæ Dominæ nostræ Elizabethæ.

By me Leonard Davies, Subdean.		Thomas Sampson.
Anthony Todd.	Anthony Harrison.	Richard Granwall.
Robert Tallentyer.	William Barns.	Crue Sharpe.
William Randall.	Thomas Madokes.	Thomas Woodsonn.
George Waterhouse.	William Lawrence.	Robert Allison.
Petor Wryght.		Tho. Goolde.

[f. 23b.]

1604. Dec. 5.

The Lord Charles Haward, High Admirall, the Lord Tho. Haward, Lo.

The Tyme of the Chapples Augmentacōn, quinto Decem. 1604.

Be it remembred by all that shall succeede us that in the yeare of our Lord God (1604) and in the second yeare of the reigne of oure most gracious soveraigne Lord James (the first of that name) by the grace of God, of Great Brittaine, Fraunce, and Ireland, *Chamberlaine, The Lo. Harrie Haward, Earle of Northampton, the Lo. Cicill, Viscount Cramborne, the Lo. Knowles, Treasurer of Houshold.* Kinge. After a long and chargable sute continued for increase of wages, in the end by the furtherance of certaine honorable persons (named in the margent) Comissioners, and by the speciall favour and help of the Right Worshipfull Doctor Mountague, Deane of the Chappell then beinge, and by the great paynes of Leonard Davies, Subdeane, and of Nathanael Gyles, then Master of the Children, with other auntientes of the place, the Kinges most excellent Majestie of his Royall bountye and regard pleased to ad to the late intertainement of the Chappell ten powndes per annum to every man, so increasinge there stipendes from thirtie to fortie powndes per annum, and allso augmented the twelve childrens allowance from six pence to ten pence p diem: And to the Sergeant of the Vestrie was then geven increase of x^{li} per annum, as to the gentlemen, and to the two yeomen and groome of the vestrie the increase of fower pence per diem as to the twelve children: His Royall Majestie ordayninge that these severall increases should be payde to the members of the Chappell and vestrie in the nature of boardwages for ever. Now it was thought meete that seeinge the intertainement of the Chappell was not augmented of manye yeares by any his Majesties progenitors *Cursed be the partie that taketh this leafe out of this booke. Amen.* (Kinges and Queenes raigninge before his Highnes), that therefore his Kinglie bountie in augmenting the same (as is before shewed) should be recordid, to be had ever in remembrance, that therby not only wee (men and children now lyevinge), but all those allso which shall succeede us in the Chappell shuld daylie see cause (in oure most devoute prayers) humblye to beseech the Devine Majestie to blesse his Highnes, oure gracious Queene Ann, Prince Henrie, and all and everye of that Royall progenie, with blessinges both spirituall and temporall, and that from age to age and everlastinglye, and let us all praye Amen, Amen.

The names of the gentlemen lyvinge at the tyme of this augmentacõn graunted:—

Leonard Davies,
Subdeane.

Barthol. Mason,

Antho. Harrison,

Robert Stuckey,

Steven Boughton,

William Lawes,

Antho. Kerbie,
Chaplaines.

Doctor Bull,
Organist.

Nathanaell Gyles,
Master of the Children.

Tho. Sampson,
Clearke of the Checke.

Robert Stone.

Willm̃ Byrde.

Rychard Granwell.

Crue Sharp.

Edmund Browne.

Tho. Woodson.

Henrie Eveseede.

Robert Allison.

Jo. Stephens.

Jo. Hewlett.

Rychard Plumley.

Tho. Goolde.

Peter Wryght.

Will. Lawrence.

James Davies.

Jo. Amerye.

Jo. Baldwin.

Francis Wyborow.

Arthur Cocke.

George Woodson.

Jo. Woodson.

Edmund Shirgoold.

Edmund Hooper.

The Officers of the Vestrie then were—

Ralphe Fletcher,
Seargeant.

Jo. Patten,
Robert Hewes, } Yeomen.

Harrye Allred,
Groome.

[f. 31.]

V.—Orders, Decrees, and Reprimands, referring to Gentlemen, &c.

1592, June 18. A perpetuall decrye made in a Chapter holden at Greenwich by Anthonye Anderson, Substitute for the presente of her Majestes Chappell Royall, and the reste of the Worshippful Companye the gentlemen thereof there assembled in the vestrye, the 18. of June, 1592. Eliz. 34.

Be it knowne to all our felows worshippful companye, as well for the presente as the tymes herafter, for all tymes to come, that in dewe consideration of our moste bounden dewties to God our heavenly Father, to our dread Soveraigne Ladye the Queenes Majestie, and the contynuance of deserved creditt to the sufficient service of God and her Majestie, in her sayd Chappell, as also in respecte that the charges or gratulation of the parties admitted hath hitherto bene of so small valewe that sondrye (some of whom not so fitt as themselves and frends supposed for so honorable a service,) have attempted to obteyne favour to be extraordinarye of our sayd Companye, and happelye some have attayned by means therunto. We nowe, in a solemne chapter assembled, havinge dewe care of the premisses, have in full consente determyned and decried that no person or persons, of what qualitie, deserte, or place soever, shalbe admitted by our consentes into our sayd companye extraordinarye herafter at any tyme but in and by the common consente by voyces in the chapter where and whensoever the Courte shall then be, and the oathe to be administred to the partie so chosen and admitted only by the Subdeane, or his Substitute, in the presence of thre at the leaste of the companye: And forther it is also by the same companye in chapter decried, that everye person or persons that herafter the date herof shalbe at their suicte (not called by the companye to our societie) admitted by oathe extraordynarye into our feloship, shall paye, or cawse to be payd, presently at and upon his sayd submission, subscription, and admission, the some of five poundes of lawfful Englishe moneye to the officer presente, or the Clercke of our Checke, for and to the use of the sayd companye, as by the officer and clercke aforsaid shall from tyme to tyme be thoghte convenyente. In witnes wherof, and of the whole premisses, and everye parte of them, we of the sayd companye, Chaplens and Gentlemen of her Majestes sayd Chappell, have subscribed our names, the 18. daye of June, 1592. Eliz. Dominæ nostræ Reginæ xxxiiij°. Greenwich.

Anth. Anderson, Substitute.
Leonard Davies.
Anthony Harrison.

William Randall.
George Waterhouse.
Jo. Hewlett.

Thomas Sampson.
Robert Stone.
Richard Granwall.
Robert Tallentyer.
Anthony Todd.
Henry Eveseede.
Isaac Burges.
John Stephines.
Richard Plumley.
Thomas Golde.   [f. 19.]

Dec. 2, 1592.
Eliz. 35.

Be it knowne, to whomsoever it may concerne, that in a chapter holden by us, the Subdeane, Chaplens, and Gentlemen of her Majestes Chappell Royall, in full porpose to avoyde a great inconvenience very moche hertofore offred, to the no small hindcrance of her Majestes service in her sayd Chappell. That whosoever of us whose names be underwritten shall at any time herafter, eyther when any place shalbe voyd in the sayd chapel, or beffore by himselffe, or with or by other or others in any sorte make frends, mocion, sewte, or private labor, to the Right Honorable the Lord Chamberlen, or to anye others by whose favor his honor might be supposed to graunte the request for any place with us, not havinge therto the consent, firste of the Subdeane for the tyme beinge, and the moste voyces of the companye in a chapter then of porpose to be holden, shall fforfeite to the use of us the sayd companye the somme of x^{li} of lawffull Englishe moneye, which sayd some of ten poundes we do apointe, graunte and decrie shal by the Subdean's apointment be stayd in the hands of the Clerke of our Check, and by him kepte to the use of the sayd companye from any and everye soche offender againste this wholsome and convenient order, from tyme to tyme herafter, owt of his bordwaiges els by him to be receyved. And if it shall happen any soche offender or offenders agenst this ordinance, or any parte therof, to use any means to be eased of this penaltie or to frustrate this order otherwyse then by a like common consent of our said companye, or to take up by any means his sayd waiges, or any parte therof, at Mr. Cofferer's office or elswhere, wherbye the sayd forffett of ten pounds, or any parte therof, sholde be deteyned from the use aforsaid, besides that he shall knowe that he is willinglye perjured, violatinge his former corporall oathe, he shall for that offence also forfett to the sayd Subdeane and this companye aforsaid the some of other 10^{li} of like Englishe money. In witnes wherof we have subscribed our names voluntarylye in the said chapter holden at Hampton Courte, in the vestrye there, the 2. daye of December, 1592. Eliz. xxxv[th].

1. Anth. Anderson,   12. Isaac Burgess.   John Bull.
     Subdeane.   13. Tymothe Greene.
2. Bartholomew Mason,   14. Edw. Pyers.   Antho. Harrison.
     Clerke.   15. Robert Allison.
3. Leonard Davies, Clerke. 16. John Hewlett.   Anthony Todd.
4. Thomas Sampson.   17. Richard Plumley.
5. Richarde Granwall.   18. Tho. Goolde.
6. Crue Sharpe.   19. Tho. Morley.
7. Robert Tallentyer.   20. Peter Wryght.
8. Thomas Woodsonn.
9. William Randall.
10. George Waterhouse.
11. John Stephines.   [f. 20 b.]

The same daye, in the same chapter there and then holden, as Dec. 2, 1592.
before on the former leaffe is sayd, it was also by the common   Eliz. 35.
consent of the Subdeane, Chaplens and Gentlemen of her Majestes
said Chappell, it was decreed, determyned and ordred for the
better service of her Majestie, that as well all and everye of us of the
sayd Chappell, as any of the vestrye which shall for that tyme kepe
the dore, or any other of them, that may or do heare us, or any
matter of what nature soever talked uttered or concluded in any
chapter by us at any tyme herafter, shall to any person or persons
utter and reveal the same, or any our lawffull secrets there concluded, by the way of reporte, talke, reproche, complainte, prejudice or otherwise to the said companye, of conclusion, matter or
matters, person or persons, comprised or concluded, or included, in
any the said chapters, shall, for the firste offence, forffett to the use
of us, the sayd companye, the somme of v^s, and for the second offence
shall forfet the somme of x^s, and if it shall apeare to the Subdeane
for the tyme beinge, eyther by the parties owne confession, or by
sufficient witnes, or by the open action, that the said partie or parties
do offend in the premisses the thirde tyme, then the sayd Subdeane,
at his discretion, shall take his surplese from him, dismiss him of

his place whatsoever, tyll he may fynde forther favor of the Right Hon. the Lord Chamberlen from tyme to tyme herafter. In witnes wherof we have subscribed our names the daye and yere above mencyoned.

Anth. Anderson, Subdeane.　　John Stephines.
Bartholomew Mason, Clerke.　　John Hewlett.
Leonard Davies, Clerke.　　Tho. Goolde.
Thomas Sampson.　　Richard Plumley.
Richarde Granwall.　　Tho. Morley.
Crue Sharpe.　　Peter Wryght.
Thomas Woodsonn.　　Isaac Burges.
Robert Tallentyer.　　John Bull.
George Waterhouse.　　Antho. Harrison.
William Randall.　　Anthony Todd.
Tymothe Greene.
Edw. Pyers.
Robert Allison.

[f. 21.]

April 13, 1593.
Eliz. 35.
An order against pretensed oathes, not to be approved for lawful oathes, and to prohibit soche unlawfull libertyes from the servisable dewtie to her Ma⟨ti⟩e in her Royal Chappel as hertofore hathe or herafter might growe by the sayd pretensed manner of oathe not to be had or suffred.

The 13. daye of Aprill 1593, in a chapter holden at St. James' upon an unkinde faction begon by sondry of the companye abowt the deverse manner of oathe taken (as they affirmed), it was presently by the Subdean, Anthony Anderson, geven to a perpetual continuance in commaund that, sence every Chaplen, Gentleman of the Chappel, and others of the vestrye have, by coreporale oathe, sworne their obedience to the Deane, Subdeane, and to his Substitute in al things for their government in the better service of her Majestie as apereth in the oathe followinge, that none nor any of them herafter at any time shold departe from the Courte and Chappel any one day, without special licence of the Subdeane for the time beinge or his Substitute or Substitutes: And therewith also was then likewise by the sayd Subdeane geven admonition to the sayd Chapleyns, Gentlemen and vestrye, that if any man of them dyd disobey this command by his absence or departure without leave as before is sayd, or havinge leave shall absent himselfe wilfully (or be absent) from the said her Majesties Royall Chappell and Service in any sorte longer then in his licence and leave (as beffore) was or shalbe geven and graunted to him, and shall not rendre to the Subdeane, or his Substitute in his absence, soche urgent cawse and necessarye busynes for his excuse, and that soche &c. so proved or probable, as to the sayd Subdeane, or Substitute in his absence, shalbe admitted lawfull or tollerable, that then every soche Chaplen, Gentleman, Yeoman, Sergeant Yeoman, or Groome of the Vestrye shall be, at the pleasure and discretion of the Subdean, checkt upon his next quarter's waiges, for the first offence xx^s, and for the seconde like offence other xx^s, more or lesse in bothe, as to the Subdean shall seme convenyent in his discretion; and for the third offence, the offender shal by the said Subdeane be dismissed of his surplice and service in chapple or vestrye tyll he cann get relieff at the hand of the Deane, and, for the present, of the Right Honorable the Lord Chamberlayne, our Cheeffe Governor, under her Sacred Majestie.   Anth. Anderson, Subdeane.

It is forther ordred and decried for ever herafter by the sayd Subdean, that none of the sayd company or persons shall at any time have leave or licence to departe, excepte he first bringe to the Subdean, or his Substitute in his absence, another of his felows at his booke, which shall promise and do kepe the service at the sayd booke as behovethe accordinglye. First geven at Hampton Courte 1592, and now recorded the 17. day of April 1593.

      Anth. Anderson. [f. 2.]

Be it remembrid the 19th daye of Aprill Anno Domini 1598, and in the forteth yeare of her Majestis Raigne, the Subdeane and the major part of the companye beinge assembled in chapter at Whitehaale did, with one assent, there agree that from hence forth all and every checke and checkes (apointed by oure statutes) which shalbe inflicted upon any Gentleman or other member of the Chappell by

1598, Apl. 19.

the Subdeane for breakinge of any of the statutes and orders, wherto wee ar all sworne : that the same checke or portion of moneye shalbe staied and taken by oure Clearke of the Checke for the tyme being out of the offender's boord wages which he is to receve that moneth wherin the offence shalbe committed, and the same monye by checke or checkes soe staied and taken upp, the Clearke of oure Checke shall accounte for and deliver the same to the Subdeane and the segniors of the companye then present at the Feast of the Nativitye of Christ every yeare, to thend the same may be devidid (with her Majestes New Yeres gifte geven us) amongst the companie which then doe wayte. In witnesse that wee have geven our free and willing consentes hereto, Wee whose names are under wreten have subscribed to this order the daie and yere above rescited.

Leonard Davies, Subdeane.

Nathanaell Giles,	Robt. Allyson.	George Waterhouse.
Master of the Children.	John Stevens.	Bar. Mason.
Richarde Granwall.	Jo. Hewlett.	Willm. Barns.
Crue Sharpe.	Richard Plumley.	Robert Stuckey.
Anthony Todd.	Peter Wryght.	
Robt. Tallentyer.	William Lawrence.	
William Randall.	S. Davies.	
J. Burges.	John Amery.	
Edw. Peers.	Edmond Browne.	[f. 24.]

1603, May 19. Be it ever remembred that uppon the 19th day of Maye in the first yeare of the raigne of our Soveraigne Lord Kinge James, at a Chapter holden at Greenwiche by the Subdeane and gentlemen of the Kinges Chappell ther assembled in the vesterie at the tyme of mynisteringe of the Othe to the Kinge, taken and receaved by all the gentlemen and yeomen of the said chappell and the officers of the vesterie, accordinge to the commaundement of the Kinge, signified by the Lord Chamberlaine, It was then and ther agreed and con cluded by a generall consent, ever after to continewe without violacõn or alteration, That whomsoever of the gentlemen and yeomen of the chappell or officers of the vesterie shall departe awaie or be absente at any tyme or tymes from the sayd chappell or vesterie when their service and attendaunce shalbe comaunded or appointed, without lysense of the Deane, the Subdeane, or his substitute: And also if they or any of them shall at any tyme disobey the lawfull comaundes and appointments of the Deane, Subdeane, or the Substitute, in any thinge that concerneth the service of the Kinge, or shall not to there best indeavoure performe the dewties belonginge to their severall places, That then the sayd gentlemen and yeomen of the sayd chappell, and all other officers of the vesterie shall willinglye and dutifullie submitt themselves, accordinge to the auncient and laudable custome of the chappell, to the check and punishment which the Deane or Subdeane shall thinke meete to impose uppon him or them, or any of them, for suche his or theirs absence, disobedience, or want of indeavoure as aforesaid, which lawdable ordinance and constitucõn agreed uppon as aforesayd, the Subdeane, gentlemen, and others whose names are heere under written, have setto ther handes faythfully and truelye to performe, fulfill and keepe. And do also by the same Chapter decree that whensoever any of the places of those of the chappell or vesterie shalbe voyde, that whomsoever shall succeade in the places aforesayd shall at the tyme of his or their admission and takinge of the othe to the Kynge, subscribe his name under his hand writinge that he will allwayes truelie and faythfully to his best indeavours performe and keepe the sayd lawfull ordynaunce and decree made as aforesayd, and that neither directly or indirectly the same be violated or broken by him or his procurement; and because the true understandinge of this decree aforesayd shalbe made manifest, the parties aforsaid doo heerby protest uppon their othe and dutie which they owe to the Kinges highnes that the true meaninge of this constitucõn and decree is only made and wholie intended to be for the avoydinge of perjurie and the better service of the Kynge, and noe waye by any intent or purpose to withdrawe themselves from ther due obedience of their officer, neither from their sayd service and daylie attendaunce which ever hathe and ought to be performed of every person accordinge to his place and qualitie belonginge to the sayd chappell and vesterie. In wittnes heerof the parties whose names are and shalbe under written have setto their handes this 19th of Maye in the first yeare of the raigne of our Soveraigne Lord Kinge James, Kinge of England, Scotland, Fraunce, and Ireland, Defender of the Faythe, &c. Annoque Domini 1603.

Leonard Davies, Subdeane.

Antho. Harrison.	Nathanaell Gyles.	George Cooke.
Robert Stuckey.	Richard Plumley.	David Hinle.
Stephan Boughton.	John Baldwine.	John Clark.
William Lawes.	Francis Wiborowe.	Hum. Bache.
Anthonie Kirkbie.	Georg Wooddeson.	Ezech. Waad.
Thomas Sampson.	John Wooddeson.	Mathew White.
Richard Granwall.	Peeter Wryght.	Thomas Peirs.
Thomas Woodson.	Edmonde Hooper.	George Sheyffeilde.
Henry Eveseed.	Edmond Sheergold.	John Frost.
Rohert Allyson.	Orlando Gibbons.	Peter Hopkins.
Jo. Stevens.	Richard Coton.	Willm. Crosse.
Jo. Hewlett.	John Amery.	William Heather.
Wm. Lawrence.	William West.	[f. 34.]
S. Davies.	Luke Jones [?]	

1603-4, Feb. 1. Mem. that the firste day of February in the same yeare 1603 the Right Worshipfull the Deane of the Chappell did commaunde and kepe a chapter in the vestrie at Hampton Courte, where it was ordered that soe often as then forwardes places shoulde become voyde in his Majestes Chappell, that the persons to be preferred should be firste harde and approved for sufficiencie of voyce and skill by the Subdeane and the major parte of the Companye, and by them to be nominated and presented unto Mr. Deane, in whose power of right it hath bene and is to admytt at his pleasure suche persons as be approved.

Also it was ordered at the same Chapter that the whole service and the songes to be performed in the Chappell shalbe appoynted by Mr. Deane or by the Subdeane of the Chappell at all tymes, and in ther absence by the Substitute, yet not without the advice of the Master of the Children, for suche songes as are to be performed by the children in the Chappell.

These two thinges were thus ordered in Chapter for the better service of the Kinges Majestie. [f. 28.]

Orders for the Attendance of the Gentlemen of his Majestes Chappell.

1. Every yeare within the twelve dayes of Christmas a list or rowle to be made new and drawne by the Subdeane and three or more of the gentlemen, to be chosen by the major parte of the fellowshipp in a Chapter called for that purpose, which gentlemen with the Subdeane shall then also dispose of their wayting in the Chappell by a monethly course, that a competent number of the gentlemen be appointed to attend the service uppon the workinge dayes throughout the yeare (except in the accustomed tymes and weekes of libertye called playing weekes) under the penalty of a check for every one absence from any in his appointed monethe.

2. Uppon Sondayes, Principall tymes at Christmas, Easter, and Whitsontide, uppon holy dayes at bothe services, uppon festivall and offerynge daye eves, at evening prayer, uppon sermon dayes at morning prayer, all that shalbe in the aforesayd list and rowle of daylie wayters, aswell out of their appoynted moneth as in it, shall attend the service under penalty of a check for every absence.

3. If any of the gentlemen chaunce to be sicke and infirme, not able therby to attend in any parte of his wayting moneth, one of the juniors of a contrary moneth shalbe called by the appointment of the Subdeane to supply the tyme of his absence under payne of check for faylinge any service.

4. If any of the gentlemen in his appointed moneth shall have any urgent busines or any impediment to be approved by the Subdeane, his absence shalbe tollerated, provided that he procure another of the gentlemen of a contrary moneth and of his parte to wayte for him, and that the partye undertakinge such supply if he be defective therein he shalbe subject to check as in his owne moneth.

5. Every of the gentlemen called to wayte uppon any occasion by the Subdeane, though out of his waytynge moneth, shall obey and attend under paine of a check.

6. If any of the gentlemen shall departe out of the chappell in service tyme without leave of the Subdeane, and returne no more that service, he shall incurr the penalty of check of absence from all service.

7. It shalbe lawfull for the Subdeane, for the ease of any of the auntientier seniors, at his discrecõn, to call the yonger juniors to wayte some parte of such senior's moneth, and they shall obey and performe the same under payne of a check.

8. If ther be above two Organistes at once, two shall allwaies attend; if ther be but two in all, then they shall wayte by course, one after an other, weekly or monethly, as they shall agree betwixt them selves, givinge notice to the Subdeane and the Clark of the Check how they do dispose of their waytinge, that therby it may be knowne who is at all tymes to be expected for the service, and they shalbe subject to such orders, and to such checks, in the same manner as the other gentlemen are.

9. The check for absence from morning prayers, holy dayes, festivall tymes, and sermon dayes, shalbe 4^d, from evening prayer uppon such dayes and their festivall eves 3^d, for absence from morninge prayer uppon workynge dayes 3^d, from eveninge prayer 2^d.

10. The check for late cominge, viz. after the first gloria patri 1^d, after the first lesson 2^d, after the second as for absent from the whole service.

11. If any one shalbe over negligent, presuming that the ordinarie

check shall excuse him from further penalty, he shalbe subject to such further check as the Subdeane shall thinke fitt to laye uppon him.

12. All the checks shall monethly be divided amongst those of the gentlemen that have bin most diligent in wayting that moneth, by the judgment of the Subdeane of the moneth's wayters.

13. If any scruple or doubt arise concerning any point in these orders, it shalbe referred to the resolucōn of the Deane of the Chappell, whose judgment shalbe theruppon obeyed.

Guil. Bartho. et Wełłe. [f. 39b.]

The Auntient tymes of lyberty and playinge weekes.

From St. Peter's daye to Michaellmas daye is the quarter of liberty, and if the gentlemen weare uppon comaund appointed to attend and wayte at any tyme in this quarter yet they wayted only uppon Sondaies and holy daies.

The weeke after Allhallowtyde.
A weeke before Christmas.
A weeke after Twelftide.
A weeke after Candlemas.
Shrove Monday and Twesdaye.
A weeke after Easter.
A weeke after St. George.
A weeke after the Rogacion weeke.
A weeke after Whitsontide.
All removinge weekes.
*At all tymes when the Kinges Majestie is from a standinge house.**

Guil. Batho. et Wełłe. [f. 40.]

Be it remembered that in the yeare of our Lord 1615, ther arose   **1615.** a controversie between the Organistes, for the manner of their

---

* The lines in italics are struck through in the original MS.

waytinge at principall feastes. It was theruppon ordered by the Reverend Father in God the Lord Bishopp of Bathe and Welles, Deane of his Majestes Chappell, that alwaies heerafter the auncient custom should be observed, which was, and still must be, that the most auncient Organist shall serve the eeve and daye of every principall feast, as namely the eeves and daies of the feastes of* Christmas, Easter, St. George, and Whitsontide, the next Organist in place to serve the second daie, and so likewise the third for the third daie, if ther be so many Organistes, and for all other festivall daies in the yeare, those to be performed by the Organistes as they shall fall out in their severall weekes of waytinge; the feastes beinge ended, he that did or shoulde begin the Saterdaie before shall finish up the same weeke, according to former custom, and the other to followe, except the feast of Christmas, for then they change every daye, as the quier dothe duringe the whole twelve dayes.

Guil. Bath. et Well.

Mem. that wheras ther is a rasure in the sixt line above written, it was rased and putt out by consent of the Lord Deane, the Subdeane, and the now Organistes Edmund Hooper and Orlando Gibbons. In testemony wherof they have subscribed their names the second of November 1615.

Leonard Davies,
Subdeane.

Edmund Hooper.
Orlando Gibbons.

[f. 33b.]

1618, July 19.   Be it remembred that uppon the 19th daye of July 1618, in a Chapter called and appointed by Mr. Davies, Subdeane, by order of the Right Reverend Father in God the Lord Bishop of Winton, Deane of his Majesties Chappell, Cuthbert Joyner, Sergeant of his Majestes Vestery, for sunderie contemptes made against the said Lord Deane and his comaundmentes (to whom he is sworne to obey), for the same his contemptes an admonicōn with a prick was

---

* " All Saints " is here erased from the MS.

sett uppon his head, as is used in his Majestes house in such lyke cases, intendinge heerby his amendment and reformacōn.

Leonard Davies, Subdeane.

Againe for misusinge the Subdeane diverse waies contemptuously, as also his fellowship. Item, for bringinge false messages to the Subdeane as from the Lord Deane. Item, his great negligences used in his service. Item, for his daily absence from his place of attendance, and that without leave desired or graunted by his officer. Item, for conveyinge certaine parcells of his Maj^{tes} goodes out of his storehouse at Greenwich, and imploying them to suche uses as he pleased, without the leave or knowledge of the Lord Deane. The like offence hath never bin formerly comitted by any Sergeant. For all these thinges it is comaunded by the Lord Deane that he shalbe checked the soīe of forty shillinges to be staied to his Majestes use out of wages next growinge and due to him.

Leonard Davies, Subdeane. [f. 35b.]

Be it remembred that uppon the 25th daye of June 1620, a Chapter was held by the Subdeane and Gentlemen for that ther was a former complaint made unto the Reverend Father in God Launcellott Lord Bishop of Winton, and Deane of his Majesties Chappell, that ther was not any lawfull Clark of the Check elected after the death of Mr. Sampson, who died five yeares before, the place beinge executed by John Hewlett, not only for that tyme, but by aprobacōn of the Company for more then eight yeares before that, uppon which complaint the said Revd Father our Deane, upon and after due consideracōn had, did pronounce the place (from the deathe of Mr. Sampson) to be actually voyd, because the sayd John Hewlett was not chosen after his sayd death: Wheruppon his Lordship referred the consideracōn therof unto the Subdeane and Gentlemen, who beinge assembled together in Chapter by the sayd Subdeane, the matter was proposed whether the place did apperteyne unto the senior gentleman or to elecōn, in which it was resolved by the

1620, June 25.

whole company that it was meerly by elecc͠on and not by senioritie, uppon which the sayd company proceaded to elecc͠on by scruteny, which being don, it was sealed up in Chapter and delivered unto our Lord Deane by the Subdeane, uppon openninge wherof by my Lord it did there appeare that by the voyces of seaventeene gentlemen then presente, John Hewlett was then and there ellected Clerk of the Check.   In testimony heerof we whose names are heer under written have subscribed our names the daie and yeare above said.

Leonard Davies, Subdeane.

Antho. Harrison. Richard Coton. John Clarke. Walter Porter.*

[f. 36b.]

1630. Actes donne in Chapter the 9th of Januarie 1630, by the Right Reverend Father in God William Lord Bishopp of London, and Deane of his Majestes Chappell, for the rectifieng and settlinge of dyvers Orders in the sayd Chappell and Office of the Vestuarie:—

1. Imprimis, That the bread and wine for the Communion, and other provisions for the service of the Chappell, shall be brought by the Groome of the Vestry (to whose office such busines belongeth) into the Inner Vestry, and by none other but by his permission, which he shall deliver to the Seargeant, to be disposed of for the service, according to the ancient costome.

2. That the Yeomen by turnes make readdy the alter, see the bookes, surplices, and plate returned to the standerd, and take care that the Kinges cussions be not made common at Communions, and not suffer woemen to be in the Chappell in seates or otherwise at Com͠union tymes but such as receave the Sacrament.

3. That the Sergeant of the Vestry shall at noe tyme attempt to gett or procure any warrant for standards and other such necessary utensills belonging to the service of the Chappell, except the ould be first adjudged unserviceable under the handes of the Deane and Subdeane for the tyme beinge, and all utensills soe ajudged past service shall be fees propper to the Sergeant of the Vestry onely, as

* The MS., probably containing other signatures, is here torn away.

anciently they have beene, unlesse it shall please the Kings Majestie to commande otherwise.

4. That the dyett, boudge of Court, as bread, beere, wood, shall be imployed in generall to the Seargeant and other offycers of the vestry, as in former tymes, the Seargent to be chiefe in orderinge the same.

5. It is likewise ordered that New Year's guifts, and other gratuityes whatsoever given to the officers of the vestry, shall be faithfully delivered to the Sergeant, to be devyded in manner and forme as hath bene accustomed, viz.: the one half moety to the Sergeant and Groome, the other halfe to be equally devided amongst the yeomen. Guil. London. [f. 41.]

Actes donne in Chapter the 29th of March 1630. By the Right   1630. Reverend Father in God William Lorde Bishop of London, and Deane of his Majesties Chappell, for reformacõn of dyvers misdemeinors committed in the sayd Chappell and office of the Vestuary:—

1. Uppon a complaynt made unto the Kinge by dyvers gentlemen of qualitie attendinge neere about the Kinges Majestie, against Silvester Wilson, one of the yeomen of the sayd vestrie, for his un- *Silvester Wilson.* civell speaches and misbehaviour towards those gentlemen and others in the Chappell, was put from his attendance in the Chappell by his Majesties speciall command, for the space of fourteene dayes, and all his paye during that tyme geven to an other for attendinge in his place, with an admonicõn to behave him selfe more civelly and respectively heareafter.

2. The sayd Silvester Wilson and Thomas Panell were then *Silvester Wilson and Thomas Panell.* admonished to give more dilligent attendaunce to the keepinge of the doores in the Chappell, not goinge in and out so often into the vestrie (without comand), but to continue in the Chappell duringe the tyme of devine service, for the better orderinge of the people in the tyme of prayer.

Mr. Sandie and Mr. Pownall.   3. Mr. Richard Sandie and Mr. Nathaniell Pownall had an admonicōn given them to be more industrious and studius, for the better increase of knowledge and performance of their duty in their facultie for the Kinges service in the Chappell.

The Gentlemen in generall.   4. Admonicōn was geven to all the gentlemen in generall that at all tymes of waytinge they bringe their psalters into the Chappell and singe at the Psalmodie, and not be sylent when it is ther duties to use theire voyces.

Mr. Warrick.   5. Mr. Thomas Warrick receaved a check of his whole paye for the moneth of March becawse he presumed to playe verses one the organ at service tyme, beinge formerly inhibited by the Deane from doinge the same, by reason of his insufficiency for that solemne service.   Guil. London. [f. 40b.]

1632.   Actes done in Chapter the 29th of Aprill, 1632. By the Right Reverend Father in God William Lorde Bishop of London, and Deane of his Majestes Chappell, for the rectifeing and setlynge of dyvers Orders in the sayd Chappell and office of Vestuarye:—

1. Imprimis, It is ordered that the gentlemen of the Chappell shall (at all such tymes as they doe attend that service) come in decent manner in their gownes and surplyses, and not in cloakes and surplyses, nor with bootes and spurres. The lyke observacōn to be used by all others that come to approve their voyces, or to be suitors for places theire.

2. Secondly it is ordered that noe man shall have his lodginge in the vestrye, or a keye to the vestry doore, without the consent of the Sergeant of that office for the tyme beinge.

3. Lastly (for dyvers good considerations) yt was ordered that Silvester Wilson should not come into the Chappell or vestrye to doe any service there, notwithstandinge hee to enjoye the Kinges Majesties entertaynment, or any other casualties belonginge to a yeoman of the vestuarie, in as ample manner as in former tyme.

                                Guil. London. [f. 41b.]

At a Chapter holden in the Vestrie at Whitehall, Aprill 5, 1637.

Whearas by experience it is founde that since the disposinge of the waitinge of the gentlemen of his Majesties [Chappell] by a monethly course the Recorde whereof appears in this booke fol. 39 B.* the attendance of his Majesties service in the Chappell many times is to much scanted, not only one the workinge daies but alsoe one Sundaies, holidaies, and sermon daies, especially if the Court lie at Greenwich or Hampton Court, It is therefore ordered, That such as upon any pretence or occasion shall at any time happen to bee absente from any service in their moneth of waitinge, although they were then checked for the same, or had leave of absence graunted to them by the Dean or Subdean, or were detayned by sicknes or any other urgent busines, yett they shall bee bounde to supplie the same by there presence and service in the month followinge, or els shalbe then checked for the same, as if it were in there appointed moneth; Provided alwaies that if any man shall not bee recovered of any sicknes by the next moneth followinge, then the supplyinge of his absences from his waitinge moneth shall bee deferred till the next by-moneth after his recovery and shall then be performed.

It was alsoe declared, That if his Majesties service be neglected one Sundaies or Sermon daies or any other tymes in which all are bound to attende, as well out of there appointed moneth as in it, in such case the ordinarie checke shall not excuse those which live neerer hand, but the same shalbe increased at the discretion of the Subdean, accordinge to the Order. (folio 40 A. paragr. 11.)

The Subdeane also is required to looke to the due observation of the Order made 1630 (as appears fol. 40-41 B. paragr. 4) touchinge the singinge of the Psalmodie, and of an other Order made 1632 (fol. 41-42 B. paragr. 1) against wearinge of clokes or cominge in with great boots and spurrs under there surplises, and if any transgress to checke them as if they were absente.

Ma. Norvic. [f. 42b.]

* See p. 71 for the record here referred to.

In the name of God, Amen.

At a Chapter holden at Whithall in the vestrie there Januarie 5, 1638, by the Reverend Father in God Mathewe Lord Bishopp of Ely, Dean of his Majesties Chappell Royall, in the presence of Stephen Boughton clarke, Subdeane, Thomas Day gentleman, Clarke of the Checke, and the rest of the Gentlemen, Priests, Deacons, and Clarks of his Majesties said Chappell.

Forasmuch as Thomas Lawton, one of the Gentlemen of the said Chappell in a countretenor's part, had sundrie tymes beene admonished, as well by the said Reverend Father the Deane as by the said Subdeane, of his disordered and debauched courses in neglectinge his service in the Chappell, and in ordinarie hauntinge taverns and alehouses and distemperinge himselfe with drincke, and in sundry other misdemenors wherein hee hath at last soe farr miscarried as that his wife is repourted to bee come to an untimely end by his hande.

It is therefore declared by the said Deane, That the said Thomas Lawton is nowe deprived of his place and privilege within the said Chappell, and is fynally expelled from his Majestes service there. And order is given to the Subdeane and Clarke of the Checke, That they fourthwith waite upon the Right Honble the Comptroller of his Majestes Houshold to give him notice of this Acte, and that they cause the same to be entred into the Registrie Booke of this said Chappell.   Ma. Elie.   [f. 43.]

This Order was made by the King with his owne hand to yt. Our Royall pleasure is, That whosoever hereafter shall be admitted into our service as a gentleman of our chappell, The said admittance shall first be In terminum probationis tantum, to endure onely but from the daye thereof unto the end of twelve months in ordinary attendance, not reconing the months of Julie, August, and September, at which time the place shall to all effects be taken for voyd againe (the sayd admittance notwithstanding) unlesse the partie shalbe found to have demeaned himselfe during the said terme of triall soe diligentlie in his attendance, and soe honestly in all his carriage, and soe well to have profited and improved himselfe in his facultie as that he may obtayne our favour to be readmitted for terme of his life. Given at Our Court at Whitehall, 7 Febr. 1639. Ma. Elie, Dec. [f. 43*b.*]

At a Chapter holden in the Vestry at Whitehall by the Reverend 1663, Dec. 13. Father in God George Lord Bishop of Winton for the better regulating of the Divine service in his Majesties Chappell Royall, the nineteenth day of December 1663, and in the fifteenth yeare of his Majesties reigne, it is thus ordered:—

1. To the end that the great neglects in God's service may be redrest in his Majesties Chappell Royall it is required that the Subdeane take care that these orders be put in due execution.

2. All the gentlemen and officers and children shall yield obedience to the Deane and Subdeane and their Substitutes in all things touching the service to be performed in the Chappell: whosoever shall refuse shall undergoe such a check as they shall impose upon him, p. 34.*

3. No man shalbe admitted a Gentleman of his Majesties Chappell Royall but shall first quit all interest in other quires, and those that relate at present to other churches besides the Chappell, shall declare their choice either to fix at their churches, or to the Chappell, by the first day of March, his Majestie not permitting them to belong to both. And all the Gentlemen of his Majesties Chappell shall have their habitations within or neer the City of London, to be ready to attend at all times when the Deane or Sub Deane shall summon them, p. 32.

4. Every gentleman and officer of the vestry shall give a note to the Sub Deane of the place of their aboad, that he may know where to send for them upon occasion.

5. The service shalbe appointed by the Deane or Sub Deane or his Substitute, with advice of the Master of the Children, for such Anthems as are to be performed by the Children of the Chappell.

* P. 69.

6. The gentlemen being decently habited in their gownes and surplices (not in cloakes and bootes and spurrs) shall come into the Chappell orderly together, and attend God's service at the hours of ten and foure on the weeke dayes, and at nine and foure on Sundayes and Sermon dayes, and not depart till prayers are ended then to returne their surplices to the Standard.

7. All the Gentlemen in Generall being placed in their seates shall use their bookes and voyces in the Psalmodies and Responsalls according to the order of the Rubricke, and in the hymnes of the Church in the time of Divine service, and answer the Amen in a loud voice.

8. None of the Gentlemen shall plead priviledge above another for absence in his month of waiting, upon any occasion whatsoever, but if any one happen to be sicke, or have occasion of busines, to be approved by the Deane or Sub Deane, whereby he cannott attend the service, he shall procure one of his owne part, who is to waite in another month to supply his roome under paine of forfeiting a double check, p. 39.*

9. All the Gentlemen in General shall give their attendance at the service in his Majesties Chappell Royall on Sundayes and Holy-dayes and their eves; whosoever shall be absent shall forfeit a double checke, v. fol. 42 B.†

10. The check for absence on ordinary weeke dayes shall be twelve pence every service; on Sundayes, Holydayes and their eves two shillings a service, p. 39.

11. Every Gentleman that shall come into the Chappell after the first Gloria Patri, shall be accounted tardy and be mulct sixpence; if he come after the first lesson, he shalbe accounted absent and pay the whole check.

12. Whosoever shall be over negligent, presuming the ordinary check shall excuse him, shalbe subject to such farther check as the Deane or Sub Deane shall lay upon him, p. 39.

13. If the Subdeane shall see cause to require any gentleman to waite, though out of his month, the said gentleman shall obey and

* P. 71.   † P. 79.

attend, under such a checke as the Subdeane with the Deanes consent shall lay upon him, p. 39.

14. Every Gentleman sworne extraordinary shall waite constantly in his Majesties Chappell, till his place fall, and shall be approv'd of both for manners, skill, and voyce, before he be admitted, p. 24.*

15. Whosoever shall be admitted into a Priest's place in the Chappell shall sweare to take on him the office of a Deacon the next Ordinacõn and to doe the service thereunto belonging, p. 36.

16. Of the three Organistes two shall ever attend, one at the organ, the other in his surplice in the quire, to beare a parte in the Psalmodie and service. At solemne times they shall all three attend. The auncientest organist shall serve and play the service on the eve and daye of the solemne feastes, viz: Christmas, Easter, St. George, and Whitsontide. The second organist shall serve the second day, and the third the third day. Other dayes they shall waite according to their monthes, p. 33.

17. The Sub Deane shall take care that an impartiall bill of perdicõns for absence be duely kept and delivered to the Clerke of the Checke at the end of every quarter, to be defalkt out of the salaries of all who are negligent, or have uppon default been mulcted, the which said summe of mulctes shall be delivered by the Clerke of the Checke into the Sub Deanes hands with all dead pay, if any shall happen to be disposed off, as the Deane shall order and direct.

18. It is ordered upon his Majesties bountifull liberallitie in augmenting the salaries of the Gentlemen and others, that since the care and labour of the Clerke of the Checke is become greater then heretofore, he shall receive 2ᵈ in the pound out of every Gentleman's salary or pension, as oft as he payes them.

19. The Sergeant, Yeomen, and Groome of the Vestry shall dayly attend the service in the Chappell at the hours of prayer; the Sergeant shall every day before prayers deliver the Gentlemen their surplices

---

* The references on this page do not tally with the folios of the Cheque Book.

out of the standard, and every Gentleman shall returne his surplice to the standard when service is ended. The Sergeant of the Vestry shall not endeavour to procure any warrant, for standards or other necessary utensills for the service of the Chappell, except the old be first adjudged unserviceable under the hands of the Deane and Subdeane for the time being, and the utensills unserviceable shall be the fees of the Sergeant, except the King's Majestie command otherwise, p. 41.

20. The Yeomen by turnes shall make ready the alter and take care that all the service and singing bookes and plate, with the surplices, be dayly returned to the standard, ibidem.

21. The officers of the Chappell shall take care that no persons be placed in the Gentlemen's seates without leave of the Deane or Subdeane.   GEOR. WINTON.

22. No man to take any booke out of the Chappell but he is to enter it into the Cheque Booke, or to leave a note with the Sergeant. [ff. 45b, 46.]

1664, Apl. 30. Orders made for his Majesties Chappell Royall for setting of formes and stooles for such persons of his Majesties family that have not seates allowed them.

1. It is ordered, That the servant to the Gentlemen of the Chappell and the servant of the Vestry are allowed to sett formes or stooles by the seate sides in such convenient places that may not hinder the passage for the service.

2. That either of them are allowed to give seats, to such persons as are his Maj. servants as shall desire them of either of them, in such convenient places as they shall desire to sitt in.

3. That his Maj. servants and their wives shalbe first placed by either of them, which they shall desire, the one not interrupting the other, for such places spoken for, and that they place not ordinary servants or strangers before them of his Maj. houshold,

and that neither of them carry forme or stoole untill they are desired.

4. That the servant to the Gentlemen of his Maj. Chappell shall attend as well as the servant of the Vestry to help put on the gowns, as well as the other the surplusses, befor service begins.

5. That neither shall interrupt other contrary to these orders without incurring the displeasure of the officers of his Maj. Chappell Royall during pleasure.

It is ordered that the two foresayd servants have each man his side to furnish with formes, viz.: The servant to the Gentlemen the Dean's side, and the other servant the Sub Dean's side, and that no stooles be set neer the desk or pulpitt on either side to hinder the free passage to the Communion table ; and it is desired that the Clerke of the Check in his discretion would oversee that no indecency be committed by the said servants in this buisines, whom if they shall not obey they shalbe lyable to such punishment as the Deane or Sub Deane shall inflict. April 30, 1664.

Walt. Jones, Sub Deane. [f. 52.]

1671, May 20.

The 20th day of May 1671.

It is ordered that the old bookes and surplices shall be to the use of the Gentlemen of his Majesties Chappell Royall, paying to the Serjant of the Vestry twelve pence for the old booke, and ten shillings apeece for their old surplices. Upon the testimony of Mr. John Harding, Gentleman for 30 years standing. As also Mr. Thomas Purcell, Mr. Alfonso Marsh and Mr. William Tucker, who averre they have often heard Mr. Nightingalle to testifie the same, as an antient privelidge belonging to the said Gentlemen. [f. 46b.]

1675, July 10.

Memorandum July 10, 1675. Mr. Blasius White was by the Subdeane discharged from his Majesties service in obedience to his Maj. pleasure so signified in this following letter from Mr. Vice Chamberlane :—

Court at Windsor Castle,
Julie y⁰ 10, 1675.

My Lord,

I am commanded by his Majestie to signify his pleasure to your Lordship that you forthwith discharge Mr. Blasius White from his Majesties service, either in his Chappell Royall or in any other service in his Maj. house. And that you give order that his name be put out of the booke of his Maj. servants under your Lordship. Thus with my best respects unto your Lordship I rest,

Your Lordship's most humble servant,

G. CARTERET.

Superscribed—
For the Rt. Reverend Father in God Walter
Lord Bishop of Worcester, Deane of his
Maj. Chappell Royall, and in his absence
to Dr. William Holder, Subdeane of his
Maj. Chap. Roy.

[f. 49.]

1680, Nov. 29.   At a Chapter holden in the Vestry at Whitehall by the Right Reverend Father in God Henry Lord Bishop of London, our Deane, the 29th day of November, 1680, it was granted that the widows and executors of the Gentlemen should have the quarters wages in which they dy, onely with this limitation, if the Deane and Subdeane thinke fitt.   [f. 46.]

1693, April 5.   April the 5th, 1693. Memorandum, That at a Vestry called by the Right Reverend Father in God Henry Lord Bishop of London, Dean of their Majesties Chapell Royal, it was ordered that whatever Gentleman of the Chapell in waiting should absent himself from the practice of the Anthem on Saturdays or other holiday eves, when the King or Queen were to bee present on the morrow, or upon any other occasions before the Wednesdays and Fridays in Lent, being thereto ordered by the Subdean to appear, should, besides the usual mulct, forfeit half a crown for every such absense.

Rh. Battell, S.D.   [f. 53b.]

August 21, 1693. Memorandum, that at another Vestry called by the Subdean, in the Dean's absense, which was occasioned by a notorious neglect of the duty of the Chapell, at which the Queen was offended, the Subdeane did then warn all the Gentlemen that in case of such scandalous omissions for the future they were to expect (besides the bare penalty of the mulct) publick admonitions, in order to suspension or deprivation, if they continued guilty of them.

Rh. Battell, S.D.   [f. 53b.]

January 20th, 1714. Memorandum, That on the day of the date above written (beinge a day of publick thanksgiving) I read prayers at St. Paul's Church, as being the King's Chappell upon this occasion, that I appointed those who read the Lessons and Litany, and likewise in the absence of the Dean of the Chappell (by whose especiall order, confirmed by the Vice Chamberlain, I officiated) that I read the Communion Service, being preceded by the Serjeant of the Vestry, and attended by the Gentlemen of the Chapell in their surplices; and that all others of our Society waited there as in the Chappell Royal.

And this I thought might be proper to insert in the Check Book in order to prevent any contest or difference which upon the like occasion might possibly hereafter arise between the officers of the Chappells Royall and the Church of St. Paul.

S. Dolben, Subdean.   [f. 54.]

In a full Vestry holden at St. James' on Saturday the 23d of April, 1720, whereat (previous notice being given) most of the Gentlemen were present, the following particulars were agreed upon and determined to be registred among the decrees and orders of the Body or Society of His Majesty's Chappell Royall by and with the approbation of the Rt. Revd William Lord Bishopp of Sarum, Dean of the said Chappel Royall (viz.) :—

1st. That when any one of the Chappel, *i.e.* of the Body or Society that immediately attends on the Sovereign, dyes, the remaining part of the salary of that quarter in which he dyes (though he should dye in the first minute of the quarter) shall goe to his widow, heirs, executors, or administrators, according to an old immemorial custom.

2dly. That one old Common Prayer Book and one old surplice in use at his Maj. Chappel Royal at St. James's, or at that Chappel where his Maj. chief and longest residence shall be throughout the year, shall be the property or proper perquisit of every Gentleman, &c. to whom they were first deliver'd, paying to the Sergeant of the Chappel, his heirs, executors, or administrators, the accustomed fee of one shilling for each Common Prayer Book, and ten shillings for each surplice when new ones shall be provided, till when the books and surplices above mentioned shall not become the perquisit as above, or be taken away without leave of the Dean or Subdean. (Note. The Dean and Subdean in like manner have their books and two surplices, paying the Serjeant as above his fee of ten shillings for each surplice, five shillings for their Bible, and one shilling for their Common Prayer Book.) And the like in proportion is to be understood of the books, surplices, furniture, and other things first delivered to the Confessor, Master of the Children, Serjeant, Yeoman or Groom, to become their perquisits to whom first deliver'd, but not to be taken away till new be provided, without leave as above.

As for the old Common Prayer Books, Bibles, &c. in use in the other Chapels Royal (viz.): Hampton Court, Windsor, Kensington, &c. where his Majesty may reside any part of the year, they shall be the proper perquisitt or property as aforesaid of the Gentlemen or members that at that time (when new ones shall be provided) compose the body of the Chappel Royal, each paying to the then Serjeant his fee as above, and likewise chuseing his book according to his seniority in the Chappel. These also have been old customs in the Chappel Royal, and now more plainly determined and registred for the removing of all doubts and disputes that possibly may arise for want of such determination or registring.

3dly. A play-week or week of Vacation from all choir attendance having been always allowed after the holydays of Christmas, Easter, and Whitsuntide, 'tis determined, for the removal of all doubts and disputes, that the first week after the above three great solemn tides or feasts which shal have holyday in it, shal be reckoned the play week or week of vacation above mentioned, and that a week wherein a holyday may fall though it were on a Monday or Saturday, only as it cannot be reckoned a week without a holyday, so is itt hereby excluded from being the week of priviledge or play-week here mentioned.   Edw. Aspinwall, Subdean.

Geo. Carleton.	John Church.	Tho. Gethin.
Tho. Baker.	Tho. Jenings.	Sam. Weely.
Wm. Turner.	Tho. Edwards.	Jam. Chelsum.
Luke Flintoft.	Bernd. Gates.	John Freeman.
Saml. Chittle.	Thomas Bell.	Peter Randall.
Sam. Bentham.	Fra. Hughes.	Talbot Young.
Thomas Blennerhaysett.	George Laye.	Franc. Goodsens.

Officers of the Vestry:—Jonathan Smith, Sergeant, John Hill, Yeoman.   [f. 57.]

Pursuant to the Memorandum on the foregoing page,* sign'd by 1724, Oct. 1. Dr. Dolben, Subdean, concerninge the attendance of the body of the Chappel Royal at the Cathedral Church of St. Paul, London, on the day of the publick thanksgiving 1714: when his Majesty K. George design'd to be present at Divine Service in order to make a solemn offering in the Collegiate Church of Windsor within the Castle, on Sunday, September the 27th, 1724, the Officers and Gentlemen of the Chappel Royal being then ready to give their ordinary attendance on his Majesty, I made application to know his Maj. pleasure concerning our attendance on his Majesty at Divine Service in the said Collegiate Church, alledging it as our duty and our right so to do: Mr. Vice-Chamberlain acquainted me that his Majesty intended to be present at Divine Service in the above-mentioned Collegiate Church as Soveraign of the Garter onely, and to present the offering requir'd of the Knights of that noble Order,

* See p. 87.

and that the performing Divine Service at that ceremony belonged onely to the members of that church. Had his Maj. honor'd that church with his royal presence at Divine Service as King on any other occasion, our claim of discharging our several duties before his Majesty would have been allow'd as in a Royal Chappel, and the whole function committed to the charge of the Officers and Gentlemen of the Royal Chappel onely. On occasion, therefore, of his Majesty's appearing in the above-named Collegiate Church as Soveraign of the Garter, the Officers, Priests, and Gentlemen of the Chappel Royal did not attend his Majesty there.

Edw. Aspinwall, Subdean. [f. 55.]

1728-9, Jany. 1.

Memorandum. When his Majesty King George the 2d from Newmarket visited the University of Cambridge, Thursday in Easter week, April the 25th, 1728, according to the custom of his royal predecessors, his Majesty gave the degrees of the University to several persons. And it was then judg'd by the Bishop of London, Dean of the Chappell, and by my Lord Viscount Townshend, first Secretary of State (whose province it was usually to draw up the list for the degrees), that the Subdean of the Chappell had a peculiar title to be set down in the list for the degree of Doctor in Divinity. And accordingly I was set down first in my Lord Townshend's list for that degree (so Sub Dean Battel obtained his degree by the favor of her late Majesty Queen Anne, when she visited the University of Cambridge). But the usual method of forming the Catalogue for the degrees not being observed as formerly, it happen'd by some mistake or accident that my name was omitted in the Catalogue (for it was a very numerous one) that was delivered to the University. So that November following, by performing all my exercises, I was admitted to my degree of Doctor in Divinity at Cambridge. This I thought proper to make a memorandum of, that my successors, by this accident, may not hereafter be depriv'd of a claim and priviledge due to them on such occasions.

Jany. the 1st, 1728-9.   Edw. Aspinwall, Subdean. [f. 55b.]

VI.—COPIES OF ROYAL WARRANTS AND PRIVY SEALS.

Presidents, &c. 1625, October.

A Warrant to the Exchequer to discharge as well the Deane, the Sub Deane, and Chaplains of his Majesties Chappell, as the Gentlemen of the same, together with the Officers of the Vestry, of all payments and sums of money due to his Majestie for the subsidies graunted him in Parliament by the clergy and temporalty of this realme. By order of the Lord Chamberlain, procured by the Lord Conwey. [f. 48.]

Charles Rex.

Wheras by our comaund at our first coming to the Crowne our ancient vestery men had direccõn to wayte in our Chappell (those that weare formerly our deare father's servants being by us discharged), to the end our said servantes might take place as all other our servants above-staires have in the like, yet notwithstanding you misconstering our meaning, have sworne our father's vestery men in ther places as before, and made our ancient servaunts (when you swore them) lowest in the vestery contrarie to our gracious intent towards them, we meaning to holde the same course with them (for their preferment) as we have don with the rest of our servants in other of our offices above staires, doe signifie unto you that our expresse will and pleasure is, and we doe heerby will and comaund you presently uppon sight heerof to sweare Thomas Meller joynt sergeant with the other, and that the same order and course be kept with them in everything as is with other our sergeants, where they are doubled; and that you likewise sweare Robt. Colman eldest yeoman of our vestery, and Silvester Wilson next yeoman to him, to whome we will have suche wages and allowances quarterly paid as the yeoman of our vestery had when we were Prince of Wales, being twelve pence a peece per diem for diet, and five powndes a peece per annum for wages (to begin from our first enterance unto

A copie of the Kinges warrant to sweare Thomas Meller, joynt Serjeant of the Vestery, and Robt. Colmann and Silvester Wilson prime Yeomen of the same.

1625, Dec. 19.

the Crowne. And these our letters shal be as well unto you the Deane of our Chappell for the procuringe and setling our said olde servants as aforesaid, as also to our cofferers and other officers for paying and allowing the foresaid wages and allowances from tyme to tyme as the same shall growe due, a sufficient warrant and discharge in that behalfe. Given at our Courte at Hampton the nineteenth day of December, 1625, and in the first yeare of our Raigne, &c.

> To our right trusty and welbeloved the Right
> Reverend Father in God the Lord Bishopp
> of Winton, Deane of our Chappell Royall,
> and to our trusty and welbeloved the offi-
> cers of our Greene Cloth, and every of them,
> and to the Subdeane and his Substitutes,
> and to every of them.

[f. 19b.]

1641, Aprill.   A warrant to the Exchequer for the discharging the Gentlemen of his Majesties Chappell, and the Officers of the Vestry, from payment of the four subsides graunted to his Majestie in this present Parliament. Subscribed by Sir Abraham Williams, upon signification of his Maj[ties] pleasure by Sir Edward Powell, procured by Sir Peter Killegrew.

These presidents were showne to the Lord Treasurer, upon sight of which his Lordship's consent was obteined, that our Privy Seale might passe, and signified to be his Lordship's pleasure in writing to the Lord Privy Seal, by Sir Phillip Warwick, Secretary to the Lord Treasurer.   [f. 48.]

1663, May 4.   Charles R.

We will and command you that immediately upon sight hereof you deliver or cause to be delivered unto our wellbeloved servant Thomas Haynes, Esq. Sergeant of our Vestry, for the use of our Chapell, these parcells following, that is to say: foure surplices of fine Holland cloath, gathered in the collar, whereof two for the Deane and two for the Subdeane of our sayd Chapell. Item, threescore and foure surplices of fine Holland cloath for the Gentlemen of our sayd Chappell, twelve surplices for the musitians, and thirty and six surplices of the like fine Holland cloath for the children of our sayd Chapell. Item, twenty ells of diaper for foure cloaths for the Communion table, in the body of the sayd Chapell. Item, twenty ells of the like Holland cloath for six towells for the Communion. Item, seven ells of broad canvas and foure yards of greene cloath. Item, three Bibles of the great volume. Item, foure Communion bookes and 34 psalter bookes. Item, one demy carpit of Turkey worke to lay before the Communion table, and one other Turky carpit of a lesser size to lay upon the alter. Item, one grosse of silke points for the coapes. Item, three standards, whereof one is for the song books of our sayd Chapell, being two setts more than formerly have bin. Item, two bare hydes of oxe leather. Item, three thousand of tenterhookes, three haṁers, one fire shovle, one pare of tongs, three black jacks, three gispins, two brushes, one perfuming pan of iron, six houre glasses, and a paire of strong iron andirons; and that you content and pay for making the premisses. And these our letters, signed with our owne hand, shall be your sufficient warrant and discharge in that behalfe. Given under our signett, at our Palace at Westminster, the 4th day of May, in the 15th yeare of our reigne, 1663.

To our Rt. trusty and Rt. wellbeloved cousin
   and councellor Edward, Earle of Sandwich,
   Master of our great Wardrobe.

May it please your Majestie,

   This conteineth your Maj. Warrant to the Master of the Great Wardrobe for necessaryes for your Maj. Chapell, and is done according to former precedents, save that there is added a Turky carpit to lay upon the alter, and two surplices for a boy added to the number of the children of your Maj. Chapell, by warrant from the Rt. Hon. the Lord Chamberlin signifying your Maj. pleasure therein.   Ex^r p Lancelot Thornton. [f. 50b.]

Charles R.
Charles the Second, by the Grace of God, &c. To the Treasurer,

Chancellor, Under Treasurer, Chamberlins, and Barrons of our Exchequer, and all other our officers and ministers there now being, and that heereafter for the time shalbe, Greeting: Whereas Doctor Walter Jones, Sub Deane of our Chappell, Ralph Amner, Thomas Peerse, Thomas Hazard, John Harding, Edward Lowe, Doctor William Childe, William Howes, Christopher Gibbons, Phillip Tynker, John Sayer, Henry Cooke, Durant Hunt, Thomas Blagrave, Gregory Thorndell, Edward Braddock, Henry Purcell, William Tucker, James Cobb, Nathaniell Watkyns, John Cave, Alfonso Marsh, Raphaell Courtivile, Edward Colman, Thomas Purcell, Henry Frost, John Goodgroome, George Bettenham, Mathew Peniall, Roger Hyll, George Yardly, Doctor John Wilson, William Jackson, Gentlemen of our said Chappell, Thomas Haines, Sarjeant of our Vestry, William Williams, and George Whitcher, Yeomen of our said Vestry, and Hugh Powell, Groome of our said Vestry, are severally charged or chargeable every one of them to pay unto us to and for the severall payments of foure intire subsidies granted to us by the temporalty of our Parliament begun and holden at Westminster the eighth day of May in the thirteenth yeare of our reigne, to be levyed and paide by such severall porcōns, and at such dayes and payments as is granted unto us and are limitted by the statute made in that behalfe at our said Parliament according as they and every of them shalbe severally taxed and assessed, as by certificate thereoff signed by the Comissr̃s for the assessing of the said payments within our household or elsewhere appointed and assigned, and in our Court of Exchequer certified and there remaining of Record, more plainely it doth and may appeare: Know yee that we of our especiall grace certaine knowledge and meere mocōn, in consideracōn of the good and faithfull service done unto us, and that during their lives they intend to doe, Have given, pardoned, remitted, and released, and by these presents for us, our heires and successors, we doe give, pardon, remitt, and release unto them and every of them abovemencōned, all such summe and summes of mony as is or shall be due by them and every of them for the said foure subsidies or any of them, to be leavyed and payde as aforesaid: Wherefore wee will and command you our said Treasurer, Chancellor, Under Treasurer, Chamberlins, and Barons of our said Exchequer, That yee doe clearly acquitt and discharge against us, our heires and successors, all our above-named servants and every of them from the payment of the said subsidies granted and payable unto us by our temporalty, and alsoe all and every collector and collectors, receivor and receivors, officer and officers deputed for the payment of any penc̃õns within our houshold or elsewhere, charged or chargeable in their account or accounts already made or to be made for the said payment and every or any of them, for the several summes of money to be paide by any the persons before menc̃õned, or taxed or assessed upon them or any of them, for the premisses and every part and parcell thereoff, although expresse menc̃õn of the particuler summes of money by them or any of them, payable for the four subsidies aforesaid, or any of them, or upon them or any of them, to the severall payments of the said four subsidies assessed and taxed, or to be assessed and taxed, be not herein particulerly menc̃õned and recited the statute of the grant of the said subsidies; or any other Act or Ordinance heretofore made, or any use, custome, auntient order, or course of our Exchequer, or any other ambiguitie, doubt, question, matter, or cause whatsoever you or any of you to the contrary moveing in any wise notwithstandinge; and theise, &c. Given, &c.

Ex^d p W. Trumbull.

This conteineth your Maj. warrant for discharging the Gentlemen of your Maj. Chappell and the Officers of the Vestrie from the payment of the foure subsidies granted unto your Maj. in this present Parliam^t.

Signified to be your Majesties pleasure by the Lord Chamberlin.

W. Trumbull. [f. 48b.]

Charles R.

Whereas Wee were gratiously pleased some time since for an encouragement to the Priests, Gentlemen, Children, and Officers of   1663, Dec. 22.

our Chappell Royall to grant severall augmentacõns to the salaries and allowances heretofore usually made them and their predecessors in the time of our late dear father, of ever glorious memory: And whereas wee have now lately, for the conveniency of the present state of our affaires, thought fitt by our Warrant of the 25th day of August, 1663, to signifie our pleasure to you, for the retrenching severall diets, entertainements, and other expences of our household, wee, graciously reflecting on the constant attendance to which our said servants of our Chappell are obliged, and willing more partiticularly to continue a just and fitt maintenance to those that serve us in that relacõn, have thought fitt to declare and signifie our royall pleasure to you, that the said augmentacõn so lately granted by us as aforesaid to the Priests, Gentlemen, Children, and Officers of our Chappell Royall be continued and paid quarterly to them for the future, with their former allowances granted unto them in the time of the reigne of our said royall father of blessed memory, our said order of the 25th August or anything therein to the contrary notwithstanding; for which this shall be your warrant. Given at our Court at Whitehall, the 22th day of December, 1663.

By his Majesties Command,

Henry Bennett.

To our Rt. trusty and well beloved Councillors Sir Charles Berkeley, Knt. Treasurer, and Sir Hugh Pollard, Knt. and Bart. Comptroller of our Household, and the rest of the Officers of our Greencloth.

This warrant is in the compting-house and entred in the booke at the compting-house, and entred also at the Signett Office.

[f. 47.]

The Coppy of our Pryvie Seal, &c.—

1664, Sept. 26.   Charles the Second by the Grace of God King of England, Scotland, France, and Ireland, Defender of the Faith, &c. To the Treasurer, Chancellor, Under Treasurer, Chamberlins, and Barons of our Exchequer now being, and which hereafter for the time shall be, and to all other the Officers and Ministers of our said Exchequer

for the time being, to whom it shall or may apperteine, and to the
Lord Steward, Treasurer, Comptroller, Cofferer, Master of our
Houshold, Clerkes of our Greene Cloath, and Clerkes Comptrollers
of our said Household now being and which hereafter shall be, and
to all other the officers and ministers there whome it doth or may
concerne, greeting. Our will and pleasure is, and wee doe hereby
require and authorize you out of such our treasure as now is, or
which hereafter for the time shall be and remaine in the receipt of
our said Exchequer, to pay or cause to be payd unto the Cofferer of
our Household now being, and to the Cofferer of the sayd Household
which hereafter shall be, the severall sums of seaventy pounds a yeare
for each of the Gentlemen of our Chappell Roiall, to be by our said Cofferer for the time being payd unto them according to our letters of
Privy Seal in that behalfe, dated the six and twentieth day of September, in the fourteenth yeare of our reigne, and also to pay unto the
sayd Cofferers the summe of thirty pounds by the yeare for the diett,
lodging, washing, and teaching of each of the Children of our Chappell Royall, the same to be by them payd unto Henry Cooke,
Master of the sayd Children for the time being, and to the Master
of the sayd Children which heerafter for the time shall be, according to our Letters of Privy Seale dated the fourteenth of
October in the thirteenth yeare of oure reigne; and our further will
and pleasure is, and we doe hereby will and command you to pay
or cause to be payd to the Cofferers of our sayd Household for the
time being, the several sums following to be by them from time to
time payd over to the Officers of our Vestry (that is to say) the
summe of seaventy pounds per annum for the wages and fee of the
Sergeant of our Vestry for the time being, the summe of forty
pounds thirteen shillings nine-pence per annum to each Yeoman,
and thirty pounds per annum to the Groome, according to our Letters of Privy Seale dated the three and twentieth day of October
in the fourteenth yeare of our reigne: And our further will and
pleasure is, that they shall enjoy their former allowances granted to
them in the time of the reigne of our late Royall Father (of blessed

memory) according to our Warrant under our Signe Manuall dated
the two and twentieth day of December one thousand six hundred
sixty and three, in the fifteenth yeare of our reigne: The sayd severall payments to commence from Michælmas one thousand six
hundred sixty three (our order of the five and twentieth of August
one thousand six hundred sixty three, or any thing therein conteined
to the contrary notwithstanding): And these our Letters of Privy
Seale or the Inrollement thereoff shall be unto you and every of you
a sufficient warrant and discharge in this behalfe. Given under our
Privy Seale at our Pallace of Westminster the six and twentieth
day of September, in the sixteenth year of our reigne.

Ex^d J. Mathew.   [ff. 49b, 50.]

1663, Dec. 10. The Coppy of the Lord Chamberlaines Warrant to the Signet for
pardon for the Subsidies, &c. the Vestry being also included:—

These are to signifie unto you his Maj^{ties} pleasure, That you pre-
pare a Bill for his Maj^{ties} signature after the accustomed forme for a
pardon to be granted from his Maj. to the Subdeane and Gentlemen
of his Maj. Chappell, being his Maj. servants in ordinary, whose
names are sett downe in the schedule annexed, that according to his
Maj. gracious intention they may be exempted from payment of any
and every of the subsidies granted to his Maj. at the Parliament
begun at Westminster the eight day of May, 1661, and for so
doeing this shalbe your warrant. Given under my hand this 10th
day of December, 1663, in the fifteenth yeare of his Maj^{ties} reigne.

E. Manchester.   [f. 48.]

To the Clerke of the Signett attending.

1665, Dec.   December, 1665.

A Warrant Dormant to the Treasurer of his Majesties Chamber
for the time being to pay to the Gentlemen and Officers of his
Docquet.   Majesties Chappell such summes of money as shalbe allowed them
by bills signed by the Lord Chamberlaine for their expences in their
extraordinary attendance upon his Matie, in removes and progresses,
to comence from Mich. last. Subscribed by Mr. Trumbull, by

warrant of the Lord Chamberlaine, and procured by Mr. Secretary
Morice. [f. 47b.]

These are to signifie unto your Lordshipp his Majesties pleasure, 1670, Aug. 11.
That you provide and deliver, or cause to be provided and delivered,
unto the Deane of his Majesties Chappell Royall at Whitehall, one
standard for the Clerke of the Checque to the Gentlemen of the
Chappell, to be placed in the vestry, as hath been formerly accustomed, and this shalbe your warrant. Given under my hand
this 11th day of August, 1670. In the 22th year of his Majesties
reigne. E. Manchester.

To the Right Honble Edward, Earle of Sandwich, Master of his Maties Great Wardrobe,
  or to his Deputy there.

[f. 46 b.]

VII.—Resignations, Dismissals, and Petitions.

Knowe all men whome theis presentes maye concerne, that I 1611, May 1.
Willm. Lawes, latelye one of the Gentlemen of his Majesties
Chappell, and in ordinarye paye, doe, for dyvers causes me there
unto movinge, make over my said place to Ezechiell Waade,
havinge first obtayned the favor and consent of the Reverend
Father in God the Lord Bishop of Bathe and Wells, Deane of his
Majesties Chappell, with the Subdeane and whole Societie, for a
certeyne some of money before hand payed. I saye I doe advisedly,
voluntarylye, and very willinglye resigne my said place in his
Majesties Chappell as aforesaid the firste of Maye, 1611. In witnes
hereof, I have subscribed to this my resignation in the daye and
yeare before written. P me William Lawes. [f. 25.

The Copye of Jo: Myners resignacōn of his place in the Churche of 1615, June 4.
    Exon: to our Lorde the Deane of his Majestes Chappell.
  Wheras I, John Myners, by the especiall favor of your good
Lordshipp, and the general consent of the Gentlemen of the

Chappell, was sworne in ordinarie to the next place that should fall
of what part soever, since which tyme, at the earnest request of
some friendes of mine (beinge as then there was no place voyd in the
Chappell), I went to Exeter, and ther was made a member of that
body, but presently after I was certified of the death of Mr. Sampson, wheruppon I cam to your Lordshipp about it, and your Lordshipp hath offered it me freely, the which then unadvisedly I refused,
but your Lordshipp more favoringe me (then I deserved) would not
take that my first deniall, but gave me longer tyme to consider
therof; afterwards uppon better advisement with my selfe of the
many inconveniences that might com unto me by my beinge at
Exeter, and of the good which might befall me heare, I returned to
your Lordship againe, cravinge your honorable favor, that I might
injoye my place, the which I was absolutely sworne unto, and your
Lordshipp most favourably graunted it me, but with this proviso,
that if I weare sworne and made one of the body of the Chappell I
should signifie under my hand and seale that I did wholy leave and
forgoe all the right and interest I had or have in Exceter, and
further, if it should so happen heerafter that I againe should
betake my sealfe to Exceter, that then I shoulde loose all the hope
and benefitt which to me belonges by my place in the Chappell, to
the which these your honorable demaundes I do most willingly con-
desend, and for the satisfaccōn of your good Lordshipp and the rest
of the Company I doe sette my hande and seale, purposinge (by
God's grace) to give over Exceter, and to doe my best endevours
for his Majestes service in the Chappell duringe life.   This 4th of
June, 1615.

Signed and sealed by the said

Jo: Myners.

Wittnesses heerof,
    Antho: Harrison, Substitute.
    Jo: Hewlett.   [f. 32.]

To the Right Reverend Father in God Lançellot Lord Bishop of 1620, Sept. Winton, and Deane of his Majestes Chappell.

The Peti͠con of the Subdeane and Gentlemen of his sayd Ma^{tes} Chappell.

A Peti͠con preferred against Henry Eveseed.

Humblie shewinge unto your Honor, that, wheras Henry Eveseed, one of the Yeomen of the Vestry, was heertofore at the speciall instance of the Subdeane and Gentlemen preferred to an extraordinarie place in the vestrye, to succeade in ordinary uppon the next avoydance, and then, uppon the misbehaviour of Aldred, at the request of your suppliantes aforesayd was admitted into ordinarie, where he hath continued now nine yeares and upward, at acceptance of which othe (by order of the Reverend our late Deane) and under his owne hand, as appeareth in our Register, he yealded himselfe to be deprived of his place if any way he misbehaved himselfe in his sayd place, since which tyme he hath misbehaved himselfe continually, either in disgrace of the whole society in generall or to sondrie of them in particuler, in such sort that it is not tollerable that he shoulde remaine longer to be indured. As first some fower yeares since he beinge infected with a fowle disease in his groine, to the great offence of all, but chiefely of those that were constrained by meanes of their service to lye neere him, uppon which the late Lord Deane thought him unfitt to serve his Majestie in his progresse into Scotland. Also since that tyme he hath very much abused himselfe through drunkennesse; for the last winter at Whithall he was drounke many daies together so that he was alwaies fightinge with his fellowes or the servauntes, to the great disquiett of the Officers of the Greencloth. At midnight, and in his mad drounkennesse, he rose out of his bed naked, and would needes run out at a glasse window, where he tare his fleshe with the broken glasse [so] that he was not hole in a good while after; in which his sayd drounkennes one night he came and vomited in a dishe of pottage which Mr. Harrison and others were eatinge of. Also at his Majestes last beinge at Greenwich, he soe still contynuinge his drounkennes that the porters complained of his continuall late cominge in drounke, at which tymes he takes occasion to quarrell and beate the servauntes. Againe upon St. Peter's day last, beinge the day of our feast, unto which were invited many Officers of the House and other our good friendes, the sayd Eveseed did violently and sodenly without cause runne uppon Mr. Gibbons, took him up and threw him doune uppon a standard wherby he receaved such hurt that he is not yett recovered of the same, and withall he tare his band from his neck to his prejudice and disgrace. Then he proceading from Mr. Gibbons mett our fellow Mr. Cooke in the chappell, wher he gave him three blowes in the face, and after that he abused our fellowe Mr. Crosse and Richard Patten, and was not satisfied with those abusinges but challenged the field of some of them, which abuse did tend to our great discreditt, contemning the Subdeane or any thing he could say or doe therin. He reported unto the sergeant that the Subdeane sate in Chapter as the knave of clubbs, and the rest of the company as knaves about him. And now on Monday last the 25th of this Sept. 1620, after many admonisions given in privat and publickly in chapter, and hopinge of his amendment did still forbeare to complain unto your Lordship, but growing still incorrigible in the sight and hearing of many of the gentlemen and all his fellowes of the vestery, and that causelesse he fell into unseemly termes with Mr. Subdeane, contemning his office, affirming it to be poore, yet himselfe to be proud therof as the divill, telling him withall that he was a base fellow intruding him selfe into their office havinge nothing to doe therin, no not the Deane nor Subdeane had any thing to doe with them in their office, and threatning our fellow Cooke to teare the fleshe of[f] his face, with many other reproachfull speeches to[o] longe heere to be spoken of. And lastly the sayd Eveseed hath bin reproved by the Subdeane and officers of the vestery to be the most negligent officer in his place that he hath knowne in his tyme, and that he is become a blasfemer and a filthy speaker in all places, that his company is rejected whersoever he cometh.

What is heere complayned of wilbe approved unto your Lord^p by the gentlemen in generall, or by some of them in particuler. In testimony wherof seventeen gentlemen have heerunto subscribed our names.*

Uppon readinge of this complaint in Chapter at Hampton Court, the 29th of September 1620, it pleased the Reverend our Deane to suspend the said Eveseed untill the feaste of All Saintes following, expecting then to receave from him better answers unto the sayd complaint as by the said suspencōn under my Lord Deanes hand more plainly appeareth in fol. 34.† Uppon consideracōn of which Henry Eveseed, yeoman of the vestery, did peticōn unto the Right Reverend Lord Deane, the third of November, in manner followinge. Humblie shewing that not long since divers occasions have happened wherby offences have bin taken wherin your peticioner doth acknowledge him selfe guilte, And albehit he doth confesse to have deserved both the losse of his place and what other punishment your Lordship shall please to impose uppon him, yet he hopeth your good Lordship wilbe favourable unto him beinge a younge man and not understandinge him selfe nor his obedience to his betters; secondly having no other meanes to live uppon but his creditt and a porcion of land given him by his friendes, which is not sufficient for his maintenance; and thirdly havinge not bin sufficiently tutered in his youth, wherby to take any course of living, but is altogether destitute both of livinge and meanes to supplie him.

His most humble suite unto your Lordship is, that your Honor wilbe pleased to be so good and favourable unto him as that he may enjoye the benefitt which all his Majestes houshold servantes have and usually had, and that your Honor will vouchsafe in regard this is the first offence that ever he committed, and for his father's sake, who somtyme was Gentle-

---

* The names of the gentlemen are not subscribed to this entry in the MS.
† See the following page.

man of this Chappell, your Lordship will shew some favor unto him, and this shalbe a sufficient warninge for him never to offend in this kinde but ever to praye for your Lordships happie preservac̃on.

Uppon reading of this petic̃on also in Chapter at Whithall before his Lordship, his Honor's pleasure was that the sayd Eveseed should submitt him selfe unto the gentlemen whome he had offended, and that his Lordship might be certified therof under their handes by Christmas following, if not, his Honor pronounced his place to be then utterly voyd.

Which submission not beinge accordingly don, ther was a proceading against him as on the next page appeareth.

[f. 37.]

1620-1.
March 3.
Henry Eveseed
deprived.

Be it further remembered that uppon the third day of March 1620, the sayd Reverend Lord Deane held a Chapter at Whithall, wher were presente 21 gentlemen and the officers of the vestery, in which Chapter Henry Eveseed for not performing his submission as was formerly enjoyned him, and for not performing his duty and service in his place, and persisting dayly in his former abuses against the Subdeane and others of the gentlemen, as was then and there provid, and his Lordship finding no hope of reformac̃on in him, did then in Chapter (according to the order of his Majestes house by former prickes sett downe) pronounce his place to be utterly voyd, and the same to be enjoyed by some other. In testimony heerof his Lordship hath caused this act to be registred, and hath heerunto subscribed his name the day and yeare above written.

[f. 38.]

Dr. Peirce his Resignation.*

1633, Aug. 31.　　In Dei nomine Amen. Coram vobis notario publico, publicaque et

* This is very incorrectly entered in the original MS.

aucthen*ticata* persona, ac testibus fide dignis, hic præsentibus Ego
Thomas Pearce sacræ theologiæ professor, unus generosorum Capellæ
(suprem*orum* q*ue*) regiæ, serenissimi in Christo principis et Domini
nostri, Domini Caroli Dei gratia Angliæ Scotiæ Franciæ et Hiberniæ
Regis, fidei defensoris, volens et affectans, ex certis causis veris et
legitimis me et animum meum in ea parte specia*liter* mov*ens* ab
onere et servitio dicti loci mei exui et exonerari, eundem locum
meum cum suis juribus et pertinen*entiis* universis in manus reve-
rendissimi in ch*risto* patris et domini, domini Guilielmi providen*tia*
divi*na* Ep*iscopi* Lond*inensis* et in Archiep*iscop*um Cant. electi decani
Cappellæ Regiæ Majestatis pred*ictæ* aut alii cujuscunque hanc meam
resignacionem admittendi *propr*ietatem habentis seu habituri non vi
metu dolo seu fraude ad hoc ductus seu seductus aut aliqua alia
machinacione sinistra circumventus sed ex mea certa scientia et
spontanea voluntate animo*que* delibe*rato* at*que* pure sponte sim-
pliciter et absolute resigno dictum*que* locum et officium meum in
Capella regia pred*icta* re et verbo dimitto jure quoque et possessione
meis in eadem capella prehabitis renuntio eisdem cedo et ab eisdem
recedo totaliter et expresse in hiis scriptis.   Tho. Peirs.

Testibus
  Willi. Pean   ⎰ Interposita et lecta fuit hujusmodi resignac*io*
  Samuele Franklin ⎱ coram me Johanne Hart notario publico
alme curiæ Cant Dñi Archibus London procur*um* generalium uno
in ædibus meis in vico vulgariter nuncupato Knightrider street Ci^{tis}
London die Sabbathi ultimo die mensis Augusti 1633 presentibus
tunc et ibidem unacum notario publico ante dicto Will^{mo} Pean etiam
notario publico et Samuell Francklene rato testibus &c.
  Ita testor ego Johannes Hart Notarius Publicus.   [f. 42.]

VIII.—Oaths of the Subdean, Gentlemen, &c.

1592.

The Othe for the Subdeane of his Majestes Chappel:—*

A. Yow shall sweare to serve the hie and moste excellent Princes

Elizabeth by the grace of God of England, Fraunce, and Yrelande,
         James

      Kinge   *their*

Qweene, Deffender of the Faythe, &c., Also *her* heirs and successors,
trewlye and faythfullye, as well in the special truste of this great
                   their

charge in the office of Subdeane of *her* Majestes Royall Chappel by
their

her highnes speciall favor bestowed upon yowe accordinge to the
same truste in yowe reposed, as in all other things towchinge her
honor and securitie. Yowe shall not conceal or kepe secrete anye
                their   *their*

tr̀easons committed or spoken againste *her* Highnes or anye *her*
successors, but shall immediatelye within 24 howrs after soche
treasons harde or knowne reveale the same to one of the Councell
for the tyme beinge, or to one Justice of the Peace nexte adjoynning
to the place whereas yow shall chaunce to heare of the forsaid
treasons: Yow shall also sweare, testifye, and declare in your con-
           Kinges

science that the *Qweens* Highnes is and oghte to be by the worde of
God the only supreme Governor of this Realme and all other her
Highnes dominions and contreys, as well in all spirituall and ecclesiasticall things and cawses as temporall: And that no forren
prince, person, prelate, State, or potentate hathe or ought to have
anye jurisdiction, power, superioritye, preheminence, or auctorite
ecclesiastical, within this Realme: And therffore yow shall utterlye
renownce and forsake all forren jurisdictions, powers, superiorities, and

---

* The words in italics are crossed out in the MS., and those written above are intended to be substituted for them. The "othe" was altered a second time for
William and Mary. Another copy occurs on f. 54, written in the reign of Queen
Anne. This was again altered to serve for the House of Hanover, the clause "his
heirs and successors" being bracketed as if for omission. It has not been thought
necessary to insert the second copy, as it differs only in the orthography.

auctorities whatsoever, and to promes that from hensfforthe yow shall beare faythe and trewe alleageance to the *Qweens* ^{Kinges and Q.} highnes, *her* ^{their} heirs and lawfull successors, and to your power should assiste and defende all jurisdictions, privileages, preheminences, and auctorities graunted or belonginge to the *Qweens* ^{Kinges and Q.} highnes, her heirs and successors, or united and annexed to the Ymperiall Crowne of this Realme: So helpe yowe God and the holye contentes of that boke.

July 26. 1592, Eliz. 34. [f. 15*b*.]

The Othe for the Gentleman of the Chappell, and other Officers therto belonginge:— *   1558.

Yowe shall sweare to serve the highe and mightye Prynces *Elizabethe*, ^{James,} by the Grace of God of Englaund Fraunce and Ire- land *Queene*, ^{Kinge} Defender of the Faythe, &c. and to hir heyres and successors, truly and faythfully, both in the offyce yowe are called unto as also in all other thynges towching her honor and suretye; yow shall not conceale or keepe secrete any treasons committed or spoken agaynste her hyghnes, or any her successors, but that im- medyatlye within xxiiij houres after such treasons harde or knowen yow shall reveale and open the same to one of the Councell for the tyme beynge, or to one justyce of the peace neixte adjoynynge to the place wheras yow shall chaunce to heare of the foresayd treasons: Yowe shall also sweare, testyfye and declare [in] youre conscience that the *Queenes'* ^{Kinges} Highnes ys and oughte to bee by the worde of God the only supreame Governor of thys Realme, and all other her highnes dominions and countreys, as well in all spirytuall or ecclesiasticall

---

* The words in italics are crossed out in the MS., as in the previous entry. Another copy of the document is given on f. 30 (temp. Caroli I.), but it was not thought necessary to include it here, as the words are the same. A third copy of the "othe," written on the accession of the House of Hanover, occurs on f. 55. The clause "his heirs and successors" is crossed out whenever it occurs in this latter copy.

thinges or causes as temporall, and that no forrayne prynce, person, prelate, state, or potentate, hath or oughte to have any jurysdiction, power, superiorytie, preheminence, or auctorytye, ecclesiasticall or spirituall, within thys Realme, and therefore yow shall utterlye renownce and forsake all forraine jurisdictions, powers, superiorytyes, and auctoryties, and to promyse that from henceforthe yowe shall beare fayth and trewe allegeaunce to the Kinges *Queenes* highnes, her heires and lawfull successors, and to your power shall assyste and defend all jurisdictions, priveleges, preheminences, and auctorytyes grauntes or belongynge to the Kinges *Queenes* hyghnes, her heires and successors, or united and annexed to the Imperiall Crowne of this Realme ; yowe shall also sweare to be obedyente to the Deane and Subdeane for the tyme beynge of her Majestyes most honorable Chappell, and unto all such lawdable orders as are or shalbee by them and the whole bodye of this Company thought meete and convenient to bee devysed for quyetnes ; and also yow shall not bee one whole day absent withoute lycence of the Deane or Subdeane, or their Substitute for the tyme beinge, so helpe yowe God and the holye contentes of that booke.

God save Queene Elizabeth.

Touching the Yeomen and Gro[o]me of the Vestrye :—

And also to bee at the commaundment of the Sergeaunte of the Vestry for the tyme beinge, touching the service of her Majestie from tyme to tyme, so helpe yow God and the hole contentes of that booke.

That is Sergeant of his Majesty's Vestery in Ordinarie, and to receave such wages and fees as unto the sayd office apperteynethe.

And that yow shall not departe from the service of the Kinge without lycence of the Deane, Subdeane, or there Substitute for the tyme beyinge.   [f. 16.]

The Oth of William Phillips,* given the first daye of October, 1604:   1604.

William Phillips, you shall sweare to serve faythfully and trulye the high and mightie Prince, James, by the grace of God Kinge of great Brittaine, Fraunce, and Ireland, defender of the fayth, his lawfull heires and successors, in the place you are called unto, that is, a yeoman for his Majesties vestrye in ordinarye, to attend the Prince with such parcells of stuffe as are or shall be committed to youre charge by vertue of this warrant signed from the King's Majestie, or otherwise, and you shall not clayme nor sue for any ordinarye place to attend in in his Majesties Chappell or Vestrie, by vertue of this oth.   All these things you shall trulye performe and keepe, and allso be obedient to and in all his Majesties service unto the Deane and Subdeane of his Majesties Chappell, so help you God and by the holy contentes of this booke.

Leonard Davies, Subdean.   [f. 26.]

I, John Croker, being to be admitted into a yeare of probacion to serve in the place of a counter tenor in his Maj. Chappell Royall, do voluntarily sweare that by the grace of God and his help I shall and will doe my best endeavour to make and approve my selfe meet every way by my temperate and sober quiet carriage in such manner as beseemeth me, and as shalbe approved by the judgment of the Deane and Subdeane and major part of the Gentlemen of the said Chappell, to be in the end of the sayd yeare taken in and made one of their Societie.   And in case I shall not soe approve my selfe, then to avoyde, yeald up, and resigne my said place of probationer in his Majestes sayd Chappell into the handes of the Deane or Subdeane of the sayd Chappell for the time being.   And further, I am willing and doe agree that, in default of the premisses touching my behaviour and carriage of myselfe, that my foresayd avoydance and resignaçõn

(marginal note:) John Croker his oathe, the xxiiij[th] of December, 1623.

* This form of oath is entered again, on f. 28b, as the " othe of Thomas Myller geven the 21st of Aprill, 1606." It was not thought necessary to repeat it, as it differs only in orthography.

shall, by these presentes, stand good and available to all intentes
and purposes against me the said John Croker, for any claime or
interest in or to the foresaid place or to the profittes any way belonging therunto, so help me God.

In wittnesse wherof I, the said John Croker, have subscribed my
name in my owne hand and that voluntarilie in the presence of the
Subdeane and diverse of the Gentlemen of the Chappell.

John Croker.   [f. 15.]

1606, Dec. 3.   I, David Henly, doe voluntarily sweare that to the uttermost of
my power I will doe my endevour by all possible meanes to make
and approve my self to the able doinge of the service required in
his Majesties Chappell in perfect and good sort, as beseemeth me in
the judgment of the Deane and Subdeane and major parte of the
Gentlemen of the sayd Chappell, and that within the space of one
whole yeare next after this my admittance into the sayd place, or els
to avoyd, yeald uppe and resigne my place of probationer in his Maj^ties
Chappell into the handes of the Deane or Subdeane of the sayd
Chappell for the tyme beinge : And further, I willbe willinge and
doe agree that in the default of the premises touchinge mine insufficiency, that my foresayd avoydance and resignaçõn shall stand
good and avaylable by these presentes against me the sayd David
Henly for any clayme or interest in or to the afforesayd place, or to
the profittes any way belonginge thereto, so healpe me God: and in
wittnes whereof I, the sayd David Henly, have subscribed my name
with mine owne hand, and that voluntarily, in the presence of the
Subdeane and many of the Gentlemen of his Highnes Chappell
afforesayd, the third day of December Anno Domini 1606.

David Henle.   [f. 27b.]

1662, Nov. 14.   I, William Jackson, Master of Arts, being to be admitted into a
Priest's place in his Maties Chappell Royall, doe faithfully promise
by the grace of God to doe my best endeavour to make my selfe
fitt by all meanes for skill with pious, discreet, and sober demeanour

for the sayd place as shall be approved of by the Deane and Sub-deane of the sayd Chappell. And in case I shall not so approve my selfe in this yeare of probation, I shall at the end of it yeild up and resigne my sayd place into the hands of the Deane or Subdeane of the sayd Chappell, which sayd resignation shall, by these presents, stand good and available to all intents and purposes against me, the sayd William Jackson, for any claime or interest in or to the foresayd place, or to any the profitts belonging therunto. In wittnes wher-of I have heerunto sett my hand this fourteenth day of November 1662, and in the fourteenth year of his Majesties reigne.

William Jackson. [f. 44b.]

I, Blaze White, Master of Arts, being to be admitted into a Priest's place in his Majesties Chappell Royall, doe faithfully promise by the grace of God to do my utmost endeavour by my skill and voice to performe and officiate the service in the sayd Chappell required of me by the Deane and Subdeane and his Substitute, according to the oath by me taken: And that I will demeane my selfe with such pious, quiett, and discreet behavour as shall be approved of by the Deane and Subdeane of the sayd Chappell : And in case I shall not approve my selfe in this year of probation, I shall at the end of it yeild up and resigne my place into the hands of the Deane or Sub-deane to be voyded to me to all intents and purposes : I doe like-wise heerby promise to relinquish all the interest I have in the Church of Canterbury, and shall not undertake any quire employ-ment in any Cathedrall Church, so long as I have relation to his Maj. Chappell Royall. In witnesse wherof I have sett my hand the fourteenth day of March in the sixteenth yeare of his Maj. reigne King Charles the Second, and in the yeare of our Lord 1663.

1663-4. March 14.

Blasius White. [f. 49.]

I, William Hopwood, doe subscribe as Mr. White hath done to all intents and purposes whatsoever. Witnes my hand the 24th of October 1664, and in the sixteenth year of his Majesties reigne.

1664, Oct. 24.

Will. Hopwood. [f. 49.]

1663-4,
March 14.

I, Thomas Richardson, being to be sworne into the next place of a lay tenor or counter tenor that shall be voyd, and into halfe pay till such a place do fall, do promise (according to a statute in that behalfe required) to give all diligence in my attendance on the service of his Maj. Chappell Royall as a probationer, and do promise and undertake for my demeanour and behavour as Mr. White above said hath done, as also that I shall not undertake any employment in any Cathedrall Church so long as I shall have relation to his Maj. Chappell Royall. Witness my hand the above sayd day of March.   Tho. Richardson. [f. 49.]

1663-4,
March 14.

I, Charles Husbands, being to be admitted into a counter tenor's place in his Maj. Chappell Royall and into halfe pay till a place shall fall voyd for Mr. Thomas Richardson, do promise for my behavour as Mr. White hath done, and when I shall have the full pay of a Gentleman of his Maj. Chappell Royall, I doe promise to relinquish all my interest in the Church of Windsor, and betake myselfe wholly to the service of his Maj. Chappell. Witnesse my hand the day and year of Mr. White's subscription.

Charles Husbands. [f. 49.]

IX.—" Benevolencies " to the Gentlemen.

Doctor Pearse.

Certayne benevolence yearelye from the Lord A[l]m[o]ner to the Gentlemen of the Chappell on Maundye Thursdaye :—

In the yeare 1580	.	.	.	.	. xx s.
In the yeare 1581	.	.	.	.	. xx s.
In the yeare 1582	.	.	.	.	. xx s.
In the yeare 1583	.	.	.	.	. xx s.
In the yeare 1584	.	.	.	.	. xx s.
In the yeare 1585	.	.	.	.	. xx s.

In the yeare 1586 . . . . . xx s.
In the yeare 1587 . . . . . xx s.
In the yeare 1588 . . . . . xx s.
In the yeare 1589 . . . . . xx s.   Doct^r Wickam,
By the Reverend Father in God Mr. Doctor Fletcher,   B. Lincolne, L.
A[l]m[o]ners
being Lord A[l]m[o]ner, in the yeare 1590 . . xx s.   Deputy.
By the Reverend Father in God Mr. Docter Fletcher,   Bishoppe of
beinge Lord Almoner, in the yeare 1591 . . xx s.   Bristowe.
In the yeare 1592 . . . . . xx s.
In the yere 1593 of the sayd L. Almoner (nowe the   To the Serg^t x^s.
To the child-
Bushoppe of Worcester) at Westm^r the Maundy there   ren 4^s. Besides
holden . . . . xx s.   y^s xx^s was also
gave.
In the yeare 1594 of the saide Lord Almoner . . xx s.
In the yeare 1595 of the Reverend Father in God the   The xxiii. of
Aprill receved
Bishop of Durham . . . . . xx s.   of the Bishop
In the yeare 1596 of the Reverend Father in God the L.   of Winchester,
x^s for St.
Bishopp of London, being L. Almoner . . xx s.   George's Day
1596.
In the yeare 1597 of the Reverend Father in God the
Lord Bishopp of Chichester, beinge L. Almoner . xx s.
In the yeare 1598 of the Reverend Father in God the
Lord Bishopp of Chichester, beinge Lord Almoner . xx s.
In the yeare 1599 of the same Lord Almoner . . xx s.
In the yeare 1600 of the same Lord Almoner . . xx s.
In the yeare 1601 of the same Lord Almoner . . xx s.
In the yeare 1602 of the same Lord Almoner . . xx s.
In the yeare 1603 of the same Lord Almoner . . xx s.
In the yeare 1604 of the same Lord Almoner . . xx s.
In the yeare 1605 of the same Lord Almoner . . xx s.
[f. 74b.]

The Continuance of the Lorde A[l]m[o]ner's benevolence to the   Doct. An-
Chappell.   drewes, B. of
Chichester.
By the Right Reverend Father in God, Mr Doctor Andros   1606.
Bushoppe of Chichester, beinge Lorde Alm[o]ner in
the yeare of our Lorde 1606 . . . . xx s.

Item of the said Reverend Father for the yeare 1607 . xx s.

Item rec. of the said Reverend Father for the yeare 1608 . . . . . xx s.

Item of the same Reverend Father for the yeare 1609 . xx s.

D. Androwes, B. of Ely. Item of the same Reverend Father nowe Busshopp of Ely for the yeare of our Lord God 1610 . . . xx s.

Item of the same Reverend Father for the Maundie beinge held the 21st of Marche 1600, beinge then Maundy Thursday . . . . . . xx s.

Item of the same Reverend Father for the yeare 1612 . xx s

Item of the same Reverend Father for the yeare 1613 . xx s.

Item of the same Reverend Father for the yeare 1614 . xx s.

Item of the same Reverend Father for the yeare 1615 . xx s.

The Maundy was kept at Durham 1617. Item of the same Reverend Father for the yeare 1616 . xx s.

Item of the same Reverend Father for the yeare 1618 . xx s.

Dr. Androwes, B. of Winton, for the Maundy. Item of the Reverend Father for the yeare 1619 . xx s.

Item of the same Reverend Father for the yeare 1620 . xx s.

Item rec. of the Reverend Father for the yeare 1621 . xx s.

Dr. Mountaine B. of Lincolne for the Maundy, and Bishop afterwards of London 1622. Item of the same Reverend Father for the yeare 1622 . xx s.

Item received of him for the yeare 1623 . . xx s.

Item received of him for the yeare 1624 . . xx s.

Item received of him for the yeare 1625 . . xx s.

Item received of him for the yeare 1626 . . xx s.

Item received of him for the yeare 1627 . . xx s.

Dr. White, B. of Norwich for the Maundy 1629. Aprill the second and March the 26, 1630. Item received of the same Rev. Father for the yeare 1628 xx s.

Item received of the Reverend Father for the yeare 1629 xx s.

Item received of the Reverend Father for the yeare 1630 xx s.

Dr. Duppa, B. of Winchester for the Maundy, Aprill 11, 1661. Item received of the Reverend Father for the yeare 1661, by Henry Lawes, Clerke of the Check . . xx s.

Item received of the Reverend Father in God Dr. Hinchman, Lord Bishop of Sarum, xx s. for the Maundy 1662 . . . . . . xx s.

Received for the Maundy in the yeare 1663 . . xx s.

Received for the Maundy in the yeare 1664 . . xx s.
Received in the yeare 1665 for the Maundy, by Thos.
Blagravé Cleark of the Check . . . . xx s.
Item received of the Right Reverend Father in God the
Lord Bishop of London, Lord Almoner, for the Maundy
in the yeare of our Lord 1666. The Maundy was kept
in the parish church at Westminster . . . xx s.
Received for the Maundy 1667 . . . . xx s.
Item received of the Reverend Father in God Dr. Lloyd,
Lord Bishop of St. Asaph's and Lord Almoner, xx s.
for the Maundy 1689, by Edw. Braddock, Clerk of
the Check . . . . . . xx s.
Item received of the Reverend Father in God Dr Lloyd,
Bishop of St. Asaph's and Lord Almoner, xx s. for the
Maundy in the yeare 1690, by Edw. Braddock, Clerk
of the Check . . . . . . xx s.
Received of the Reverend Father in God Dr. Lloyd, An. 1691.
Bishop of St. Asaph's and Lord Almoner, xx s. for the
Maundy in the yeare 1691, by Edward Braddock,
Clerk of the Check.
Received of the Reverend Father in God Dr. Lloyd Ann. 1692.
Bishop of St. Asaph's and Lord Almoner, xx s for the
Maundy in the yeare 1692, by Edw. Braddock, Clerk
of the Checke.
Received of the Reverend Father in God, Dr. Lloyd, An. 1693.
Bishop of Litchfeild and Coventry and Lord Almoner,
xx s. for the Maundy in the yeare 1693, by Edward
Braddock, Clerk of the Check.
Received of the Reverend Father in God Dr. Lloyd, An. 1694.
Bishop of St. Asaph's and Lord Almoner, xx s. for the
Maundy in the yeare 1694, by Edward Braddock, Clerk
of the Check.
Received of the Reverend Father in God Dr. Lloyd An. 1695.
Bishop of Litchfeild and Coventry and Lord Almoner,

xx s. for the Maundy in the yeare 1695, by Edw. Braddock, Clerk of Cheque.

An. 1696.   Received of the Reverend Father in God Dr. Lloyd,
Bishop of Litchfeild and Coventry and Lord Almoner,
xx s. for the Maundy in the yeare 1696, by Edw. Braddock, Clerk of the Cheque.

An. 1697.   Received of the Reverend Father in God Dr. Lloyd,
Bishop of Littchfeild and Coventry and Lord Almoner,
xx s. for the Maundy in the yeare 1697, by Edw. Braddock, Clerk of the Cheque.

An. 1698.   Received of the Reverend Father in God Dr. Lloyd,
Bishop of Worcester and Lord Almoner, xx s. for the
Maundy in the yeare 1698, by Edw. Braddock, Clerk
of the Check   .   .   .   .   [f. 75.]   xx s.

An. 1699.   Received of the Reverend Father in God Dr. Lloyd,
Bishop of Worcester and Lord Almoner, xx s. for the
Maundy in the yeare 1699, by Edw. Braddock, Clerk
of the Check   .   .   .   .   .   . xx s.

An. 1700.   Received of the Reverend Father in God Dr. Lloyd,
Bishop of Worcester and Lord Almoner, xx s. for the
Maundy in the yeare 1700, by Edward Braddock,
Clerk of the Check   .   .   .   .   . xx s.

An. 1701.   Received of the Reverend Father in God Dr. Lloyd,
Bishop of Worcester and Lord Almoner, xx s. for the
Maundy in the yeare 1701, by Edw. Braddock, Clerk
of Check   .   .   .   .   .   . xx s.

An. 1702.   Received of the Reverend Father in God Dr. Lloyd,
Bishop of Litchfeild and Lord Allmoner, twenty
shillings for the Maundy for the yeare 1702, by me
Edw. Braddock, Clerk of Check   .   .   . xx s.

An. 1703.   Received of the Reverend Father in God Dr. Sharp,
Archbishop of York and Lord Allmoner, twenty
shillings for the Maundy in the yeare 1703, by me
Edward Braddock, Clerke of the Check.

Received of the Right Reverend Father in God Dr. Sharp, Archbishop of York and Lord Almoner, xx s. for the Maundy in the yeare 1704, by me Edward Braddock, Clerk of the Check. An. 1704.

Received of the Right Reverend Father in God Dr. Sharp, Arch Bishop of York and Lord Allmoner, xx s. for the Maundy in the yeare 1705, by me Edward Braddock, Clerk of the Check. An. 1705.

Received of the Right Reverend Father in God Dr. Sharp, Arch Bishop of York and Lord Allmoner, for the Maundy in the yeare 1706, by me Edward Braddock, Clerk of the Check An. 1706.

Received of his Grace of York, now Lord Allmoner, twenty shillings for the Maundy. An. 1707.

Received of his Grace of York, now Lord Allmoner, one pound for the Maundy, by me Dan. Williams, Clerk of the Check An. 1708.

Ditto		1709.
Ditto		1710.
Ditto	by me Daniel Williams, Clerk of Cheque.	1711.
Ditto		1712.
Ditto		1713.

Received one pound, D. W^{ms} — Clerk of the Cheque.
Received one pound, D. W^{ms} —   [f. 76.] 1715.

Docter Horne, Docter Watson, Docter Cooper, Byshoppes of Winchester. Certayne benevolences yearely from the Bishoppes of Winchester, prelates of the Garter, to the Gentlemen of the Chappell at the feaste of St. George.

In the yeare 1581	.	.	.	.	. xx s.
In the yeare 1582	.	.	.	.	. xx s.
In the yeare 1583	.	.	.	.	. xx s.
In the yeare 1584	.	.	.	.	. xx s.
In the yeare 1585	.	.	.	.	. xx s.

Docter Cowper.

Doctor Cooper.	In the yeare 1586	xx s.
	In the yeare 1587	xx s.
	In the yeare 1588	xx s.
	In the yeare 1589	xx s.
	In the yeare 1592	xx s.
	In the yeare 1593	xx s.
	In the yeare 1594 he dyed, leavinge the fee unpaide .	Nil.

Doctor Wickam.

Doctor Wickam.	In the yeare 1595	xx s.
Doctor Daye.	Item of the Revd. Father in God Docter Daye, Lord Bishop of Wynchester, Anno 1596 . . .	xx s.
Doctor Bilson.	Item of the Revd. Father in God Doctor Bylson, Bishop of Wynchester, Anno 1597 . . .	xx s.
	Item of the Reverend Father in God Doctor Bylson, Bishopp of Wynchester, Anno Domini 1598 . .	xx s.
	Item of the Reverend Father in God Doctor Bilson, Bishopp of Winchester, Anno Domini 1599 . .	xx s.
	Item of the Reverend Father in God Doctor Bylson, Bishopp of Wynchester, Anno Domini 1600 . .	xx s.
	Item of the Reverend Father in God Doctor Bylson, Byshopp of Wynchester, Anno Domini 1601 . .	xx s.
	Item of the same Reverend Father for the yeare of our Lord 1602	xx s.
	Item of the same Reverend Father for the yeare of our Lord 1603	xx s.
	Item of the same Revd. Father for the yeare of our Lord 1604	xx s.
	Item of the same Revd. Father in God for the yeare of our Lord God 1605	xx s.
	Item of the same Revd. Father for the yeare of our Lord God 1606	xx s.
	Item of the aforenamed Reverend Father in God for the yeare of our Lord God 1607	xx s.

Item of the sayd Revd. Father for the yeare of our Lord
God 1608 . . . . . **XX S.**

Item of the same Revd. Father for the yeare of our Lord
God 1609 . . . . . . **XX S.**

Item of the same Revd. Father for the yeare of our Lord
God 1610 . . . . . . **XX S.**

Item of the same Revd. Father for the yeare of our Lord
God 1611 . . . . . . **XX S.**

Item of the same Revd. Father for the yeare of our Lord
God 1612 . . . . . . **XX S.**

Item of the same Revd. Father for the yeare of our Lord
God 1613 . . . . . . **XX S.**

Item of the same Revd. Father for the yeare of our Lord
1614 . . . . **XX S.**

Item of the same Revd. Father for the yeare of our Lord
1615 . . . . **XX S.**

Item of the same Revd. Father for the yeare of our Lord
1616 . . . . **XX S.**

Item received of the Revd. Father in God James Mount-
ague, Lord Bishop of Winchester, for the fee due this
St. George's feast, beinge held at Winsor, the 13th of
September, 1617 . . . . . **XX S.**

Doctor Mount-
ague.

Item recd. of the same Revd. Father for the yeare of our
Lord 1618 . . . . . . **XX S.**

Item received of the Revd. Father in God Lancellott
Lord Bishopp of Winton, for the fee due at St. George's
feast, beinge kept at Greenwich, the 26th of Maie, 1619 **XX S.**

Doctor An-
drewes.

Item recd. of the Revd. Father for the yeare of our Lord
1620 . . . . **XX S.**

Item recd. of the Revd. Father for the yeare 1621 . **XX S.**

Item rec. of the same Rev. Father for the yeare 1622 . **XX S.**

Item received of him for the yeare 1623 . . . **XX S.**

Item rec. of the same Rev. Father for St. George's feast,
held at Winsor, the 28th of Aprill, 1624 . . **XX S.**

Item rec. of the same for the feast held at Winsore the 14
   of December, 1625 .   .   .   .   . xx s.
Item rec. of him for the feast held at Whithall the 27 of
   Aprill 1626 .   .   .   .   .   . xx s.

Doctor Neale. Item rec. of the Rev. Father in God Richard Lord
   Bishopp of Winton, for the fee due at St. George's feast,
   being kept at Windsore, the 26 of Sept. 1628 . . xx s.
Item rec. of the same Rev. Father for the feast held the
   23 of April 1629 .   .   .   .   . xx s.

Doctor Curle. Item rec. of the Rev. Father in God Walter Lord Bishopp
   of Winton, for the fee due at St. George's feast, being
   kept at Whithall, the 23 of Aprill 1634 . . xx s.

Doctor Duppa. Item rec. of the Rev. Father in God Lord Bishop of
   Winton, for the fee due at St. George's feast, being kept
   at Windsor the 15 of Aprill, 1661 .   .   . 3 li.

Doctor Morley. Item received of the Rev. Father in God George Lord
   Bishop of Winton, for the fee due at St. George's feast,
   being kept at Windsor, the 23d of Aprill, the sum of
   xx s. and x s. for the children, Anno Domini 1663 . xxx s.

Dr. Morley. Recd. for St. George's feast, kept at Whitehall, in the yeare
   1667 .   .   .   . xx s.

                                [ff. 72b. 73.]

Benevolences given to the Gentlemen of the Chappell by Bishopps
at the tyme of their Consecraçõns as heerafter doe followe,
viz. :—

Imprimis, Receaved of the Reverend Father in God Doctor
   Mountague, Bishopp of Bathe and Welles, at the tyme
   of his Consecraçõn, given to the Gentlemen of the Chap-
   pell, the some of .   .   .   .   . 5 li.
Item, Receaved for the benevolence of D. Tompson
   Bishopp of Gloster, and of D. Buckridge Bishopp of
   Rochester, given to the Gentlemen at the tyme of their
   Consecraçõns, the some of 4li viz. of eyther of them . iiij li.

Item, Receaved of D. Kinge, Bishopp of London, for the
lyke benevolence, given at the tyme of his Consecracõn,
the some of　.　.　.　.　.　. xl s.

[f. 71*b*.]

The Lord High Treasurer of England gives to the Gentlemen of
the Chappell for their New Year's Gift forty shillings.

The Right Reverend the Deane of his Maj. Chappell for the time
being gives to the Gentlemen of the Chappell for their New Year's
Gift forty shillings.

The Right Reverend Father in God Dr. Henry Compton, Lord
Bishopp of Oxford and Deane of his Maj. Chappell Royall; gave to
the Gentlemen of his Maj. Chappell (at his coming in to be their
Deane) a buck and ten pounds in gold to drinke his Lordship's health,
which was accordingly done at Windsor the 16th day of August
1675.

The Lord Allmoner for the time being giveth to the Gentlemen
of the Chappell every Maunday Thursday twenty shillings, and five
shillings every New Year's Day.

The Right Reverend Father in God Doctor John Robinson, Lord
Bishop of London and Dean of his Majesties Chappell Royall, gave
to the Gentlemen of his Majesties Chappell ten guineas to drink his
Lordship's health, and (buck venison being out of season,) his Lordship was pleased to give a guinea to buy venison, which was accordingly done; and as many Gentlemen as wear in toun mett and din'd
at the Bell Tavern in Westminster the 22d day of October 1719.

The Right Revd. Father in God Dr. Wm. Talbot, Lord Bishop of
Sarum, upon his being made Dean of his Majesties Chappells Royall,
gave a buck and tenn guineys to the Gentlemen of the said Chappell
to drink his Lordship's health, which was accordingly done at the
Rummer at Chearing Cross, the　　　day of August 1718.

[f. 74.]

X.—Records of the " Chapel Feast."

A Warrante for three powndes geven by her Majestie to the Chappell Feaste:—

By the Queene.

Right trustie and welbeloved Councellor, wee greete you well, and lett you wytt our will and pleasure is that upon the sighte hereof youe paye and deliver, or cause to be paide and delivered, to the Gentlemen of oure Chappell Royall the some of three powndes currante money in this our realme, to be taken unto them as of our guifte towardes their feaste, as aboute this tyme in former yeares hathe bene geven unto them oute of our threasure remayninge in your custodie as Threasorer of our Chamber. Wherof faile youe not: and these our lettres shalbe your sufficient warrante and discharge in this behalfe. Geven under our signett, &c.

To our trustie and welbeloved Thomas
Henneage, Knight, Threasorer of
oure Chamber.

To our right trustie and welbeloved Councellor the Lord Stanhope, Treas^r of our
Chamber.

[f. 85.]

We will and command that uppon the sight hereof you deliver, or cause to be delivered, to the Gentlemen of our Chappell Royall, or to the bearer hereof in their names, two bucks of this season, to be taken of our guifte, within Chynkeford Walke, within our Forreste of Waltham, in our Countye of Essex, anye restrainte, preevie token, or commaundment heretofore geven to the contrarye notwithstandinge. And these our lettres shalbe your discharge in that behalfe. Geven under our signett at our Mannor House of, &c.

2 buckes, Henald Chappell. [sic.]

1 bucke, Enfield Chase. [f. 85.]

1619, June 27.   Mem. that at a Chapter held the 27th daie of June, 1619, It was there agreed uppon by generall consent that alwaies heerafter ther shalbe allowed unto the stewardes of the Chappell Feast of every gentleman attendant the some of three shillinges fower pence, whether the feast be generall or devided, and that the sayd monies be paid out of June bord wages, which comonly is paid at the breakinge up of the Chappell, and such of the Gentlemen as are growne aged or taken with sicknes, so that there is no expectacōn of their service any more, they to pay yearly sixe shillinges eight pence a peece towards the same feast: Provided alwaies, that if any of the Gentlemen by any occacōn shall have cause to be absent from the sayd feast, then any such gentleman may and shall lawfully appoint and send any cople of his friendes to supplie his absence at that feaste: and likewise if any of the Gentlemen shall bringe or send any frinde or friendes more than he ought to doe he shall paye unto the stewardes for every such guest the some of two shillinges sixe pence, to be taken out of his or their borde wages for the monethe of September next followinge. In testimony heereof we the Gentlemen now attendinge have heerunto subscribed our names the daie and yeare above written.   Leonard Davies, Subdeane.

Antho. Harrison.	George Wooddeson.	Willm. Crosse.
Richard Coton.	Orlando Gibbons.	Edmund Nelham.
Ezech. Waad.	Will. West.	Walter Porter.
Jo. Hewlett.	George Cooke.	Peter Hopkins.
John Amery.	John Frost.	George Sheffeilde.
		Nathanaell Gyles.

[f. 36.]

Warrants for Buckes graunted by Kinge Charles:—

Our will and Pleasure is that uppon sight heerof you deliver or cause to be delivered unto the Gentlemen of our Chappell Royall, or to the bearer of this for them, one fatt buck of this season, and this our warrant shalbe your discharge. Given at our Court at Greenwich this 25th of June, 1626.   1626

To the Ranger, Keeper, or Underkeeper, of
    our Chase of Enfield.

Our will and pleasure is that uppon sight heerof you deliver or cause to be delivered unto the Gentlemen of our Chappell Royall, or to the bearer heerof for them, two fatt buckes of this season, and this our warrant shalbe your discharge. Given at our Court at Greenwich this 25th of June, 1626.

To the Keeper and Underkeeper of our Parke
of Mariebone.   [f. 85.]

The warrant for the 3 was as above is written.

1632, June 3 A Decree made in a Chapter holden at Grinwich by Stephan Boughton (Subdeane of his Majesties Chappell Royall) and the Gentlemen of the Company there assembled togeather in the vestry beeing twenty in number, touching the choice of the Stuards of the Chappell Feast for the tyme to come, this third of June Anno Domini 1632:—

Be it remembred that it is agreed and concluded by the Subdeane and Gentlemen assembled the day and yeare above written, that from hence forward the stuardes of the Chappell Feast are yearely to be elected and chosen by the company or major part thereof, being for that porpose yearely assembled by the Subdeane or Substitute's appoyntment: And every gentleman soe chosen and elected as aforesayd refusinge the sayd office of stuarde or stuardes shall paye xx^s apeece, to be taken out of his wagis by the Clarke of the Checke for the tyme beinge, for the use of the company, to be expended at the sayd feast or otherwise, as the company shall thinke fytt: It is lykewise agreed on and concluded by the consent of the gentlemen aforesayd, that every one of the sayde company shall paye to the stuards out of June boardwagis for the sayd feast sixe shillings eight pence yearely for him selfe and his wife, the said vj^s viij^d to be taken out of the sayd moneth aforesayde by the Clarke of the Checke to the use aforesayd: And such of the gentlemen as are exemted from dayly attendance shall paye to the use aforesayd xiij^s iiij^d out of his boord wagis in the month before expressed. It is further concluded and agreed on by the assent and consent of the gentlemen aforesayd, that yf any of the companie (whether maried or unmarried) shall bringe to the sayd feast any other person or persons except his owne wyfe, shall paye (over and above all other paymentes before expressed) ten shillings for each person so brought, to be taken out of his wagis as before is expressed : And, lastly, it is concluded and agreed on by the gentlemen, that the stuardes shall yearely yeald a just and true accompt to the companie howe they have disbursed the moneys that they have receaved for the sayd feast, if the companie shall requier it at their handes. In wittnes heerof wee have heerunto subscribed our names the day and yeare first above written. [f. 69.]

Be it remembred, That whereas Captain Henry Cooke, Master of 1662. the Children of his Majesties Chappell Royall, was chosen by the Gentlemen of the said Chappell at their feast held in the yeare 1662, to [be] one of the stewards for the feast to be held in the next yeare following, viz. 1663, he, the said [Capt. Henry] Cooke accepted of that stewardship on condition that this choise should be no precedent to binde [him or] his successors for the future whilst they are Masters of the sayd Children, to take upon [them any] more the sayd stewardship, it being never the custome of former yeares nor now . . . .* meet or convenient for the Master of the Children to beare that office. [f. 36.]

Charles R.

Our will and pleasure is, that you forthwith paye or cause to be 1666, July 28. payed to the Gentlemen of our Chappell Royall the summe of twenty pounds as of our free guift, and in lieu of three deere which of custome wee have been pleased to grant yearly unto them: For which this shall be your warrant. Given att our Court att Whitehall the 28th day of July in the 18th yeare of our reigne 1666.

By his Maties command,

ARLINGTON.

To our trusty and wellbeloved Sir
    Edward Griffin, knt our Treasurer
    of our Chamber.

£20 to the Gentlemen of the Chappell in lieu of 3 deere. [f. 47b.]

---

* A piece of the MS. is here torn away.

1690. Memorandum, that in the yeare 1690, being the second yeare of the reigne of our Soveraigne Lord and Lady King William and Queene Mary, there Majesties were graciously pleased to restore unto the Gentlemen of there Chappell Royall there antient annuall feast which for some years beffore they had lost, and instead of three bucks which they allways had at the said feast did then grant unto them twenty pounds in money to be yearly paid unto them out of there Majesties Treasury Chamber, with these perquisitts following, viz. :—

At the Salsary, fine flower 1^{bs} 1^d. At the Poultry, butter 36^{pd}.
At the Pantry, Cheat fine 2 doz. Coarse 2 doz.
At the Buttry, beer 1 h^{hd}. At the Cellar, clarrett 2^{gs} 2^{ps}.
At the Larder, a sir loyne of beef 46^{pd}. [f. 84b.]

XI.—APPOINTMENTS OF THE DEANS.

1618-9, January 1. Lancelott Lord Bishop of Winton sworne Deane of the Chappell. Be it remembred that uppon the first daie of Januarie 1618, the Right Honorable Lancellot Lord Bishopp of Winton and one of his Majestes Privie Counsell was sworne Deane of his Majestes Chappell in the vestery at Whithall, whose othe was ministred by Leonard Davies then Subdeane, in the presence of the gentlemen then there attendinge. [f. 28.]

1626, Oct. 6. Wm Lord Bishop of Bathe and Welles sworne Deane of his Maj. Chappell. Be it remembred that uppon the sixte day of October 1626, the Right Reverend Father in God William Lord Bishopp of Bathe and Welles was sworne Deane of his Majestes Chappell in the vesterie at Whitehall, whose othe was ministred unto him by Stephan Boughton, Subdeane, in the presence of the Right Hon. the Erle of Montgomarie, Lord Chamberlaine to his Majestie.

Stephan Boughton, Subdeane. [f. 38b.]

Deanes of the Chappell Royall since the yeare 1660 to 1687.

Gilbert Sheldon, Lord Bishop of London, afterwards translated to Canterbury.

George Morley, Lord Bishop of Winchester.

Herbert Croft, Lord Bishop of Hereford.

Walter Blandford, Lord Bishop of Worcester.

Henry Compton, Lord Bishop of London.

Nathaniel Crewe, Lord Bishop of Durham.

Henry Compton, Lord Bishop of London, was againe made Deane of the Chappell Royall in the first yeare of the reigne of there Majesties William and Mary, and in the yeare of our Lord 1689.   1689.

John Robinson, Lord Bishop of London, was, by her Majesty Queen Anne, made Dean of the Chappell Royall the 17th day of July 1713.   1713.

William Talbott, Lord Bishop of Salisbury, was, by his Majesty King George, made Dean of his Maj. Royall Chappells the 15th day of March 1717-8.   1717-8.

Edmund Gibson, Lord Bishop of Lincoln, was, by his Majesty King George, made Dean of his Maj. Royall Chapells the 17th day of Novr 1721.   [f. 53.]   1721.

XII.—THE NAMES OF THE SUBDEANS, PRIESTS, AND GENTLE-MEN AT VARIOUS CORONATIONS.

A note of the names of the Subdeane, Gentlemen and others of the Chappell, at the tyme of the Coronation of Kynge James the First.   Anno Domini 1603.

Leonard Davies, Subdeane.

Bartholomew Mason.	Stephen Boughton.	
Anthony Harrison.	William Lawes.	Mynisters.
William Barnes.	Anthony Kirckbye.	
Robert Stuckley.		

Nathanaell Gyles, Master of the Children.
Thomas Sampson, Clerke of the Check.
Jo. Bull, Doctor in Musicke.

Robert Stone.	William Randall.	James Davies.
William Birde.	Robert Allison.	William Lawrence.
Richard Granwall.	Jo. Stevens.	Jo. Amery.
Crue Sharpe.	Jo. Hewlett.	Jo. Baldwine.
Edmond Browne.	Richard Plumley.	Francis Wyborough.
Tho. Wooddeson.	Tho. Goulde.	Arthur Cocke.
Henry Eveseede.	Peter Wright.	George Wooddeson
		Jo. Wooddeson.

} Gentlemen.

Ralphe Fletcher, Sergant.
Jo. Patten, Yeoman.
Robert Hewes, Yeoman.
Henry Allred, Groome.

} Officers of the Vestry.

[f. 87.]

1661, Apl. 23. The Names of the Subdeane, Gentlemen, and others of his Majesties Chappell Royall, at the tyme of the Coronation of King Charles the Second, Aprill 23, being St. George's Day, 1661.

Doctor Walter Jones, Subdeane.

Roger Nightingale.	John Sayer.	Henry Smith.
Ralphe Amner.	Durant Hunt	William Tinker.
Phillip Tinker.	George Low.	

} Ministers.

Henry Cooke, Master of the Children.
Henry Lawes, Clarke of the Checke.
Thomas Peers, Thomas Hazzard, John Harding, Gentlemen.
Edward Low, William Chylde, Christopher Gibbons, Organists.

William Howes.	James Cob.	Edward Coleman.
Thomas Blagrave.	Nathaniell Watkins.	Thomas Purcill.
Gregory Thorndell.	John Cave.	Henry Frost.
Edward Bradock.	Alphonso Marsh.	John Goodgroome.
Henry Purcill.	Raphaell Courtevile.	George Betenham
		Mathew Pennell.

} Gentlemen.

Thomas Haynes, Sergeant of the Vestry.

William Williams, Yeoman, Georg Whitcher, Yeoman, Augustine Cleavland, Groome.

At which time every Gentleman of the Chappell (in orders) had allowed to him for a gowne, five yards of fine scarlet, and the rest of the Gentlemen, being laymen, had allowed unto each of them foure yards of the like scarlet. [f. 44.]

The names of the Gentlemen of the Chappell at the Coronation of 1685, April 23. our Sovereigne Lord King James the Second, Aprill the 23rd, 1685.

Dr. William Holder, Sub Deane.

John Sayer,	James Hart,	John Sharold,	⎫
George Yardley,	Andrew Trebecke,	John Gostling,	⎪
Blase White,	Stephen Crespion, Confessor,	Leonard Wooddeson,	⎬ Ministers.
Henry Smyth,	William Powell,	Samuel Bentham,	⎪
Dr. William Child,			⎭

Thomas Blagrave, Clearke of the Cheque.

Dr. John Blow, Master of the Children.

Edward Braddocke.	William Turner.	John Abel.
James Cobb.	Richard Hart.	Morgan Harris.
Nathaniell Watkins.	Michaell Wise	Henry Purcell.
Henry Frost.	(was then suspended	Josias Boucher.
John Goodgroome.	and did not appear).	Nathaniell Vestment.
George Bettenham.	Alphonso Marsh.	Edward Morton
Thomas Richardson.	Thomas Heywood.	(extraordinary).

Thomas Heynes, Sergeant of the Vestry.

Marmaduke Alford, eldest Yeoman of the Vestry.

Morice Morer, Yeoman of the Vestry.

George Oldner, Groome of the Vestry, George Wyatt, Common Servant.

At which tyme was allowed scarlett as at the Coronation of King Charles the Second, p. 44. [f. 52b.]

1689, Apl. 11. The names of the Sub Dean, Gentlemen, and others of their Majestyes Chappell Royall, at the time of the Coronation of King William and Queen Mary, Aprill the 11th, 1689.

The Revd. Mr. Ralph Battell, Sub Dean.

Mr. Blaze White.   Mr. Stephen Crispion.
Mr. Sayr.   Mr. John Gostling.   } Ministers.
Mr. James Hart.   Mr. Leonard Woodeson.
Mr. Andrew Trebeck.   Mr. Samuel Bentham.

Doctor William Child, Organist.
Doctor John Blow, Organist and Master of the Children.
Mr. Henry Purcell, Organist.
Mr. Edward Bradock, Clerk of the Cheque.

Mr. James Cobb.   Mr. William Turner.
Mr. Nathaniel Watkins.   Mr. Alphonso Marsh.
Mr. Henry Frost.   Mr. Morgan Harris.
Mr. John Goodgroome.   Mr. Josiah Bouchier.
Mr. George Betenham.   Mr. Nathaniel Vestment.
Mr. Thomas Richardson.

Officers of the Vestry.

Henry Parker, esq. Serjeant.
Marmaduke Alford, Yeoman.   George Oldner, Groom.

[f. 54b.]

XIII.—NOTICES APPERTAINING TO THE SERJEANTS, YEOMEN GROOMS, AND OTHER OFFICERS.—*List I.*

A remembrance of the deathes and incombe of the Officers of the Vestery :— *

1592. John Dison, Sergeant of the Vestery, died in December 1592, and Ralfe Fletcher was sworne Sergeant in his roome the 24th of the same.

    * This List occupies f. 3 and the reverse in the original MS.

1591. John Burchall, eldest Yeoman, died at Chichester in the Queen's Progresse the   of August, and John Patten was sworne Groome in his place in the same progresse, by the Gent. Ushers, but was new sworne by the Sub Dean at his returne, before he could be receaved into wages.

1593. Wm. Pike, second Yeoman, died the 12 of Maye, and Henry Alred was sworne Groome in his place the same daye, and Robt. Hewes sworne younger Yeoman the viij[th] of June following.

1608. John Patten, eldest Yeoman, made over his place the first of Maye unto Christopher Clark, who was sworne then Groome.

1608. Sergeant Fletcher made over his place to Cuthbert Joyner the 26th of June.

1610. Christopher Clark, Groome of the Vestery, resigned his place the 22th of December to Wm. Lowther, who was sworne Groome the same daye.

1611. Henry Alred for many disorders, and for suspicōn of stealing 3 coapes out of his Maj[tys] Vestery at Greenwich, was put out of his place the vij[th] of June, and Wm. Lowther was sworne Yeoman that daye, and Henry Eveseed the younger was sworne Groome of the Vestery in his place, the 19th of the same June followinge.

1615. Jhon Nicholas, eldest Yeoman of the Vesterie, sold his place unto Richard Patten, who was sworne Groome thereof the 30th of Sept. and Wm. Lowther and Henry Eveseed were sworne Yeomen.

1620. Henry Eveseed, for many disorders comitted and proved against him, was deprived of his Majestes service the third of Marche, and Thomas Pannell was sworne Groome in his place the 20th of the same, and then was Richard Patten raised to the Yeoman's place.

1624. Wm. Lowther, eldest Yeoman, died the 3 of July, and Thomas Walker, servant to the Lord Bishop of Winton, and

Deane of the Chappel, was sworne Groome in his place the xxvth of the same followinge.

1625. Memorandum, that uppon the xixth of November, by King Charles['s] warrant, under his hand signed, was Thomas Meller sworne Joynt Sergeant of his Ma^{tes} Vesterie, and Robt. Colman and Silvester Wilson Yeomen of the same, and Thomas Meller to receave suche wages as doth belonge to the Sergeant from his Majestes first entrance unto his Crowne, and Robt. Colman and Silvester Wilson to receave xij^d a peece per diem, and x^{li} a peece per annum for the fee, and they to have prioritie of place above the Sergeant and Yeomen as other his Ma^{tes} servantes had.

1625. Cuthbert Joyner, Sergeant of the Vesterie, died the vj daye of Januarie, and was buried in the Savoy Churche the daye followinge.

1636. Thomas Meller, Sergeant of his Maties Vesterie, dyed the 25 day of June, and Thomas Walker, then eldest Yeoman of the Vesterie, was sworne Sergeant in his place on Christmas following; and John Powntney, the youngest Yeoman, was sworne eldest Yeoman, and Hugh Jenkins, being then Groome, was sworne youngest Yeoman, and Roger Judd, servant to the Bushop of Norwich, then Deane of his Maties Chappell, was sworne Groome, uppon Shrove Tuesday followeing.

1660. Thomas Haynes was sworn Sergeant of his Maj^{ties} Vestry, the vth day of November 1660; the same day at the same tyme William Williams was sworn the eldest Yeoman, and Whitell sworn youngest Yeoman, and Augustine Cleavland Groom.*

1665. Mr. William Williams, eldest Groom of [his Maties] Vestry, departed this life the 28th of July [1665]; in whose place was sworne Owen Phillips y^e   of August 1665, by warrant from Dr. [Morley] Bishop of Winton, Deane of his Maties Chappell.

* This entry has been crossed out in the MS.

1671. Mr. Hugh Powell, Groome of the Vestry, [departed] this life the 28th of February 1671.

1671. Richard Ouldner sworne Groome of the Vestry the 20th day of March.

1675. Capt. Owen Phillips, Yeoman of the Vestry, departed this life at Richmond, in Surrey, the 26 of August 1675.

1675. Mr. Marm. Alford was sworne Yeoman of the Vestry the 30 of August 1675.

1675. George Oldner sworne Groome of the Vestry the 29th of September, being Michælmas Day, at Whitehall.

1678. Mr. Adam Watkins, Bellringer, departed this life the third day of September 1678.

1680. George Whitcher, eldest Yeoman of the Vestry, departed this life the 4th of February 1680, in whos place was sworne Morice Morer the 5th of Febr. 1680; the said Morice Morer was sworne youngest Yeoman, but it was not to be a president to hinder the Groome of his right for the future.

1685. Thomas Heines, esq. sworne Serjant of the Vestry the 28th day of March.

1685. Mr. Marmaduke Alford sworne eldest Yeoman of the Vestry the 28th day of March.

1685. Mr. Morice Morer sworne youngest Yeoman of the Vestry the 28th day of March.

1685. Mr. George Oldner sworne Groome of the Vestry the 28th day of March.

1686. Mr. Morice Morer, youngest Yeoman of the Vestry, departed this life the   day of Novr. 1686.

1687. Serjant Thomas Haynes, Serjant of the Vestry, departed this life the 30 of June 1687.

1695. Mr. George Oldner, Groom of the Vestry, departed this life the 14 of January 1694-5.

1697. Mr. Isaac Cook, Groom of the Vestry, departed this life the 5th day of April 1697.

1704. Mr. Nicholas Phipps, Closet Keeper in the Chapel at White Hall, departed this life the 20th of January 1703-4.

1708. Mr. Mathew Fairless departed this life (Groom of the Vestry) the 14 of July 1708.

1715. Henry Parker, esq. Serjeant of the Vestry departed this life the 13th of March 1714-5.

1715. Marmaduke Alford, esq. Serjeant of the Vestry departed this life the 10th of May 1715.

1718. Mr. Daniel Farmer, Closet Keeper in the Chappell of White Hall, departed this life the 16th day of May 1718.

1719. Mr. John Lenton, Groom of the Vestry, departed this life the day of May 1719.

XIV.—Notices appertaining to the Serjeants, Yeomen, Grooms, and other Officers.—*List II.*

Ordinarye.

11 Dec. 1592.   The 11th daye of December, 1592, at the speciall commaunde of the Right Honorable the Lord Chamberlen, was sworne by Antho. Anderson, Subdeane, Henry Alredd, into ordinarye, without waiges, and without forther suicte to his Lordship, to be sworne Groome of the Vestrye into waiges at the nexte avoydance. Thes beinge witnes['s] of the oathe.

Antho. Anderson.
Bartholomew Mason.
Leonard Davies.
Thomas Sampson.
Robert Tallentyer.   [f. 21<i>b</i>.]

25 Dec. 1592.   Upon Christmas Daye, the 25th of December, 1592, were sworne into ordynarye William Pike, the elder Yeoman of her Majestes Hon. Vestrye, and John Patten, that was Groome before, sworne the

same daye the yonger Yeoman of the same Vestrye, and thirdlye Robert Hewes, the Right Hon. the Lord Chamberlen's man, was likewise sworne Groome into the sayd Vestrye, and everye of thes by the apoinctment and commaundment of the said Right Hon. Lord Chamberlen, in witnesse whereof we the Subdeane and other the Gentlemen of her Majestes Chappell have subscribed our names the daye and yere abovesayd.

And likewise Raphe Fletcher, beinge the eldest Yeoman at the deathe of the last Sergeant, Mr. John Dison, was by her sacred Majestie apointed, upon the forsaid Lord Chamberlens presentinge to her Majestie (his ho. by her Majestie ordeyned our cheefe governor havinge no other Deane) was by the Subdeane likewise sworne Sergeant of the sayd Vestrye the 24. of December aforsayd, beinge Christmas even. In witnes of the whole premisses, we, as before, have subscribed our names.

Anth Anderson, Subdeane.

*	William Randall.	Leonard Davies.
Thomas Sampson.	Henry Eveseed.	Antho. Harrison.
Crwe Sharpe.	Tymothe Greene.	John Bull.
Thomas Woodsonn.	John Stephens.	Anthony Todd.
Robert Tallentyer.	Bar. Mason	[f. 21*b*.]

The 12. daye of May 1593, William Pike, late Yeoman of her Majestes hon. Vestrye, departed, according to a former order and comaundment, geven by the Right Hon. the Lord Chamberlen to her Sacred Majestie, geven the 11th daye of December, as aperethe in the other paige, was sworne into ordinarye Groome of the sayd Vestrye Henrye Alred, a longe attendant in the said Vestrye, and sworne extrordinarye therto beffore. His oathe was geven him by me Antho. Anderson, Subdean of her Majestes Chappell Royall, in the parishe churche of Stebinhithe the daye and yere abovesayd, in

Maye 12, 1593.

* A signature occurs occurs here which it is impossible to decipher.

the presence of two Gentlemen of the Chappell and the Serjeant of the Vestrye aforsaid.   Anth. Anderson, Subdean.

Richarde Granwall, Peter Wryght, Gentlemen.

Rafe Fletcher, Sergeante.   [f. 22.]

June 8, 1593.   The 8th daye of June was sworne the yonger Yeoman of hir Majestes most hon. Vestrye Robert Hewes, before beinge the Groome therof, and was sworne by me in the parishe churche of Stepneye in the morninge, then beinge present sondry persons, 1593.   Anth. Anderson.

Samuel Totsford, Preacher and Curate ther.

John Salisburye, Groome of her Majestes C.

Tho. Hoare, and others.

25 Jan^y, 1594-5.   The Right Honorable the Lord Chamberlayne uppon the 25th day of Januarye Anno Domini 1594, did comaund me, Leonard Davies, Subdean, at Greenwich, to sweare Richard Hemyngwaye extraordinarye Groome of her Majesties Vestrie, comaundinge further that I shoulde recorde in this booke of remembrance, that his honor's pleasure is that the saide Rich. Hemyngwaye shoulde be placed Ordynary Groome in the Vestrye at the nexte avoydance whensoever without further suite to him: And the same his honor's graunte was at the earneste sute of Mr. Morgan, her Majesties chiefe apothecarie: The day and yeare above written the saide Rich. Hemyngwaye was sworne extraordinarye for the nexte Groomes place in a chapter kepte for that purpose as was commaunded.

Leonard Davies, Subdean.   [f. 22b.]

1595-6. January.   An Order sett downe by the Officers of the Vestrie with the Sub-deanes consent.

Wheras the two Yomen of the Vestrie are by dewtie to see her Majesties stuffe meete for her Chappell, to be trussed upp at everye remove and sent to her highnes nexte house of waytinge.   Uppon sufficient cause it is agreed uppon by Mr. Fletcher, Sergeant of the Vestrye, and Robert Hewes, Yoman ther, and Henrye Alred, Groome, that John Patten, Yoman also (of that office) shall for the some of vj s. viij d. beinge bye equall porcons quarterlye paide to the Sergeante (by the saide John Patten) be discharged at every remove throughout the yeare of his personall beinge present to see her Majestes stuffee so trussed upp and removed, as belongeth to his place. In testimonye that we the above named officers of the vestrie doe joyntlye consent hereto, We have subscribed our names to this order agreed uppon the   of Januarye Anno Domini 1595, and in the 38th yeare of her Majestes Raigne.

[f. 23.]

Be it remembred that the 22th daye of June Anno Domini 1601, and in the 43th yeare of the reigne of our Soveraigne Ladye Queene Elizabeth, Henry Alred, Groome of the Vestrie, for his manye and great disorders committed, recevid this his first admonition and warninge (with a pricke sett uppon his head) and that done in open Chapter by the Subdeane and all of the gentlemen of the company then present, beinge eighteen in number, intendinge hereby his reformation and amendement, as he regardeth his continuance in her Majestes service.

Leonard Davies, Subdeane.*

The said Henry Alred appearinge before the Subdeane and the rest of the Gentlemen in Chapter the 29th of the same June in the yeare afore said dyd then and there make his humble submission with promise of amendment hereafter of his former misdemeanors, and was there uppon accepted, and accordinge to the power which lyeth in us wee have reversed the said admonition and taken away the prick formerly sett uppon his heade.

Leonarde Davies, Subdeane. [f. 16b.]

* This entry is erased in the MS.

1603.

The 29th daye of Aprill Anno Domini 1603, the Subdeane and Gentlemen meetinge in Chapter to take order for the service of the Kinges Majestie as they weare comaunded, at which meetynge the Sergeante of the Vestrie did then and there to the greate disturbance of the sayd companie unreverently and undutifully behave himselfe towardes the Subdeane and gentlemen then present, for the which the Subdeane and gentlemen then presente, beinge 21 in number, doe thinke meete that his Check for his contempt and disobedience as aforesayd shall be twentie shillinges to the Kinges Majestie, to be taken out of his next quarter's wages. [f. 16*b*.]

1606-7, Jany. 6.
Hen. Eveseede sworne Groome of the Vestrie extra- ordinarie.

Be it remembred that uppon the sixt daie of Januarie 1606, and in the fourthe yeare of his Majestes raigne that now is, was Henry Eveseede the yonger sworne a Groome of the Vestrie extraordinarie for the next place that shall fall therin, whensoever or by what meanes soever, by the order and gift of the Right Worshipfull Mr. Doctor Montague, Deane of his Majestes Royall Chappell. In testimony the Subdean and Gentlemen of the Chappell who were then presente have subscribed their names the daie and yeare above said. Leonard Davies, Subdean.

J. Bull.	Francis Wiborowe.	John Amery.
Thomas Sampson.	Richard Granwall.	Anthony Harrison.
Richard Plumley.	Henry Eveseed.	Stephen Boughton.
John Baldwine.	Jo. Hewlett.	[f. 29.]

1606-7, Jan. 6.
Jo. Davies sworne Yeoman of the Vestrie extra- ordinarie.

Be yt also remembred that uppon the daie above mencioned John Davies, by the order and gift of the right wors[l] Mr. Doctor Montague, Deane as above said, was sworne a yeoman extraordinarie of his Ma[tes] Vesterie at the same time. And in testimonie therof the gentlemen who were present have subscribed their names the daie and yeare first above written. Leonard Davies, Subdean.

Anthony Harrison.	John Baldwine.	Jo. Hewlett.
Stephen Boughton.	J. Bull.	Richard Plumley.
Thomas Sampson.	Richard Granwall.	Francis Wiborowe.
John Amery.	Henry Eveseed.	[f. 29.]

Be it remembred that uppon the 23rd of Februarie 1606, and in the fourth yeare of his Majestes raigne that now is, Robert Bicknar was by the free guift and comaunde of the right Worsh^l Mr. Doctor Mountague, Deane of his Maj^tes Chappell, sworne Bellringer for his Maj^tes householde, in the vesterie at Whitehall, by Leonard Davies, Subdeane, in which othe amonge other partes as to the supremacie &c. he was sworne to obedience to the Deane and Subdeane of the sayd Chappell, and to the Confessor of his Majestes housholde for the tyme beinge, in all matters and thinges apperteyninge to his said place and service. *(margin: 1606-7. Feb. 23. Robt Bicknar, Bellringer.)*

Leonard Davies, Subdeane. [f. 29b.]

Be yt remembred that Thomas Miller uppon the 26th daie of Maye 1607, was by the order of the right worshipfull Mr. Mountague, Deane of his Majestes Chappell, sworne Yeoman of the Kinges Ma^tes Vestery, and to attend the Prince. And he received his othe then as Yeoman after the same manner and forme as he did beinge sworne Groome, as above appearethe.* In testimony heerof I Leonard Davies, Subdeane, have heerunto subscribed my name the daye and yeare above written. *(margin: 1607, May 26. Thos. Miller sworne Yeoman for the Princes Vestery.)*

Leonard Davies, Subdeane. [f. 28b.]

Be it remembred that uppon the 28th of Marche 1608, Henry Alred, Yeoman of the Vestrie, for his fearefull blasphemies, wicked execracons and threatninges to spill bloud, and that at the tyme and place when the holy sacrament was to be administred the Wednesday before Easter, beinge the 27th of the sayd monethe, to the great offence of many well disposed, received in Chapter, kept by the Subdean and Gentlemen the sayd 28th daie by the comaundment of the Right Worshipfull Mr. Doctor Mountague, Deane of his Majestes honorable Chappell, an admonicōn with a prick sett uppon his head, as is used in his Majestes house in such lyke cases, intendinge theerby his reformacōn and amendment as he regardeth his continuance in his Majestes service. *(margin: 1608, March 28.)*

Leonard Davies, Subdeane. [f. 29b.]

* See p. 109.

1608, May 15.
Wm. Dale
Groome of the
Prince's
Vestrie.

Be it remembred that uppon the fifeteene daie of May 1608, (beinge Whitsondaie) William Dale, by the order and appointment of the Reverend Father the Lord Bishop of Bathe and Welles, and Deane of his highnes chappell, was sworne Groome of the Kinges Majesties Vesterie, to attend the Prince. And he then receaved his othe in the selfe same manner and forme as did Thomas Miller, as appearethe in the page next before. In testimonie heerof I Leonard Davies, Subdean, have heerunto subscribed my name the daie and yeare above sayd. Leonard Davies, Subdean. [f. 29.]

1608, Nov. 2.

Be it agayne remembred that at a Chapter helde by the now Reverend Father in God James Lord Byshopp of Bathe and Welles, and Deane of his Majestes Chappell, the second of November 1608, Henry Alred, Yeoman of the Vestrie, for drounkennes, many greate disorders, and threatninge the spillinge of the Subdeanes bloude, receaved this second admonicon by his Lordshipp's order in the said Chapter, with an other prick sett uppon his head, still intendinge his reformacon of lyfe, or heerby shewinge him the cause of his just expulsion according to the auncient orders of his Majestes house. Leonard Davies, Subdeane, [f. 30b.]

1608, Nov. 2.

Be it remembred that in the yeare 1608, the Sergeant and Officers of the Vesterie for the tyme beinge, did by way of peticon complayne unto the Right Reverend Father in God the Lord Bishopp of Bathe and Welles and Deane of his Ma^{tes} Chappell, That the Subdeane and Gentlemen of his Majestes sayd Chappell that then weare did oppresse and molest them in their sayd office as they affirmed, beseeching therefore the sayd Reverend Deane, that by his order the Subdeane and Gentlemen might not have entrance or accesse into the Vestery, but only at the howers of service in the Chappell, nor that the Subdeane nor any with him should eyther dyne or supp in the sayd office as they have don, neyther that he nor any of the gentlemen should have eyther bed or trunck to stand in the vestery, but to have the place private unto themselves. Uppon this their complaint it pleased the sayd Reverend Father the Deane to holde a Chapter in the sayd vestery the second day of November the yeare above sayd, wherto were called the Subdeane and gentlemen then attendinge, beinge 24 in number, and also the Sergeant and officers of the Vestery: wher the sayd Deane examininge howe that office had byn used in tymes tofore, he founde that whiles that syxe Lord Chamberlaines had the government of the Chappell (in the vacancy of a Deane) that the Subdeane and Gentlemen did injoye in the vestery those privileges which the officers now would abridge them of, and therfore the said Reverend Father the Deane out of his wisdom (to conserve order and quiett) did then in Chapter thus order the matters in question: First that the vestery should be used by the Subdeane and Gentlemen (as a place of repose) all the daye for their severall exercises and comfort as had bin, and further that the Subdeane with fower or five quiett and sober gentlemen with him should dayly dyne and supp in the vestery as they had accostomed: And agayne for the matter of lodginge and placinge of the gentlemen's truncks in the vestery his Lordship pleased to referr the conveniency therof unto the discrecõn of the Subdeane and Sergeant of the vestrie for the tyme beinge.

The which his Lordshipp's sayd orders he hath caused to be registred in this our booke of recordes the day and yeare above sayd, Wherto for the better confirmacõn it hath pleased his Lordshipp to putto [*sic*] his hand, &c.

Ja. Bath: et Well: [f. 35.]

Be it remembred the third tyme, that at a Chapter held and so appointed by the now Reverend Father in God James Lord Bishopp of Bathe and Welles, and Deane of his Majestes Chappell, the one and twentithe of Marche 1610, Henry Alred, Yeoman of the Vestery, for blasphemy, for whoredom, for threatninge the spillinge of blood of certaine persons, for contemptes, and for many other great disorders committed, hath caused to be layd uppon him this third and last prick, by his Lordshipp's order in the sayd Chapter,

1610-11, March 21.

therby shewinge the cause of his just expulcõn accordinge to the order and auncient customs of his Majestes house.   [f. 31*b*.]

1611, June 19.   Henry Eveseed the younger sworne Groome of the Vestrie the 19th of June 1611, with this addicõn.

Also I do voluntarilie take this as a part of my othe, that I will behave my selfe in my place, obediently, orderly, and quietly from tyme to tyme, or else to yeald my selfe to be put out of his Majestes service.   In testimony heerof I subscribe my name the daie and yeare above written.   Henry Eveseed. [f. 24*b*.]

1613, Nov. 11.
Wm. Phillipps othe to Prince Charles.

Be it remembred that William Phillipps was sworne Yeoman of the Kinges Ma[tes] vestery the 11th of November 1613, by warrant from the Revd. Father the Lord Bishopp of Bathe and Welles, and Deane of his Highness Chappell, directed to the Subdeane of his Majestes sayd chappell, or to his Substitute, bearinge date the 9th daie of the foresayd monethe of November, to serve Prince Charles in that place in suche manner and sorte as formerly he was sworne to serve Prince Henry, which was donne accordingly as above said, and accordinge to his othe formerly taken as in foll. 26 appearethe,* the oathe of supremacie not beinge omitted.   In testimony theerof I, Anthony Harrison, Substitute, have heerunto subscribed my name the daie and yeare as above said.

Anthony Harrison, Substitute.   [f. 28*b*.]

1613-14,
Feb[y]. 6.
Rob[te]. Colman, his othe to serve Prince Charles.

Mem. that Roberte Colman uppon the sixte daie of Februarie 1613, was sworne Groome of his Majestes vestery by warrant from the Reverend Father the Lord Bishopp of Bathe and Welles, and Deane of his highness Chappell, directed to me Leonard Davies, Subdeane of his Majestes sayd Chappell, bearinge date the fifte daie of the same, to serve Prince Charles in that place in suche manner and sorte as Thomas Miller, next under neath writt, was sworne to serve Prince Henry, which was accordingly done as above said, the oathe of supremacie not beinge omitted.   In testimony

* See p. 109.

heerof I have heerunto subscribed my name the daie and yeare above said.   Leonard Davies, Subdeane. [f. 28*b*.]

Mem. that uppon the 16th daie of June, 1615, Henry Eveseed, Groome of the Vestery, for many negligences and abuses comitted by him in his place and service, received an admonishion by the Subdeane, at the direccōn of my Lord Deane of his Majestes Chappell, for the amendment of his former negligences and abuses, for the avoyding of further courses to be taken against him tendinge to his expulsion. Presente   La. Bath et Well.
Subdeane, Hewlett, Wiborowe, Crosse. Nicholas (Yeoman).
[f. 32.]

1615, June 16.

Be it remembred that uppon the fifte daye of November, 1615, William Ward (by warrant from the Reverend Father in God the Lord Bishopp of Bathe and Welles, and Deane of his Ma^tes Chappell), was sworne Groome of his Majestes Vestery Extraordinarie, for the tuninge and mendinge of his Majestes organes when he shalbe therunto required by those that have the charge therof : And it is a parcell of his othe to be obedient to the Deane and Subdeane of his Majestes Chappell for the tyme beinge, and not to sue or claime any place to attend in his Majestes sayd Chappell or Vestrie, otherwise then for the service above expressed. In testemony heerof I have heerunto subscribed my name the daie and yeare above written.
[f. 33*b*.]

1615, Nov. 5.
Willm.Wardes Oathe.Groome.

Be it remembred that a Chapter was held the 29th of September 1620, by the Right Reverend Father in God Lancellott Lord Bishop of Winton, and Deane of his Majestes Chappell, uppon a peticōn preferred by the Subdeane and Gentlemen of his Majestes sayd Chappell against Henry Eveseed, Yeoman of the Vestery, for many and sundrie abuses committed by him against the sayd Subdeane and fellowship, upon readinge wherof and examininge the particulers of the complaint, and findinge the slender answeres of the said Eveseed therunto, did deferr this Chapter untill the Feast of All

1620, Sept. 29.

Saintes next followinge, to the intent his Lordship might be the better informed by his further answere therin. And in the meane tyme his Lordship's pleasure was to suspend him from exercisinge his office, bothe in Chappell and Vestery, and that he should have nothinge therin to do, and that all his wages should be stayed in the handes of the Clark of the Check untill he had satisfied his Lordship with better answers therunto. La. Winton. [f. 34*b*.]

1624, April 20.
Sampson Row-
den sworne
Bellringer.

Mem. that uppon the 20th daye of Aprill 1624 (uppon the death of Robt. Bicknar) Sampson Rowden by the free guift and comaund of the Right Reverend La. Lord Bishop of Winton, Deane of his Majestes Chappell, was sworne bellringer for his Majestes Houshold, and tooke his oathe in all respectes as Robert Bicknar did, as on the other side appearethe.*   [f. 29.]

1625, June 20.
William
Hewes dis-
placed from
being our
Comon Ser-
vaunt.

Mem̃ that at a Chapter held the 20th of June 1625, it was there agreed by the Subdeane and Gentlemen ther assembled, that for as muche as William Hewes, our comon servant, being often times formerly admonyshed of his ill behaviour and carriage towards his sayd masters and himselfe, and would not receave nor regard his sayd admonicions, but still growing worse and worse in dronkennes and other disorderly behaviour, was then in Chapter, by a generall consent, dismissed from his sayd place and service. In wittnes heerof the Subdeane and Gentlemen have caused this to be entered into the register booke to be a testimony of their so doinge.

Stephan Boughton, Subdean. [f. 22.]

1626, Apl. 20.   Roger Evans, by warrant from the Right Reverend Father in God Lancellott Lord Bishop of Winton, and Deane of his Ma^tes Chappell, was sworne Bell ringer the 20th daie of Aprill, uppon the deathe of Sampson Rowden, who was bell ringer before him.

[f. 33*b*.]

1626, July 9.   Mem. that uppon the 9th of July John Burward was sworne Groome of the Vestery extraordinary, for the tuninge and mendinge

See p. 139.

of his Majestes organs when he shalbe therunto required, as doth more largly appeare by our Lord Deanes warrant for that purpose.
[f. 33*b*.]

Thomas Haynes was sworn Sergeant of his Majesties Vestry (by Dr. Jones the Subdeane) on the eight of November 1660, the same day at the same tyme William Williams was sworn elder Yeoman, and George Whitcher younger Yeoman, and Augustine Cleavland, Groome, in the presence of Mr. Roger Nightingale and Mr. Henry Lawes, Clearke of the Check. [f. 8.] 1660.

Augustine Cleveland, Groome of the Vestrye, was killed with the violence of horses drawing a coach over him, June 3, 1662, at Hampton Court, and Hugh Powell was admitted into his place June 15th. [f. 8.] 1662.

This day Hugh Powell was admitted and sworne Groome of the Vestry by the Right Worshipfull Dr. Walter Jones, Subdeane of his Maties Chappell Royall, in the roome of Austin Cleveland who unfortunately dyed by the violence of horses and coach running over him at Hampton Court on the first day of this month, and was buried in Hampton Parish Church, June 3, 1662. Ita testor Philippus Tinker, Regiæ familiæ Confessor. [f. 44*b*] 1662. June 15.

Be it remembred that Mr. Thomas Dunkley was this day sworne Yeoman of his Majesties Vestry extraordinary, to waite closett Keeper in ordinarye, by the Reverend Subdeane, Dr. Walter Jones, in the presence of March 21, 1663. At Whitehal

Thomas Blagrave, Clerk of the Checke.
Tho. Haines, Serjeant of the Vestry. [f. 45.]

Samuell Blayton, Bellringer, suspended by my Lord of Winchester, Dean of his Majestes Chappell Royall, the 5th of Aprill 1666. [f. 86*b*.] 1666.

1672, Dec. 23.   I George Wyatt, being admitted and entertained Common Sergeant to the Gentlemen of his Majesties Chappell Royall, doe promise and bind my selfe and my heires (not to embezell or pawne my Badge) in the sum of forty shillings, but to leave it when I dy to the Gentlemen my masters for the use of my successor. Witnes my hand the 23ʳᵈ day of December 1672.

George Wyatt. [f. 1.]

Adam Wat-
kins, Bell-
ringer, the 4th
of January
1672.   Be it remembred that upon the fourth day of Jauuary 1672, Adam Watkyns was by the free guift and command of the Right Reverend Father in God Walter Lord Bishop of Worster, and Deane of his Majesties Chappell, sworne Bellringer for his Majesties Houshold, in the Vestry at Whitehall, by the Reverend Dr. Richard Colebrand, Sub Deane, in which othe among other parts of the same as to the supremacy &c. he was sworne to obedience to the Deane and Sub-Dean of the said Chappell, and to the Confessor of his Majesties Houshold for the time being, in all matters and things apperteineing to his said place and service.

Ric. Colebrand, Sub-Dean. [f. 1.]

Henry Wat-
kins, Bell-
ringer the 26th
of November
1678.   Be it remembred that upon the 26. day of November 1678, Henry Watkins was by the free gift of the Right Reverend Father in God Henry Lord Bishop of London, and Deane of his Majesties Chappell Royall, sworn Bellringer for his Majesties Houshold, at Whitehall, by the Reverend Dr. William Holder, Sub-Deane, in which oath among other parts of the same as to yᵉ supremacy &c. he was sworn to obedience to the Deane and Sub-Dean of yᵉ said Chappell, and to the Confessor of his Majesties Houshold for the time being, in all matters and things apperteining to his said place and service.   [f. 1.]

1684-5.
March 23.   March the 23ᵗʰ, 1684-5, at Whitehall. Be it remembred, That Mr. Thomas Dunkley was this day sworne Yeoman of his Majesties

Vestry extraordinary, to waite Clossett Keeper in ordinary, by our
Reverend Subdeane, Dr. William Holder. [f. 45.]

November 28. Mr. Richard Keyes was sworn Common Serjant, 1693.
renouncing all profits. R^h Battell. Witnes Edw. Braddock, Clerk of
the Check. [f. 10.]

Jany 23. By vertue of a warrant from the Right Reverend Dean 1694-5.
of the Chappell, I swore and admitted Mr. Isaak Cooke Groom of
the Chapel or Vestry, in the place of Mr. George Oldner, deceased.
R^h Battell, S.D. Wittnes Edw. Braddock. [f. 10.]

April 14. Mr. Matthew Fairles was sworn Groom of the Chapel 1697.
in the place of Mr. Isaac Cook, deceased, by mee R^h Battell, Witnes
Edw. Braddock, Clerk of the Check. [f. 10b.]

May 18. By vertue of a Warrant from the Right Reverend the 1703.
Lord Bishop of London, Mr. Isaak Ellis was sworn in Bellringer to
her Ma^tys Chapels at Whitehal, by mee R^h Battell, S.D., Wittnes
Edw. Braddock, Clerk of the Checke. [f. 11b.]

Jan. 28. By warrant from the Lord Bishop of London, Dean, 1703-4.
Mr. Daniel Farmer was sworn Closet Keeper of Whitehal Chapell,
in the place of Mr. Nicholas Phipps, deceased, by mee R^h Battell,
S.D. [f. 11b.]

Mr. Mathew Fairles dyed the 14th of July, 1708, Groom of the 1708.
Vestry. [f. 12.]

Mr. John Lenton was sworne Groom of the Chappell, in the 1708.
place of Mr. Mathew Fairles, deceased, by me Rd. Battell, S.D.
Wittness Daniell Williams, Clerk of the Check. [f. 12.]

March 15, 1710-11 To prevent any dispute that may hence- 1710-11.
March 15.

foreward arise betwixt the Yeoman and Groom of the Vestry, in relation to the right of keeping the doors of the chappel, I do declare that the care of the outward doors and parts of the chappel is in the Groom and not in the Yeoman of the Vestry. And that if there be any occasion for an assistant, the Groom shall employ some person whose deportment shall give no offence to any, and who shall submissively and readily comply with the directions of the Sergeant and Yeoman.   H. London. [f. 53b.]

1710-11.   March the 24th. By vertue of a warrant from the Lord Bishop of London, Mr. Thomas Brookes was sworne in Bellringer to her Majestys Chappels at Whitehall, by mee R^h Battell, S.D. Witness Daniell Williams, Clerk of the Cheque.

1714-15.   Henry Parker, Esq. Sergeant of the Vestry, dyed the 13th of March 1714-15, and Mr. Marmaduke Alford, Yeoman, was sworne Sergeant, and Mr. Jo. Hill, my Lord's Gentleman, was sworn Yeoman, by the Right Reverend John Lord Bishop of London, Dean of his Majesties Royall Chapels.   [f. 13.]

1715.   Marmaduke Alford, Esq. Serjeant of the Vestry, dyed the 10th of May 1715, and Jonathan Smith, Esq. by vertue of a warrant from the Right Reverend John Lord Bishop of London, Dean of his Majesties Chappell, was the next day following sworne Serjeant in his place, by me Dolben, Subdean, Wittness D. Williams, Clerk of the Cheque.   [f. 13.]

1716-17.   Mathew Shelley, Organ Blower, dyed the 9th of February
Feb. 9.   1716-17, and Samuel Clay, a Servant to the Dean, was on the 12th of the same month sworne Organ Blower in his place.
             Wittness Daniel Williams, Clerk of ye Cheque. [f. 1.]

1718.   Mr. Daniel Farmer, Closet Keeper in the Chapel of Whitehall, dyed the 16th day of May 1718, and by vertue of a warrant from the Rt. Revd. the Lord Bishopp of Sarum, Dean of his Majesties Royal Chapells, Mr. Philip Bennet was sworn Closet Keeper in his place this 12th day of June 1718, by me Edw. Aspinwall, Subdean.

[f. 13*b*.]

Mr. John Lenton, Groom of the Vestrey, dyed the   day   1719. of May 1719, and by vertue of a warrant from the Rt. Revd. the Lord Bishopp of Sarum, Dean of his Majesties Royal Chapels, Mr. William Duncombe was sworn Groom in his place, this   day of May 1719, by me Edw. Aspinwall.   [f. 13*b*.]

February 9th, 1732-3. By virtue of a warrant from the Rt. 1732-3, Feb. 9. Revd. Edmund Lord Bishop of London, Dean of his Maj. Chapels, John Herring was admitted into the place of Bell ringer of his Maj. Chapels Royal, vacant by the death of Thomas Brooks (having first (as usual) sworn obedience to the Dean, Subdean, and Confessour of his Majesty's Houshold for the time being).

Geo. Carleton, Subdean.   [f. 57*b*.]

By virtue of a warrant from the Rt. Rev. Edmund Lord Bishop 1737, Oct. 10. of London, Dean of his Maj. Chapels Royal, I have sworn and admitted John Martin into the place of Bell Ringer of his Maj. Chapels Royal, vacant by the resignation of John Herring.

Geo. Carleton, Sub Dean.   [f. 58*b*.]

By virtue of a warrant from the Lord Bishop of London, Dean   1743, of Maj. Chapels Royal, I have sworn and admitted Mr. John   March 30. Martin into the place of Chapel Keeper of his Maj. Chapel at Whitehall, now vacant by the death of Mr. John Richardson.

Thos. Baker.   [f. 59*b*.]

By virtue of a warrant from the Lord Bishop of London, Dean 1743, April 19. of his Maj. Chapels Royal, I have sworn and admitted Mr. John Williams into the office of Bell ringer (now vacant by the resignation of Mr. John Martin) of his Maj. Chapels Royal.

Thos. Baker.   [f. 59*b*.]

XV. —ROYAL CEREMONIES.

Aprill 15,
Estreday 1593.
The Princelye comminge of her Majestie to the Holy Communion
at Estre [Easter].

The moste sacred Queene Elizabethe upon Estre day, after the
Holy Gospell was redd in the Chaple at St. James, came downe
into her Majestes Travess: beffore her highnes came the gentlemen
pencioners, then the Barons, the Bushopps, London and Landaffe,
thErls, and the ho: Councell in their colors of State, the Harolds
at Arms, the Lord Keeper bearinge the Great Seal himselfe, and
the Erle of Herefford bearinge the sword beffore her Majestie.
Then her Majesties Royal person came moste chearfully, havinge as
noble supporters the Right Honorable thErle of Essex, Master of
her Majestes Horse, on the right hande, and the Right Hon. the
Lord Admyral on the lefte hand, the Lord Chambrelen to her
Majestie (also nexte beffore her Majeste) attendante al the while.
Dr. Bull was at the organ playinge the Offertorye. Her Majestie
entred her travess moste devoutly, there knyelinge: after some
prayers she came princely beffore the Table, and there humbly
knielinge did offer the golden obeysant, the Bushop the hon.
Father of Worcester holdinge the golden bason, the Subdean and
the Epistler in riche coaps assistante to the sayd Bushop: which
done her Majestie retorned to her princely travess sumptuously sett
forthe, untyl the present action of the Holy Communion, con-
tynually exercysed in ernest prayer, and then the blessed Sacrament
first receyved of the sayd Bushop and administred to the Subdean,
the gospeller for that day, and to the Epistler, her sacred person presented her selfe beffore the Lord's Table, Royally attended as beffore,
where was sett a stately stoole and qwssins [cushions] for her Majestie,
and so humbly knielinge with most singuler devocion and holye
reverence dyd most comfortablye receyve the most blessed Sacramente
of Christes bodye and blood, in the kinds of bread and wyne, accor-

dinge to the laws established by her Majestie and Godly laws in Parliament. The bread beinge waffer bread of some thicker substaunce, which her Majestie in most reverend manner toke of the Lord Bushop in her naked right hand, her setisfyed hert fixinge her semblant eyes most entirely uppon the woorthye words Sacramental pronounced by the Bushop, &c. that with soche an holye aspecte as it did mightelye adde comfforts to the godlye beholders (wherof this writer was one very neare): and likewise her Majestie receaved the cuppe, havinge a moste princely lynned clothe layd on her cushion pillowe and borne at the four ends by the noble Erle of Herefford, the Erle of Essex, the Erle of Worcester, and thErle of Oxford: the side of the sayd clothe her Majestie toke up in her hande, and therewith toke the ffoote of the golden and nowe sacred cuppe, and with like holy reverend attention as beffore to the sacramentaon words, did drinke of the same most devoutly (all this while knielinge on her knies) to the confirmation of her faythe and absolute comfforte in her purged conscience by the holy spirit of God in the exercise of this holye Communion, of her participation of and in the merits and deathe of Christe Jesus our Lorde, and the perfecte communion and spiritual ffoode of the verye bodye and bloode of Christe our Lord Saviour: and so retorninge to her sayd Travess their devoutly stayed the end of prayers, which done her Majestie Royally ascended the way and stayrs into her presence, whom the Lord blesse for ever and ever. Amen.

Ant. Anderson, Subdean. [f. 14b.]

Be it remembred that in the second yeare of his Majestes raigne, Augt. 1604. and in the monethe of August, came an Embassador out of Spaine to take the Kinges othe for the maintenance and continuance of the League betweene them, which was don in this manner and forme followinge, viz.:

In the Chappell weare two Traverses sett up of equall state in all thinges as neare as might be.

Then was there a table sett up at the halfe pace before the Communion table, neare the Kinges Traverse, wheruppon ther laye writinges and a standishe with pen and incke.

Then his Majestie cominge into the Chappell, on his righte hand went the Constable of Spayne, and on his left the Spanishe lidger Embassador, and so they went up to the Communion table together.

Then his Majestie went into his Traverse where he usually sitteth, and the Constable into the other, and there they bothe remayned till an Anthem was ended, which beganne so soone as his Majestie and the Embassador weare in their Traverses, till which time the Organs played.

Then the Kinge and the Constable cominge out of their Traverses stoode neare together uppon the halfe pace, turninge their faces the one to the other: beinge so placed, my Lord Vicounte Cranborne Principall Secretarie read the Oath, the Kinge puttinge his hande within the Embassador's in the beginninge of the Oath, and layd his handes uppon a Lattin Bible of the vulgar translaçõn the other part of the othe, the Bible beinge held by the Deane of the Chappell in a Coape all the while the Oath was reade.

Then after the takinge of the Oath the Kinge and Constable kissed each other, and then they went againe into their Traverses, and ther staied till an other Anthem was songe.

That ended, they went out of the Chappell in the same manner that they came in, the organs playinge till they weare gone out of the Chappell. [f. 69*b*.]

1610-11,
Jan. 27.

John Beaumanoir, Lord of Laverdin, Baron of Tusse, Asse, Millexe; and Anthonis, Earle of Negreplisse, Launat et Mouxvoux in Guyenne, Governor and Lieutenant Generall for the French Kinge in his contries of Mayne, Lavall et Perche, and one of his Privie Counsell, Marshall of Fraunce, Knight of thorder of the Holy Ghost, and Ambassadore from the Christian Kinge to the King's

Majestie of Great Brittaigne, in the monethe of Januarie 1610, to take his Highnes Oath for the maintenaunce and continuance of the league betweene them, which was don the 27th of the same in this manner and forme as followethe, viz.:

In the Chappell weare two traverses sett up of equall state in all thinges as neare as might be.

Then was there a table sett up at the halfe-pace before the Comunion Table, neare the King's traverse, wheruppon ther laye writings and a standishe with pen and incke.

Then his Majestie cominge into the Chappell, the Prince wente before him with the Embassador, and so they went up to the Comunion Table.

Then his Majestie went into his traverse wher he usually sitteth, and the Embassador into the other, and ther they both remayned tyll an Anthem was ended, which beganne so soone as his Majestie and the Embassador weare in their traverses, till which tyme the Organs played.

Then the Kinge and the Embassador cominge out of their traverses stood neare together uppon the halfe-pace, turninge their faces the one to the other. Beinge so placed, my Lord Treasurer read the oath, the Kinge putting his hand within the Embassador's in the beginning of the Oath, and layd his handes uppon a Lattin Byble of the vulgar Translation the other part of the Oath, the Byble beinge held by the Bishopp of Bathe and Welles Deane of the Chappell, in a Coape, all the while the Oath was read.

Then, after the takinge of the Oath, the Kinge and Embassador kissed eache other, and then they went againe into their traverses, and there stayed till another Anthem was songe. That ended, they went out of the Chappell in the same manner that they cam in, the Organs playinge till they weare gone out of the Chappell.

[f. 70.]

1625, May 7. The Order of the Funeralls of Kinge James, who was buried the vijth daye of Maye Anno Domini 1625.

He departed this life the 27th of March 1625, beinge Sondaye. His dead corps were brought from Theobalds to Denmark House, the   of the same moneth, where all his officers attended and wayted duringe the tyme that his corps lay there, except the Chappell, who wayted uppon Kinge Charles at Whithall.

At Denmark House the hall there was made a chappell for the tyme, where the Confessor read morninge prayer daylie, and uppon Sondayes one of the Chaplaines preched: the deaske was covered with black clothe.

Two dayes before the daye of the funeralls the corps were brought into the sayd Chappell in greate solemnitie with an Anthem, and sett under an hearse of velvett, and the Gentlemen of the Chappell from that tyme wayted there, and performed solemne service with the Organs brought thither for that purpose; they also wayted with the corps by course night and day: by night, first Decany syde, and next Cantoris syde, and twise in the night, viz. at nine of the clock and at midnight, they had prayers with a first and second Chapters, and ended with an Anthem. The hall or Chappell was hunge with blacks after this manner: the upper end, as farr as the baye window on the one syde and the dore on the other syde, was hunge with black clothe, all the other partes with black bayes. At the upper end stood the Communion table, and was covered with fine black cloth adorned with two faire fronts of black velvett: uppon bothe sydes of the hall from one end to the other were sett tables, and uppon bothe sydes of the tables were formes; bothe tables and formes were covered with black bayes, all which velvett cloth and bayes, as well that which covered the tables and formes as that wherewith the walls were hanged, were adjudged to be fees unto the gentlemen of the chappell, and was divided amongest them, wherin the Officers of the Vestery had also part accordinge to their places. Kinge Charles resided all the tyme that the corps lay at Denmark House at Whithall, beinge attended by his officers and servantes as he had while he was Prince, and there the Gentlemen of the Chappell wayted: the Chappell there was also hunge as that at Denmark House, the upper parte to the seates with black cloth, all the rest with black bayes, the Comunion table with black cloth, and adorned with two frontes of black velvett; the foot pace before it was covered with black cloth, the rayles rounde aboute it with black bayes; uppon one syde was sett up a fayer traverse of black taffata, and in it a chaire of black velvett, in the chayer a short cushion and a longe cushion, both of black velvett: before the chayer a black velvett footstoole, a forme covered with a fayer large carpett of velvett, a longe velvett cushion upon the forme for the Kinge to leane uppon, and another befor it for him to kneele uppon: against the wall stood another forme covered with black velvett, uppon it two longe black velvett cusshions with two velvett carpetts sutable for the Kinges offeringes. All the pavement within the traverse was covered with black clothe: ther was also a faire large foote carpett which reached from the Communion table to the halfe-pace risinge from the seates, for the offeringe. The pulpitt was covered all over from the topp to the ground with black vellvett: uppon the deske was a faire deskcloth of black vellvett fringed. All these aforesayd hanginges, tafata, traverse, chayer, footestoole, cusshions, carpetts, pulpitt clothe, deske cloth, &c. were fees to the Gentlemen of the Chappell, and divided amongest them, wherin the Officers of the Vestery had also their partes accordinge to their places. The Deanes stall in the said Chappell had over it a faire state of black vellvett of fower breads of vellvett and fringed with a fayer silke fringe; before him was a fayre vellvett carpett of fower breads; in his state was a longe vellvett cusshion to sitt uppon, another to kneele uppon, and a third laye uppon the deske before him, all which state, carpett and cusshions were the Deane of the Chappell's fee, and he had them to his owne use after the funeralls were ended. Ita est, STEPHAN BOUGHTON, Subdeane.

Memorandum that Kinge Charles was him selfe in person the

cheife mourner, and followed the corps of his father on foote from Denmark House unto Westminster Churche: and the Wardrop being unprovided of a traverse and other necessaries for Westminster Church, which could not sufficiently be provided, a warrant from the Lord Chamberlaine to the Deane of the Chappell was procured to borrow the traverse in the Chappell at Whitehall, some of the cusshions and carpetts, all which were restored back againe by the Lord Chamberlaines commaund unto the Gentlemen of the Chappell, as their propper fees and duties. Likewise at the funeralls of Queene Elizabeth all the mourninge ornamentes in the Chappell were adjudged to be fees unto the Gentlemen of the Chappell, and they had them to their owne proper uses.

Ita est, STEPHAN BOUGHTON, Subdean.

Be it also remembered that at the funeralls of Kinge James, Stephan Boughton, Subdeane, and tenn other gentlemen being Ministers, had allowance of nine yards apeece of blackes for themselves, and two yards apeece for their servantes.

Also that Natha: Giles, Doctor and Master of the Children, William Heather, Doctor, John Hewlett, Clark of the Check, John Steephens, Recorder of Songes, and Orlando Gibbons, senior Organist, had the lyke allowaunce of nine yards apeece for themselves as the ministers had, and two yards apeece for their servauntes.

The rest of the gentlemen, beinge 17, had for their blacks every one seven yardes, and for every of their servauntes two yards apeece.

Extraordinarie gent: had as the 17 ordinarie gentlemen had.

Cuthbert Joyner, Serjeant, had for himselfe seven yardes and fower yards for two servauntes.

The two Yeomen and the Groome of the Vestrie had 4 yards apeece.

Sampson Rowden, bellringer, had four yards.

The common servaunts of the Chappell and vestery had for eache of them four yards.

The Organ Blower had 4 yards.

Ita est, STEPHAN BOUGHTON, Subdean. [ff. 70b, 71.]

The Order of the Chappell's service at the Coronac̃ōn of our Soveraigne Lord Kinge Charles, uppon Candlemas Day, in the first year of his raigne, Anno Domini 1625.

Upon which day all the Chappell mett at the Colledge Hall in Westminster, wher they had a breakfast at the charge of the Colledge, from thence they went by a back way into the Church, and so into the vestrie, where together with the Quier of Westminster they putt on surplesses and copes and went into Westminster Hall, and there wayted untill the Kinge came thither, who came from White-hall by water, and landinge at the Parliament stayres came into the Great Hall, wher was a large scaffold covered all with cloth, and uppon it a throne and chayer of estate, wher the Kinge sate untill the whole trayne weare marshaled in their order. The Chappell followed the Knights of the Privie Counsell, who went next after the Knights of the Bath, the Sergeant Porter with his black staff and Sergeant of the Vestry with his virger goinge before them; next the Quier of Westminster, then the Chappell, who went singinge through the Pallace yard and round about the Church, through the great Sanctuarie till they came to the west dore of the Church: when all the Chappell were within the Church they began the first Anthem.

I was glad when they sayd unto me we will goe into the house of the Lord, for thither the tribes goe up, even the tribes of the Lord, to testifie unto Israell, to give thankes unto the name of the Lord. For there is the seate of judgment, even the seate of the House of David. O pray for the peace of Jerusalem: they shall prosper that love thee.

1. Anthem,
Psal. 122.

After the Archbishop hath don at the corners of the scaffold, and the people's acclamac̃ōn ended, the Quire singeth

Strengthened be thy hand, and exalted be thy right hand. Righteous-nes and Peace be the preparac̃ōn of thy seate, mercy and

2. Anthem.

judgment ever goe before thy face.   Allelujah: my songe shalbe alwaies of the lovinge kindnes of the Lord.   Glory be to the Father, &c.

When the sermon is ended, and after the Kinges Othe is taken, the Archbishop beginninge Come Holy Ghost, the Quire singeth

3. Anthem.

Come Holy Ghost, eternall God, proceeding from above,
Both from the Father and the Sonne, the God of peace and
    love,
Visitt our mindes, and into us the heavenly grace inspire,
That in all truth and Godliness we may have true desire.
Thou art the very Comforter in all woe and distresse,
The heavenly guiftes of God most high, which no tong can
    expresse,
The Fountain and the lyvely Spring of joy celestiall,
The fire so bright, the love so cleare, and unction spirituall.

After a prayer is read by the Archbishop, two other Bushops singe the Litany.   And the Quire singethe the Answeres.

Whiles the Archbushop is annoyntinge the Kinge, the Quier singeth

4. Anthem.

Sadock the priest and Nathan the Prophett annoynted Salamon Kinge, and joyfully approchinge they cryed, God save the Kinge, God save the Kinge, God save the Kinge, for ever and ever.   The Kinge shall rejoyce in thy strength, O Lord. Allelujah.

When the Crowne is sett uppon the Kinges head and the Arch- bushop hath ended the exhortation: Be stronge and of a good courage, &c., the Quier singeth

5. Anthem.

The Kinge shall rejoyce in thy strength, O Lord, exceeding glad shall he be of thy salvation: for thou hast given him his hartes desire and hast not denied him the request of his lipps.   Thou hast prevented him with the blessinges of goodnes, and hast sett a crowne of pure gould uppon his head.   Allelujah.

When the Kinge hath done at the Alter, and is goinge to his Throne, the Quier singeth the Te Deum.

After the homage is done to the Kinge by the Lordes, and the Archbushop goeth to begin the Comunion, the Quier singeth

Behould, O God our Defendor, and looke uppon the face of thine 6. Anthem.
    Annointed, for one day in thy Courtes is better then a thousand.
    O how amiable are thy tabernacles, thou Lord of Hostes.
    Allelujah.

Then followeth the Comunion, and when the Epistle and Gospell are ended, being read by the Bushops, the Quier singeth the Nicene Creed, the Archbushop beginning yt.

After the Offitorie vearse is read by the Archbishop, the Offitorie beginneth with this Anthem, beinge songe by the Quier:

Lett my prayer be sett forth in thy presence like unto the incense. 7. Anthem.
    Lett the liftinge up of my handes be as an eveninge sacrifice.
    Allelujah.

After this then is ended, the organs playe till the Offitorie be ended. Then the holies and the Et in terra pax, &c., as in the Comunion book, to be songe by the Quier, except the Archbushop will read them. After the Comunion is finished, the Quier singeth

O hearken then unto the voyce of my callinge, my Kinge and 8. Anthem.
    my God, for unto Thee will I make my prayer.

Then the ordinarie collects in the Comon Prayer Booke after the Comunion beinge read by the Archbushop, and the prayer of God, &c., so all is ended.

After all the ceremonie in the Church was ended, the Kinge returned back againe into Westminster Hall in the same manner as he went, the Chappell goeinge in their former order, and singinge all the waye till they came to Westminster Hall dore, and their they stayed, makinge a lane for the Kinge and all the Lordes to passe betwixt them, and continued singinge till the Kinge was within the Hall: and from thence they returned back into the Church, where in the vestry they putt of their copes and surplusses, and came to White hall, wher they had some allowance of diett for their suppers.

All the way from the scaffold in the Great Hall, through the Pallace yard and the street in the Great Sanctuarie, unto the scaffold in the Quier of the Church, was strowed with russhes and uppon the russhes covered with blew broad cloth.

[ff. 71*b*, 72.]

XVI.—Royal and Noble Marriages.

Mariages solemnized in her Majesties Chappell and Closet as followethe.

1. The Lorde Marques of Northampton was maried to Mrs. Frohelin at Westminster, in the Closet, in the monethe of May, in the yeare of owre Lord God 1571. xl s.

2. The Lord Ambrose Dudley, Earle of Warwycke, was maryed to the Earle of Bedford hys daughter, at Westmynster, in the Closet, in the yeare 1573. One bucke, xl s.

3. Sir Thomas Leyghton, Knyghte, was maryed to Mrs. Elizabeth Knoles, in the Chappell at Westmynster, in the yeare 1578. One bucke and xl s.

4. Syr William Drewery, Knyghte, was maryed to Mrs. Elizabeth Stafford, in the Chappell at Greenewytche, in the yeare 1579. One bucke and xl s.

5. The Earle of Pembrooke was maryed to Mrs. Mary Sydney at Westminster, in the Closet, in the yeare 1580. One bucke and xl s.

6. Sir Phillipp Harbert, Knight, was maryed to Susanna Vere, daughter of the Earle of Oxford, in the Chappell at Whitehaule, 1604, wher was payd for fees to Mr. Deane of the Chappell x li. and to the gentlemen of the sayd Chappell v li. December the 27th in the second yere of the reigne of oure Sovereigne Lord Kinge James.

7. The younge Earle of Essex was maryed to Frances Howard, daughter to the Earle of Suffolke, Lo. Chamberlaine, in the Kinges Chappell at Whitehall, the 5 or 6 of January 1605 (the Kinges Majestie givinge her in maryage), wher was paid for fees to the Deane of the Chappell, he maryinge them, 10 ƚi. and to the gentlemen of the Chappell then ther attendinge 5 ƚi.; which mariage was solemnized in the third yeare of the Raigne of our Soveraigne Lord Kinge James.

8. Be it remembred that uppon the 6th daye of Januarie 1606, (being twelfe day) and in the 4th yeare of his Maj. Raigne that now is, was the right hon the Lord James Haye married in the Kinges Chappell at Whitehall, unto Honor, the daughter and heire of the Lord Dennie (the Kinges Maj^{tie} givinge her in marriage). And Doctor Mountague, Deane of the Chappell, marryinge them, had for his fee 10 ƚi. And the Gentlemen of the Chappell for their extraordinary service and attendance 5 ƚi. as before had byn payd them in and for the lyke service.

9. Be it remembred that uppon the 9th daie of February 1607, beinge Shrove Tuesday, the Lord Vicount Haddington was maryed in the Kinges Chappell at Whithall, unto Elyzabeth the eldest daughter of the Earle of Sussex (the Kinges Majestie givinge her in maryage), wher was layd downe one the booke for fee for the Deane of the Chappell who maryed them 10 ƚi. And the gentlemen of the Chappell had for their fee as before had bin used the some of 5 ƚi.   [f. 76*b*.]

The Order of askinge the banes betweene the two greate Princes the Prince Palatine and the Ladie Elizabeth her Grace.

I aske the banes of matrimonie betweene the two great Princes, Fredericke Prince Elector Count Palatine of Reine of the one partie, and the Lady Elizabethe her Grace, the only daughter of the highe and mightie Kinge of Great Brittanny of the other partie. If any man can shew any cause why these two Princes may not be lawfully joyned in matrimony, let him speake, for this is the, &c. First asked in the Chappell at Whithall the last daye of Januarie 1612, and there also the second of Februarie next followinge the second tyme, and the third tyme at Winsore the 7th daie of the foresaid Februarie. The Prince Palatine beinge installed Knight of the Garter the same daie.   [f. 76.]

The order of askinge the banes.

I aske the banes of matrimony betweene Phillip Harbert, Knight, gentleman of his Majestes most honorable bedd Chamber, of the on[e] partie, and the Ladye Susanna Vere, of her Majestes most honorable Privye Chamber, of the other partie.   Yf therefore ther be any that that can shew any lawfull impediment why these two honorable persons may not be joyned together in the holye estate of matrimony, accordinge to God his holye institucōn, and the lawes of this Realme, let them now speake, for this is, &c.   [f. 76.]

The Banes of Roberte Earle of Somersett.

I aske the banes of matrimony betweene the Right Honorable personages, Roberte Earle of Somersett, of the on[e] partie, and the Ladie Francis Howard, of the other part: if any man can shewe any just cause why these may not lawfully be joyned together, lett him speake; this is, &c.

These banes weare solemply asked three severall times in his Maj. Chappell at Whithall: first the 19th daie of December 1613, the second time the 21th of the same, and the third time on Christmas daie, and married the daie followinge.

I aske the banes of matrimony betweene Sir John Villiers, Knight, gentleman of the Prince his highnes bed-chamber, of the one partie, and Frauncis Cooke, youngest daughter of the Right Hon. Sir Edward Cooke, Knight, one of hys Majestes most hon. Privie Councell, and of the Hon. Ladie Elizabeth Cooke his wiffe, of the other partie. If any man can shew any just cause why these may not lawfully be joyned together in the holy state of matrymonye, lett him speake, for this the, &c.

The first tyme these banes were asked was the 27th of September 1617, beinge Saturdaie at night, the second was Sondaye morninge the 28th of September, and the third and last tyme was the 29th daie followinge in the morninge, after which in the said morninge they were marryed at Hampton Courte.   [ff. 76, 83*b*.]

The Order and manner of the solemne celebracõn of the marriage of the two great Princes, Frederick Prince Elector Counte Palatine of Rheine, and the Ladie Elizabeth, the only daughter of the right highe and mightie Prince the Kinge of Great Brittaine, in his Majestes Chappell at Whithale, uppon Sondaie the 14th daie of Februarie 1612, in the 10th yeare of his Maj. raigne, and in the 17th yeare of the age of the two yonge Princes.   1612-3. Feb. 14.

10. First the Chappell was in royall sorte adorned, the upper end of it was hunge withe very riche hanginges, conteyninge a part of the storie of the Actes of the Appostells, and the Communion table furnished with riche plate.   Then a stately throne or seate was raysed in the middest of the Chappell, some five foote in height and some twenty foote in lengthe, haveinge stayers to assend or descend at eache end, spred with riche carpettes under foote, and rayled one both sydes, the rayles covered with clothe of tissue, but open at topp that the whole assemblie might see all the ceremony the better. Uppon the sides of the Chappell from the stales up to the Communion table weare a duble rowe of seates made for the Gentlemen of the Chappell, arayed withe tapstery very comely. The place beinge thus furnished, the hower approchinge, which was betweene 11 and 12, his Majestie, to make his cominge to the Chappell more solemne and stately, proceaded from his Privie Chamber, throughe the presence and garde chambre, and throughe a new bankettinge house erected of purpose for to solemnenize this feast in, and so

doune a paire of stayers at the upper end therof hard by the Courte gate, wente alonge uppon a stately scaffold to the great chamber stayers, and throughe the greate Chamber and lobby to the clossett, doune the staiers to the Chappell, into which this royall troupe marched in this order. First came the bridgroome arrayed in clothe of silver, richly imbroydered with silver, with all the younge gallants and noblemen of the Courte ; but ther entred the Chappell only 16 noble younge men Bachylers, so many as he was years olde, the rest of the noblemen and gentlemen by his Majestes expresse command entred not the Chappell. The Bridgroome thus beinge placed in his seate, next came the Bride. Before her went the Lord Harrington. She was supported or ledd by the Prince Charles on the righte hand, and the Earle of Northampton, Lord Privie Seale, on the left hand, attended with 16 younge Ladies and Gentlewomen of honor bearinge her traine, which was of cloth of silver as her gowne was, her hayre hanginge doune at length dressed with ropes of pearle, and a Coronett uppon her head richly dect with precious stones. The gownes of all the younge Ladies that followed her weare of cloth of silver. Immediatly after the yonge Ladies followed the Lady Harrington, wiffe of the Lord Harrington, who had bin Governesse to the Lady Elizabeth for the space of tenne yeares. Then came all the greate Ladies of the Courte: with this traine she ascended the throne and tooke her place. Immediatly followed the Kinge and Queens Majestes, attended with their Officers of honor, and the Lords of his Majestes Privie Counsell and divers Ladies. The Kinge and Queene enteringe the Chappell and assendinge the Throne, thei sate in this order. First, on the right hand sate the Kinge in a Chayer most royally and richly arrayed. The diamondes and jewells uppon him weare not lesse worth by good estimacŏn then sixe hundred thousand poundes in valewe. The Earle of Arundell bearinge up the sworde stood close by the chayer; next the sword sate the Bridgroome on a stoole, and after him Prince Charles sate uppon a stoole, and then Comte Henry stood by him, who is brother to Counte Maurice and unckle to the Palatine. On the other side sate the Queene in a chayer, most gloriously attired in a white sattin gowne; the jewells on the attire of her head and the rest of her garmentes weare valewed at fower hundred thousand poundes: hard by her sate the Bride on a stoole; ther stood by the Bride the Lady Harrington bearinge up her traine. The Lord Chamberlaine for the Kinge stood at the one end next the alter, the Lord Chamberlaine for the Queene stood at the other end, the Lord Privie Seale stood uppon the stayers of the Throne hard by the Kinge. The Kinge and Queene placed in their seates, the Lordes and Councellors of the Kinge, and the Lordes and Councellors of the Prince Palatine, tooke their seates on the left hand of the Chappell, the Ladies of Honor tooke the other side of the seates, the younge Lordes and gentlemen of Honor and younge Ladies and Bride-woemen, with the necessarie officers and attendantes uppon the Kinge and Queene, stood all belowe uppon the pavement. This one thinge is remarkable, that by the great and extraordinarie care and diligence of the Earle of Suffolke, Lord Chamberlaine, the Chappell was so kept, as ther came not within the Chappell one person but of honor and great place. This Royall assemblie beinge in this sort settled in their places, then began the Gentlemen of the Chappell to singe a full Anthem, which ended, the Bisshopp of Bathe and Welles, Deane of His Maj. Chappell, went into the pulpitt, which stood at the foote of the stepp before the Communion table, and preached uppon the second of St. John, the marriage of Canaa of Galilea: the sermon beinge ended, which continued not muche above halfe an hower, the Quier began an other Anthem which was the Psalme, Blessed art thou that fearest God, &c. While the An-them was in singinge, the Arch Bisshopp of Canterburie and the Deane of the Chappell went into the Vestery, and putt on their riche Coapes and came to the Communion table, wher standinge till the Anthem was ended, they two assended the Throne, wher these two great Princes weare married by the Bishopp of Canterburie in all pointes accordinge to the booke of our Common Prayer, the Prince Palatine speakinge the wordes of marriage in Englishe. After the Arch Bishopp had ended the Benediccõn, God the Father, God the Sonne, &c. the Quier sange the same benediccõn in an Anthem made new for that purpose by Doctor Bull: this Anthem ended, the Arch Bisshopp and the Deane descended the Throne, and the Bridgroome and Bride followinge them kneeled before the Communion table, where the versickles and prayers weare sunge by the Arch Bisshopp and answered by the Quier. The prayers beinge ended, began an other Anthem; that don, Mr. Garter, Principall Kinge at Armes, published the stile of the Prince and Princess to this effect. All health happines and honor be to the highe and mightie Princes Frederick the fourth, by the grace of God, Count Palatine of the Rhine, Arch Sewer and Prince Ellector of the Holy Empire, Duke of Bavier, and Elizabeth his wiffe, only daughter to the highe mightie and Right Excellent James, by the grace of God Kinge of Greate Brittaine. Which beinge ended, ther was brought out of the vestery, by divers of the Lordes, wine and wafers, which when they had eaten, they departed after the same manner as they cam in, beinge led back from the Chappell by the Duke of Lennox and the Earle of Nottingham Lord Admirall. The Kinge and Queene, leavinge the Bride and Bridgroome in the great Chamber, went to their privie lodginges, and left the Bride and Bridgroome to dine in state in the new banquettinge House with the Prince, the Embassadours of Fraunce, Venice, and the States, Count Henry, and the whole troupe of Lordes and Ladies. [ff. 77, 77b.]

11. After that the Earle of Essex and his Wiffe the Ladie Frauncis Howard had byn maryed eight yeares, ther was by a Commission of Delegates an anullity found to be in that maryage *propter latens, incurabile et perpetuum impeditum quo ad hanc:* wheruppon they beinge sundered, ther was a maryage solemnized betweene the Earle of Somersett and her uppon the 26th of December 1613, at Whithall, in the Chappell, beinge St. Steeven's daie, at which maryage was present the Kinges Majestie and the Queene, with the Prince and all the Lordes and Ladies of the Court and about London.

The Bride was given by the Earle of Suffolke, Lord Chamberlaine, her Father. And the gentlemen of the Chappell had for their fee as before had been used, the somme of five poundes.

12. Memorandum that uppon the 29th daie of September 1617, Sir John Villiers, Knight, Gentleman of the Prince his Highnes bedchamber, was married in the Chappell at Hampton Courte unto Frauncis Cooke youngest daughter of the Rt. Hon. Sir Edward Cooke, Knight, one of his Maj. most Hon. Privie Councell, wher the Kinges Maj. (receavinge her from Sir Edward her father) gave her in marryage. And the Gentlemen had for their fee the somme of five poundes. [f. 78.]

XVII.—ROYAL AND NOBLE BAPTISMS, CHURCHINGS, CONFIRMATIONS, &c.

The order and manner of the service performed in and by the ^{1605, May 5.} Chappell at the Christninge of Marye the daughter of the Mightie ^{At Greenwich.} Kinge, James, &c. the fyfte of Maye, Anno 1605.

At the tyme when the Royall Infant should be brought to the Chappell, the gentlemen of that place (after many companies goinge before) went out of the Chappell two and two in ther surplesses unto the nurcerie doore, there following them the Deane of the Chappell, next after came the Arch Bishop of Canterbury, bothe in rich copes of Needellworke. Then all returninge, came the noble Babe, who was carried under a cannapee of cloth of goold, and all the waye as it came towardes the Chappell ther was a generall scilence, neither voyce nor instrument was heard in the waye. When the Royall Infant was thus brought unto the lower Chappell doore, there did the Archbishop and the Deane of the Chappell receave the Babe and came next before it into the higher Chappell. At the same instant did the Organest begine and continew playinge aloude untill the Child was placed in the Traverse, and the Gosipps one the right side without the cell, upon three severall rich stooles, and the rest of the honorable trayne, as thus: his

Majestie (with the Prince) in his clossett above, and tharells [the Earls], Bishops and Lords Barons on the one side, and the great Ladies on the other side of the Chappell. When all were placed, then begane an Antheme, shewinge the dedication of the Royall Infant unto Allmightie God by baptisme (the Chorus whereof was filled with the help of musicall instrumentes): the which Antheme beinge endid the child was brought from the Traverce to the Font, whome the Arch Bishop baptised with great reverence (beinge still in his rich cope), who was assistid in the administracõn of the Sacrament by the Deane of the Chappell (he allso beinge in his cope). Under the cell (compassinge the font) were onlye the Archbishop, the Deane of the Chappell, the Gosypps (the Duke Vanhulston, the Ladye Arbella, the Countis of Northumberland,) the Great Countesse which held the Babe, and a Countisse bearinge her trayne, and the two supporters, which were the Duke of Lyniox and the Lord Treasurer. And fower Earles sonnes wayted without at the fower corners of the cell. In the tyme of the Baptisme the Kinge sent a Gentleman Usher to the Gosipps signifyinge his pleasure what the name of the Child should be, which Babe beinge named accordinglye, the Lord's Grace signed Marye, the Christened Infant, with the signe of the Crosse. And the Baptisme beinge ended, an other Antheme was songe of thankesgeevinge to God for the ingraffinge of the Blessed Infant into Christ his Holy Church by Baptisme. Then the heroldes put on there coates, and Garter the Kinge of Heroldes standinge neere the rayles which inclosed the Font, and turninge his face towards the Kinges Majestie, did with a loud voyce proclayme what was his dutie to doe. That ended, the Trumpetors sounded cherefully, standinge in the Lower Chappell. Then began an offertorye to be played, in which tyme the noble baptised Infant was brought to the Holye Table and there it offered, by the person of the Lord Treasurer. Then the God Father and God Mothers did severallye offer allso, beinge fett [fetched] from ther seates by the Lord Chamberlaine, the Deane of the Chappell receavinge ther offeringes at the Communion Table in his cope.

Then followed a full Anthem (Singe joyfullye), in the singinge wherof the.Gosipp's great giftes weare brought out of the vestrie (by certaine Knightes) and placed uppon the Communion Table, at thend of which Antheme the Collect for the Kinge was read, and therwith the service ended. Then cartaine Lords Barons brought up from the Lower Chappell a bason and ewer and towells, and the Gosipps washed, and after that a great bankquet was brought allso out of the Lower Chappell by Lords Barons in to the higher Chappell, and there first presentid unto the Gosypps, and then to other great personagis (the organes playinge aloud all that tyme). When the same Banquet was endid, all the Companyes went out of the Chappell in order, and in ther due places as they came in, att which there returne with the Royall Baptised Infant, the Chappell and the Musitions joyned together, makinge excellent hermony with full Anthemes, which continued so doinge untill the Child came unto the nurcerye doore, where it was first receavid.

[f. 32*b*.]

The Order of the Queen's Highnes Churchinge, which was in the 1605, May 19. Chappell, uppon Whitsondaye 1605.

First at the Kinges cominge to his Closett to here the Sermon, ther was a full Anthem songe, and after the sermon was ended then was songe an Anthem for a Childe. Immediatlye after that, began an Offertorye to be played, in which the Kinges Matie came downe and offerred, and then went in to his Travase: forthwith certaine Knightes of the Garter and other honorable persons went up and did fetche the Queen's highnes downe in to the Chappell, she beinge supported by the Duke Vanhulston and the Duke of Lynneox, and the Lady Arbella bearinge her trayne, who also did there betake her selfe to her travase, all which tyme the Organest continued the offertory. When the Kinge and Queene weare so seated, then ended the offertory, and a full Anthem (beginninge Blessed art thou that fearest God) was songe, at the end whereof the Bishop of Canterbury, beinge assisted by Mr. Deane of the Chappell (and

both in rich copes) did read the ordinary service of Churchinge of
woomen, appointed by the booke, her highnes kneelinge the
while in her Travase. The churchinge beinge ended, the Queene
rose up and cam forth and offered at the Holye Table, as the Kinges
Majestie had formerly done, Mr. Deane receavinge both their
offeringes in his cope, and the Organes playinge at each tyme.
Then after the Queene had offered she retired herselfe in to her
Travase, and presentlye began an Anthem of thankesgevinge, prepared of purpose for the Churchinge: that ended, the Collectes, one
for the Kinge, the other for the Queene, weare read, and therwith
ended the whole service. Then the Organest playd againe, whilst
the Kinges Majestie, the Queene, and the whole trayne, departed
out of the Chappell.   [f. 33]

1606, June 22.   Be yt remembred with thankes gevinge to Almightie God, that
uppon the 22d day of June (beinge Sundaye) Anno 1606, betweene
the howers of three and fower of the clocke in the morninge of the
same daye, Oure gratious Queene Anne by the help and goodnes of
God was safelye delivered of a Royall Daughter at Greenwich, in his
Majesties howse there. The daye followinge beinge Mundaye the
23th of the same moneth, the Royall Babe growinge verye weake,
yt was baptized privately by Doctor Mountagew, Deane of his
Majesties Chappell (by the name of Sophia), betweene the howers
of 6 and 7 of the clocke in the eveninge of the same daye, the
Countisse of Suffolke and the Ladye Walsingam beinge her suerties
or witnesses at her Baptisme. Allso the same nobell Infant beinge in
thend overcome by the power of Death, yealdid her sweete soule into
the handes of the Holye geiver therof, betweene the howers of 8 and 9
in the eveninge of the same Mundaye the 23th of June. The dead
corpes of the Royall Babe was removed by water from Greenewich,
and was interred in the Abbey Church of Westminster, the 26th
daye of the same moneth beinge Thursdaye, attended by most of
the Lordes of his Majestes Privie Counsaile, and many other great
Lordes and Ladyes, all clad in blacke, but not in murninge weedes.

Her Highnes second Churchinge.

Be yt further remembred that upon the third daye of August beinge Sundaye, Anno 1606, the Queenes highnes was churched pryvatlye in her privie Chamber at Greenwich, by Doctor Mountagew, Deane of his Majesties Chappell, who also baptised the Royall Babe Sophia (latelye buried), which was the second Child her Highnes bare unto the Kinges Majestie after ther cominge unto this Kingdome. [f. 39.]

The Order of the Prince's Confirmacōn in the Chappell, the third of Aprill 1607, beinge then Good Fridaye. 1607, Apl. 3.

On which daye Henrie Prince of Greate Brittaine was attended on by sondrie honorable persons into the Kinges Chappell at White-hall, and in the tyme of singinge of the first Anthem before the sermon began, wher, at the lower step in the Quier there, a carpett and cushions beinge prepared, he there kneelinge was confirmed in his faithe in Christe, by the Reverend Father the Arch-bishop of Canterbury (the Deane of the Chappell assistinge him, and bothe in riche copes). At which Confirmacōn were attendinge also with the Arch Bishop sixe grave Bishops (the Kinges Majestie remayninge that while in his greate Closett): the which beinge don accordinge to the booke of Comon Prayer, and an Anthem songe, the Prince returned againe with his honorable traine unto the great closet, wher the Kinges Majestie still remayned, and then began the sermon, &c.

The 5th of Aprill then next following (beinge Easter daye) 1607, Henrie Prince of Great Brittaine did after his confirmacōn pub-licquely receave the Holy Comunion, with the Kinges Majᵗⁱᵉ his father, in the Chappell at Whitehall, a cushion beinge prepared wheron he kneeled on the leafte hand of the Kinge his Father, a little belowe the Kinge. And after that Mr. Deane had ministred the

Comunion unto him selfe and his Assistantes, in one sorte of bread and cup, he then ministred the holy Comunion unto the Kinges Majestie in bread and cupp prepared for him selfe alone, and lastly unto the Prince in bread and cupp prepared only for his grace: when the Kinge had receaved the bred, then the Prince had the bread administred unto him, and in lyke sorte the cupp. This holy Comunion was receaved by the Kinges Maj^{tie} the Prince and the rest all reverently kneelinge in their severall places, before the Comunion Table. [f. 78b.]

1610-11, Mar. 22.

The Order of the Ladie Elizabeth her Grace's Confirmacõn in the Chappell the 22th of Marche 1610, beinge Good Frydaye.

On which daye her Grace was attended on by sondry Hon. persons, bothe of Lordes and Ladies, into the Kinges Chappell at Whitehall, and in the tyme of singinge of the first Anthem, before the sermon began, wher at the lower step in the Quier there, a carpett and cushions beinge prepared, she there kneelinge was confirmed in her fayth in Christe by the Reverend Father the Bishopp of Bathe and Wellcs, Deane of his Maj. Chappell, the Subdeane therof assistinge him, and bothe in riche copes; the Kinges Majestie and the Queene remayninge that while in their greate clossettes: the which beinge don accordinge to the booke of Comon Prayer, and an Anthem songe, her Grace returned againe with her hon. traine unto the greate clossett where the Queens Majestie still remayned, and then began the sermon.

The 24th of Marche then next followinge (beinge Easter daie) the Ladie Elizabethe receaved the Holy Comunion in like sorte as the Prince in the other syde did, &c. [f. 79.]

1613, Ap. 5.

Prince Charells Confirmacõn in the Chappell the 5th of Aprill 1613, beinge then the Mondaie in Easter weeke.

On which daie Charells Prince of Great Brittaine was attended on by sondrie honorable persons into the Kinges Chappell at Whithall, and in the singinge of the first Anthem, wher at the

lower step in the Queere there, a carpett and cusshions beinge prepared, he there kneelinge was confirmed in his faithe in Christe by
the Reverend Father in God the Bishopp of Bathe and Welles,
Deane of his Majesties Chappell (assistinge him, and
bothe in riche coapes.) At which confirmacōn weare attending
also the Arch Bishopp of Canterburie and   grave Bisshopps,
(the Kinges Majestie remayninge that while in the greate closett):
the which beinge don accordinge to the booke of Comon prayer,
the Prince returned againe with his hon. traine unto the greate
closett, wher the Kinges Majestie still remayned, untill the end of
divine service.

The 23th of Maye then next followinge (beinge Whitsondaye)
Prince Charells receaved the Holy Comunion at Greenwich, in lyke
manner as Prince Henry and the Ladie Elizabeth her grace
did, &c.   [f. 79.]

The Names of the Children Baptised in the Chappell in the raigne
of our Soveraigne Ladye Queene Elizabeth.

Elizabeth, the daughter of the Lord Cobham, was baptised in the
Chappell in the second yeare of her Majestes raigne, when was
payd to the Gentlemen of the Chappell for fees 5 ťi.

Edwardus Fortunatus, sonne to the Ladye Cicilia, was baptised in
the Chappell in the seventh yeare of her Maj. raigne, when was
payd to the Gentlemen of the Chappell for fees 5ťi.

The Names of the Children Baptised in the Chappell in the raigne
of our Soveraigne Lord Kinge James.

Anna, the daughter of the right honorable Therll of Southampton, Baptised in
was baptised in the Chappell in the second yeare of his Majestes April 1604.
raigne, when was payd to the Gentlemen of the Chappell for The Deanes
Fee 10 li.
fees 5 ťi.

James, the sonne and heire of the right honorable the Earll of Baptized in
Southamton, was baptised in the Chappell in the third yeare of his March the 26
daye 1605.

Maj. raigne, when was payd to the Gentlemen of the Chappell for fees 5 li.

James, the sonne of the right honorable the Earle of Nottingam, was baptised in the Chappell at Whitehall the 25th of Marche 1607, and in the 5th yeare of his Maj. raigne, the Kinges highnes, therle of Suffolke (then Lord Chamberlaine), and the Ladie Arbella beinge sureties. For which was paid unto Mr. Deane for his fee , and to the Gentlemen of the Chappell for their fees 5 li.

James Lord Matrevers, the sonne and heire of the Right Hon. the Earle of Arundell, was baptised in the King's Chappell at Whitehall the 17th of July 1607, and in the 5th yeare of his Maj. raigne. The Kinges highnes, the Earle of Suffolke (then Lord Chamberlayne), and the Ladie Arbella, deputie for the olde Cometesse of Shrosburie, beinge sureties, for which was payd unto the gentlemen for their fee 5 li.

James, the sonne of the Right Hon. the Earle of Arguile, was baptised in the King's Chappell at Greenwich, the 25th of September 1610, and in the 8th yeare of his Majestes raigne. The Kinges highnes (the Prince beinge his substitute), the Earle of Sarum Lord Highe Treasurer, and the Ladie Marquesse of Winchester beinge sureties. For the which was paid unto the Gentlemen of the Chappell for their fees five poundes. The Deane absent from the Christenninge.

Anna, the daughter of the Right Hon. the Earle of Salisburie, was baptised in the Chappell at Whitehall the 23d of February 1612, and in the tenthe yeare of his Majestes raigne (the Queen's Majestie, the Countisse of Darbie the younger, and the Earle of Shrosburie beinge sureties), for which was paid unto the Gentlemen of the Chappell for their fee five poundes.   [ff. 75b, 76.]

James Stuart, sonne of the Lord Aubigny, one of his Maj. bed-chamber, was christened in the Chappell at Whithall, on Wensday the 29th of Aprill 1612. The Kinges Majestie, the Duke of Linox, and the Ladie Elizabethes grace weare wittnesses therunto. For which was given to the Gentlemen for fees [five poundes].

Henry, sonne of the abovesaid Lo. Aubigny, was baptised in the Chappell at Whitehall the second daye of Aprill 1616. The Queene beinge godmother, the Prince and the Earle of Mar godfathers. For which was given unto the gentlemen for their fees five poundes.

James, sonne of the Right Hon. the Lord Haddington, was baptised in the Chappell at Whithall the 11th daye of March 1616. The Kinges Hignes, the Earle of Sussex, and the Ladie of Bedford beinge sureties. For which the gentlemen receaved for their fees 5 ƚi.

James, sonne of Sir William Feildinge, Knight, was baptised in the Chappell at Whithall the 13th daie of March 1616. The Kinges Majestie, the Earle of Buckingham, and the Ladie of Bedford beinge sureties. For which was given to the gentlemen for their fees 5 ƚi.

Charles, second sonne of the Right Hon. the Lord Haddington, was baptised in the Chappell at Whithall the 17th of May 1618. Prince Charles, the Lord Marquesse of Buckingham, and the Ladie of Hartford beinge sureties. For which was given to the gentlemen for their fees 5 li. [f. 79b.]

XVIII.—FORMS OF PRAYER, &c.

A Prayer for her Majestie and the Lordes of the most hon. Ordre 1593, Apl. 23.
of the Garter.

O moste mightie and mercyfull Father, the absolute Protector of all puissant Princes, noble Lords and valerous Knyghts, whose power hathe ever shewed it selfe in the prowes and wonderfull acts of thy holye worthies, We humblye besече the still to save and deffende thy moste noble worthye our dread Soveraigne Ladye Elizabeth, whom thowe hast raysed up an admirable Deborah for thy holye Churche with us and farre abroad. O Lord, encrease her heroical power and strengthe in thee, her princelye herte and hands for thee against all thyne and her enymies, that thes her dominions may daylye flourishe in thy trewthe and trewe nobilitie. Graunt also, O Lorde, to the noble societie of the most honorable Ordre of the Garter, Josua's holynes, David's integritie, Salamon's wisdome, and Gideon's good successe, in all their loyall services for and under thyne anoynted Elizabethe our Qweene, that so their peaceable practises and martial feates beinge begun, contynued, and ended in thee, may be so prospered by thee as still we may wondre at thy mightie works, and magnifye thy mercye, throughe Jesus Christe our Lorde. Amen.

ANTH: ANDERSON, Subdeane, Aprill 23, 1593, Eliz. 33.

[f. 84*b*.]

The Order for the Memory and Commendation of the Queenes Majesties Progenitors, Founders of the most noble Order of the Garter, to be used at the Feast of St. George.

Oure Father, which arte in heaven, &c.;
> then

O Lord, open thow my lippes, &c.
> Certaine psalmes.

The first lesson the 44 of Ecclesiasticus, or the
> then

We prayse thee, O God, etc.	First Lessons.	Second Lessons.
> then	2. ecclesiasticus	2. Chap. of the 2.
I beleeve in God, etc.	4. ecclesiasticus	the Phillippians.
	5. ecclesiasticus	3. Chap. of the
The answeres.	7. ecclesiasticus	epystle of St. Jhon.
	8. ecclesiasticus	1 Peter, 2. chap.
	11. ecclesiasticus	Epistle of Jude.
O Lord, heare oure prayer;	14. ecclesiasticus	1 Timothye, 2. chap.
And graunt our petition, etc.	25. ecclesiasticus	
	37. ecclesiasticus	

The Collect for the Sonday;

The first night { First lesson, Judges 6 Chap. begin at 11th verse. Second lesson, Ephesians vj.

> then

Morninge { 1 Lesson, Ecclesiasticus 44. 2 Lesson, John 15.

Eveninge { 1 Lesson, Ecclesiasticus 46. 2 Lesson, Acts 25.

Anth. Anderson, Subdean, Apl. 23, 1593.

(left margin, vertical:) We prayse and thanke thee, O Lord, in all the noble Kinges patrones of this Order, and our benefactors.

O Lord God our Heavenly Father, and oure mercifull Saviour Jesu Christe, assiste James our most worthie Kinge continuallye with thie holie spirytt, that as he is auncientlie and trewlie descended from the noble Princes of this Realme and the bountifull patrones and founders of this noble order, so he may proceede in all good woorkes (namely) for sustentation of learninge and helpe of povertie, and that all noble men of this Realme (speciallie suche as be the Companions of this most honorable Order of the Garter) may like-wyse dispose them selves in honor and vertue at all tymes, that God therby may be the better honored, the common wealth served, and there good fame remayne to ther posteritie, and that wee all may continewe in the true fayth, and walke in good woorkes that God hath appoynted us, throughe Jesu Christe our Lord and Saviour. Amen.

O Lord, save James our Kinge and all the companions of this most noble order of the Garter. Amen.* [f. 85b.]

Be it remembred with thankesgeivinge to Allmightie God, that upon the eight daye of Aprill in the yeare 1605, our gracious Queene Ann, by the helpe and goodnes of God, was safelye delivered of a Royall daughter at Greenewich in his Majestes howse there. [1605, Apl. 8]

A publicke Thankesgeivinge to God for the same, used in his Majestes Chappell.

O Lord our God, Mercifull and Gracious, Wee render unto thy divine Majestie our most humble and hartie thankes for thy goodnes this last night past extended unto our most gracious Queene in givinge her so happie a deliverye of a blessed Infant. Wee most humblye intreate thy Majestie still to continew thy Fatherlye protection over her and it, that wee maye ever gyve praise unto thy Holye Name, through Jesus Christ our Lord. Amen. [f. 38.]

---

* This Prayer again occurs, f. 82b, the only difference being in the spelling of certain words.

A Prayer now to be used at the Feast of St. George.

O Lord save our Kinge, and mercifully heare us, &c.

Allmightie and most mercifull Father, we humblie beseeche thee in the name of thy sonne Christ Jesus our Lord and Saviour, to direct and endew Kinge James, our most Godlye and worthie Soveraigne, with the continuall and plentifull grace of thine Holy Spirite, that as he is aunciently and rightly descended from the most puissant and prudent Princes of this Realme, the first founders and erectors of this most noble order of the Garter, so he may abound and excell in all thinges acceptable to thee, namely, in the maintenance of pietie, peace, justice, and equity, in the supporte of good learninge, and the reliefe of the poore and oppressed: and graunt, most gracious Lord, that all the noble men of this Realme, especially suche [as are] companions of this most honorable order of the Garter, may be thoroughly devoted to trew godlines, valour, and vertue, so as God may therby the better be honored, their Soveraigne served, the Common wealth secured, and the memoriall of their well doinge remaine to their posteritie: and that wee all may live and die in thy fayth and feare, and walke in those workes whiche thou hast appointed us, through Jesus Christ our Lord. Amen.

O Lord, longe preserve James our Kinge and all the Companions of this most noble order of the Garter.   Amen.   [f. 83.]

The Order of the Maundy.

The Subdean begins the Exhortation, Confession, and Proper Psalm for the occasion, Psal. 41.   Then the Lesson, St. John, cap. 13th from verse 1st to verse 18; which ended, his Matie (attended by the Lord Almoner and the white staves) goes to the poore men in order, sprinkles their feet with a sprig of hyssop dipt in water, wipes them and kisses them; which ended, his Majestie returns to his chair of State.

Then begins the first Anthem, which let be, Hide not thou thy face from us, O Lord, &c.; which done, the Lord Almoner distributes the shoes and stockins. He being returned, sing the second Anthem, which let be, Prevent us, O Lord, in all our doings, &c.; which done, he distributes the cloaths, woollen and linnen. Being return'd, sing the third Anthem, which let be, Call to remembrance, O Lord, thy tender mercyes; which done, he distributes the purses; and being return'd, sing the fourth Anthem, which let be, O praise the Lord all ye Heathen, &c.; which done, he distributes the fish and bread. After which, being returned, the Gospell is read, St. Mat. 25th from ver. 14th to the end; which ended sing the last Anthem, which let be, O Lord, make thy servant King Charles, &c.

Then this Prayer.

Be present with us, O Lord, by this gracious acceptation in the discharge of this our duty and service: and in as much as thou vouchsafedst to wash thy disciples' feet, and didst command us to follow thy blessed steps till thy coming again, looke down graciously we beseech thee on the worke of thyne own hands performed this day (by thy servant our Gracious Soveraigne Lord the King) in imitation of thee and obedience to thy commands, and as by the outward washing by water the spots and stayns of the body are done away, so let all the corruptions and defilements of our souls through sin be cleansed by thy most precious bloud. Grant this, O blessed Jesu, who with the Father and Holy Ghost livest and reignest ever one God, world without end. Amen.

Then Prayers for the King, Queen, &c.

After the blessing, the Lord Almoner calls for wyne, and drinkes to all the poore the King's health, and bids them be thankfull to God and pray for the King.

A Prayer at the Maundy.

O most blessed Jesu, who, being the son of the ever living God, didst not only not disdeine to take our humane nature and the forme of a servant upon thee, but, haveing determined to lay downe thy life as a Ransome for the sins of the whole world, didst on the night before thy sufferings leave to thy disciples that admirable patterne of profound humility which men and angells might have stood amazed at, to see thee the God of Heaven and Earth wash and wipe and kisse the feet of thy Disciples: looke downe we beseech thee upon our Gratious Soveraigne thy good servant, and us, this day, who, to preserve the memory of this thy inimitable goodnesse, are heer assembled to praise thee for those thy high expressions of love to thy unworthy creatures, and earnestly to pray that this great example of thee, our Heavenly Master, may make such impressions in us that we may with humble minds and charitable affections be alwayes ready to descend to the lowest offices in relieving the necessitys of the meanest of our Brethren : that we haveing learnt of thee to be meeke, and humble, and charitable, may be the better fitted to receive the Holy Sacrament, and to reigne with thee in all the glories of thy Kingdome.   Grant this, O deare Jesu, and mediate for us with thyne Eternall Father, with whom and thy Holy Spirit thou livest and reignest for evermore.   Amen.

[ff. 75b, 76.]

[*The following entries occur at the end of f. 80b, in other respects a blank leaf.*]

1662. Lisbona, the daughter of unknowne parents, accidentally found shortly after its birth in a private place of Hampton Court, but conceived to be the child of a Portugall woman, was baptized in a private chamber there, June 20, 1662.

1663. A Blackmoore baptised in the Chappell at Whitehall, 1663.

FINIS.

NOTES.

Page 1. *Mr. Angell, Subdean.*—John Angell, whose name occurs in the lists of Gentlemen of the Chapel in the reigns of Edward VI. and Mary. He died August 17, 1567 (p. 2).

Ibid. *Robert Parsons.*—Morley spells his name Persons. See Catalogue at the end of Introduction to Practicall Musicke, 1597. He was born at Exeter, but no particulars of his life are known. He is erroneously said to have been organist of Westminster Abbey. John Parsons, who was appointed organist of that establishment in 1621, may possibly have been his son. The epitaph upon " Master Parsons, organist at Westminster," printed in Camden's Remains (edit. 1674, p. 549), relates to this John, not to Robert, as has been supposed. In The First Booke of Selected Church Musick, published by John Barnard, a Minor Canon of St. Paul's Cathedral, in 1641, is contained a Morning, Communion, and Evening Service, by Robert Parsons. Many of his compositions are extant in MS., particularly in the library of Christ Church, Oxford ; and the words of some of his anthems are given in James Clifford's Divine Services and Anthems, 1664. He was unfortunately drowned at Newark-upon-Trent, Jan. 25, 1569, and a record of the event is entered in the Cheque-Book (p. 2).

Ibid. *Mr. Walker.*—William Walker, Gentleman of the Chapel in the reigns of Edward VI. and Mary.

Ibid. *William Mundy.*—A musician of some eminence, the father of John Mundy, organist of the Chapel Royal, Windsor, who died in 1630, and was buried in the cloisters of the establishment with which he was connected. Both musicians are mentioned in some verses at the end of a MS. collection of Motetts and Madrigals, transcribed, A.D. 1591, by John Baldwine, " singing man of Windsor." Recounting the celebrated composers of his time, he says :—

> " I will begine with White, Shepperd, Tye, and Tallis,
> Parsons, Gyles, Mundie, th'oulde one of the Queenes pallis ;
> Mundie yonge, th'oulde man's sonne, and likewyse others moe,
> There names would be to[o] longe, therefore I let them goe."

Sir John Hawkins has confounded father and son, making William the son of John, whereas the reverse was certainly the case. Had he observed the entry in the Cheque-

Book, showing that William was sworn a member of the Chapel Royal, Feb. 21, 1563, he could not have supposed that John, who took his degree of Mus. Bac. in 1585, and his Mus. Doc. degree in 1624, was the elder of the two. (See Wood's Fasti, i. 236, 415.) It is hardly necessary to say that Hawkins has been copied in this mistake by all subsequent writers. We learn from the Cheque-Book that William Mundy was received into the Chapel Royal from the choir of St. Paul's, a fact hitherto unnoticed. Nothing is known of his biography ; even the date of his death is unrecorded. A service of his and four anthems are printed in John Barnard's First Booke of Selected Church Musick, 1641, and a number of his compositions exist in MS. (See also Clifford's Divine Services and Anthems, 1664, for the words of several of his anthems.) The anthem in Boyce's Cathedral Music (also in Barnard), " O Lord, the Maker of all things," incorrectly attributed to Henry VIII. by Aldrich and Boyce, is the composition of William Mundy. The words being contained in the Complin Service in Henry the Eighth's Primer has probably given rise to the error.

Ibid. *Richard Farrant.*—Gentleman of the Chapel in the reigns of Edward VI., Mary, and Elizabeth. He resigned his post to accept that of Master of the Children of St. George's Chapel, Windsor. Hawkins says he was also lay-clerk, and one of the organists of the same establishment. The following entries from the Office-book of the Treasurer of the Chamber (temp. Eliz.) relate to Farrant in his capacity of Master of the Children. They are extracted from Cunningham's Account of the Revels at Court (Shaks. Soc. 1842, p. xxix.) :—

" Payde upon the Counsayles Warrante dated at Westm^r the xxvth of Februarye, 1568, To Richarde Farrant, Scole M^r to the Children of Wyndsor, for presentinge a playe before the Quenes M^{tie} on Shrove Tewsdaye at nyght laste paste, by way of, &c., vj li. xiii s. iiij d."

" Payde upon the Counsayles Warrante dated at Windsor the ij of Jauuarye, 1569, To Richarde Ferrante, Scolem^r to the Childeren of Wyndsor, by waye of, &c., for presentinge a playe before her Highnes this Christmas upon St. John's daye at nighte laste paste, vj li. xiij s. iiij d."

On Nov. 5, 1569, Farrant returned to his old appointment, and was reinstated Gentleman in the room of Thomas Causton. The entry (p. 2) expressly says " From Winsore." He died Nov. 30, 1580 (p. 3) ; another entry (p. 65) gives the date Nov. 30, 1581. At all events he died in one of these years, not in 1585, as Hawkins supposed. Hist. of Music, edit. 1853, p. 465.

As a Church composer Farrant has great merit, an assertion borne out by his works printed in Barnard and Boyce's collections. Two of his anthems, " Call to remembrance " and " Hide not thou thy face " (the last adapted by Aldrich), were for a long period used at Whitehall Chapel on Maunday Thursday, when the Sub-Almoner (attended by the organist in waiting and the Gentlemen and children of the Royal Chapels) distributes the Royal charity among certain aged applicants.

Farrant is popularly known at the present day by the association of his name with the anthem " Lord, for thy tender mercies' sake." The history of this beautiful little anthem is involved in some obscurity, both as regards the words and the music. The former may be found, with some variations, in Prayers, commonly called Lydley's Prayers, reprinted by the Parker Society in Bull's Christian Prayers and Meditations, p. 174. So far as the music is concerned, it is extremely doubtful if Farrant was its author. It seems from internal evidence to be the production of a somewhat later era, and may possibly be the composition of John Hilton. In the old MS. Part-books preserved in Ely Cathedral it is ascribed to him; and Dr. Blow, when transcribing, in the year 1686, a large collection of the compositions of his predecessors and contemporaries, unhesitatingly attributed it to John Hilton. It was considered to be his by Dr. Tudway, and also by James Hawkins, organist of Ely Cathedral from 1682 to 1720. The words of the anthem appear in the second edition of Clifford's Divine Services and Anthems, 1664, but with the name of Thomas Tallis attached to them as that of the composer. They next occur in Thomas Wanless's Full Anthems and Verse Anthems, printed at York in 1703, but without any name of composer. They are not found in any subsequently printed book of words of anthems until that of Mason (also printed at York) in 1782, when the name of Farrant is appended to them. The music of the anthem first appeared in print under Farrant's name in Page's Harmonia Sacra, published in 1800. But the mistake, if mistake it be, of attributing the anthem to Farrant, is of an earlier date. A copy exists in the handwriting of Dr. Aldrich, who has written the name of Richard Farrant at the end, afterwards crossing it out and substituting in its place that of John Hilton.

Ibid. *Thomas Byrd, or Bird.*—Gentleman of the Chapel in the reigns of Edward VI. and Mary. He is supposed to have been the father of the celebrated William Byrd. If so, he was, in all probability, also connected with the musical establishment of the Cathedral of St. Paul, in which choir his son was certainly educated. See the Life of William Byrd, prefixed to his Mass for Five Voices, printed by the Musical Antiquarian Society.

Ibid. *Robert Moorcocke.*—Gentleman of the Chapel in the reigns of Edward VI. and Mary. He died June 15, 1581 (p. 3).

Ibid. *Richard Bower.*—He seems to have succeeded William Crane, who was Master of the Children of the Chapel in the latter years of Henry VIIIth's reign. In the Household Book of Henry VIII., A.D. 1530, printed in the Trevelyan Papers (Camd. Soc. p. 161), we find :—

" Item, to Mr. Crane, for playing before the King with the Children of the Chappell, in reward, vj li. xiij s. iiij d."

And in the Household Book of Edward VI., A.D. 1548 (ibid. p. 201), the following entry occurs :—

" Item, to Richard Bower, for playing before the Kings majestie with the Children of the Chappell, in rewarde, vj li. xiij s. iiij d."

Rymer's Fœdera (xv. 517) shows that his salary was 40*l.* a-year. Strype, describing the old church at Greenwich (Stowe's Survey, ii. 92, Circuit Walk), says : " Within the rails are three flat stones, with brass plates. One for Richard Bower, late Gentleman of the Chapel, and Master of the Children to K. Henry the Eighth, K. Edward the Sixth, Q. Mary, and Q. Elizabeth. He deceased 26 July, 1561." [1563?]

Ibid.   *Richard Edwards.*—This celebrated poet, musician, and dramatist is called by Wood a " Somersetshire man." He was born in 1523, and on May 11, 1540, admitted a scholar of Corpus Christi College, Oxford. On the foundation of Christ Church, in 1547, he became a student there, and in the same year took his degree of M.A. Wood tells us that he was also a member of Lincoln's Inn. The period of his leaving the University is not known, but in his early years he appears to have held some appointment about the Court. This is evident from the following passage in one of his poems in The Paradise of Dainty Devices :—

> " In youthfull yeares when first my young desires began
>   To pricke me forth to serve in Court, a slender, tall young man,
>   My father's blessing then I ask'd upon my knee,
>   Who, blessing me with trembling hand, these words gan say to me:
>   My sonne, God guide thy way, and shield thee from mischance,
>   And make thy just desartes in Court thy poor estate to advance," &c.

His experience of Court life is further confirmed by a small volume of MS. Sonnets in the Brit. Mus. (Cott. MSS. Titus A. xxiv.), signed with his initials, addressed to some of the beauties of the Courts of Mary and Elizabeth. Warton says that " in the year 1561 he was constituted a Gentleman of the Royal Chapel by Queen Elizabeth, and Master of the Singing-boys there," but this does not appear from the Cheque-Book. We have no means of ascertaining the date of his admission to this establishment ; but upon the death of Richard Bower, in 1563, he was appointed to fill his place as Master of the Children.

Edwards is well known as a writer of songs and ballads; and as the chief contributor to The Paradise of Dainty Devices. Many of his pieces have been quoted by Warton, Ellis, and Brydges, and his beautiful " Soul's Knell," supposed to have been written on his death-bed, is admired even to this day. He was the author of two dramatic pieces, Damon and Pythias, and Palemon and Arcite. The first was acted at Court, and printed, probably in 1568 or 1570, although the earliest edition that has come down to us is dated 1571. The latter was acted before Queen Elizabeth in the Hall of Christ Church, Oxford, Sept. 3, 1566. Wood tells us that its performance gave Her Majesty " so much content " that she sent for the author, and, after commending him, " gave him promise of reward." Poor Edwards did not live to reap the benefit of this promise, as the Cheque-Book records that he " died on the last day of October, 1566 "—a few weeks after the performance of his play.

Edwards was on friendly terms with most of the poets of his time. Copies of verses were frequently addressed to him. One of these, by Barnabe Googe, extracted from his rare volume, Eglogs, Epitaphes, and Sonettes, 1563, we shall quote:—

"Of Edwardes of the Chappell.

"Devyne Camenes, that with your sacred food
    Have fed and fosterde up from tender yeares
A happye man, that in your favour stoode—
    Edwardes in Courte that can not fynde his peeres—
Your names be blest, that in the present age
    So fyne a head by Arte have framed out,
Whom some hereafter, healpt by Poets rage,
    Perchaunce may matche, but none shall passe (I doubt).
O Plautus ! yf thou wert alyve agayne,
    That comedies so fynely dydste endyte ;
Or Terence, thou that with thy pleasaunt brayne
    The hearers mynde on stage dydst much delyght,
What would you say, syrs, if you should beholde,
    As I have done, the doyngs of this man ?
No worde at all, to sweare I durst be bolde,
    But burne with teares that which with myrth began,
I meane your bookes, by which you gate your name,
    To be forgot you wolde commit to flame.
Alas ! I wolde, Edwards, more tell thy prayse,
    But at thy name my muse amased stayes."

In Turberville's Epitaphs, Epigrams, Songs and Sonnets, 1570, are two elegies on his death, one by Thomas Twine (one of the translators of Virgil), and the other by George Turberville, the editor of the book. Both pieces are interesting, but the former contains passages most deserving of quotation. Here we have an allusion to the place of his early education :—

" O happie House ! O place
    of Corpus Christi, thou
That plantedst first, and gavste the roote
    to that so brave a bowe ;
And Christ Church, which enjoydste
    the fruite more ripe at fill,
Plunge up a thousand sighes for griefe,
    your trickling tears distill," &c.

The subsequent mention of his two dramas is valuable as coming from a contemporary :—

" Thy tender Tunes and Rimes,
    wherein thou woonst to play,
Eche princely Dame of Court and Towne
    shall beare in minde alway.
Thy Damon and his Friend,
    Arcyte and Palemon,
With moe full fit for Princes eares,
    though thou from earth art gone,
Shall still remain in fame," &c.

These are valuable records of his poetical and musical character, and bear testimony to the estimation in which his talent was held by his brethren.

Richard Edwards has been confounded with another poet of the same name, who may have been his son. In the Registers of the Stationers' Company, xxiij° die Febr. 1581-2, Richard Jones entered "The Mansion of Myrthe, penned by C. Edwardes." This was, perhaps, the same " Mr. Edwardes " who wrote an epitaph on the Earl of Pembroke in 1569-70. At any rate the epitaph could not have been written by Richard Edwards who died in 1566, as Ritson supposed. (See Bibl. Poet. 195 ; and Collier's Register of Stat. Com. i. 221 ; ii. 158)

As a musician we have little means of judging of Edwards' talent, but few specimens of his skill remaining to us ; but he probably excelled in the art. He was educated under George Etheridge, who is said to have been "' one of the most excellent vocal and instrumental musicians in England." (Pits' Angl. Script., Paris, 1619, 784.) The music of the beautiful choral song, " In going to my naked bed," is assigned to him by Hawkins, but without authority, as the MS. from which he printed it has no composer's name attached to the piece in question. The MS., however, Thomas Mulliner's Booke for ye Organ or Virginals, is contemporary with Edwards, and contains several of his compositions.

Page 2. *William Hunnis.*—This poet-musician was a Gentleman of the Chapel in the reigns of Edward VI. and Mary. He was a court poet of the Sternhold-and-Hopkins school, contributing largely to the rhyming literature of his day. Under the happy title of A Handful of Honeysuckles, he published Blessings out of Deuteronomie, Prayers to Christ, Athanasius's Creed, and Meditations, in metre. But, as Warton says, " his spiritual nosegays are numerous ; to say nothing of his Recreations on Adam's banishment, Christ his Cribb, and the Lost Sheep, he translated into English rhyme the whole book of Genesis, which he calls a Hive full of Honey." (Hist. of Eng. Poet. edit. 1840, iii. 158.)

Hunnis's works may be thus briefly enumerated :—1. An Abridgement, or brief Meditation on certain of the Psalms in English Meeter, *n. d.* 2. Certain Psalmes chosen out of the Psalter of David, and drawen forth into Englyshe meter, 1550. 3. A Hyve full of Hunnye : contayning the Firste Booke of Moses, called Genesis, turned into English Meetre, 1578. 4. Seven Sobs of a Sorrowfull Soule for Sinne : comprehending those Seven Psalmes of the Princelie Prophet David commonly called Penitentiall ; turned into a forme of familiar Praiers and reduced into Meeter, 1585. 5. Hunnies' Recrea-

tions : conteining foure godlie and compendious discourses, 1588. Of these works the
two last-mentioned were the most popular, and editions were multiplied, especially of
the Seven Sobs, down to a comparatively late period. The Handfull of Honeysuckles contained in this volume was printed as early as 1579, although no copy of
that date has descended to our times. For a more particular account of the works of
this writer, see Collier's Bibliographical Account of Early English Literature, the
Registers of the Stationers' Company, and W. Carew Hazlitt's Hand-Book of Old
English Literature.

In the Office Books of the Treasurers of the Chamber during the reign of Elizabeth
are many entries of payments to Hunnis, chiefly for presenting plays, in conjunction
with the Children of the Chapel, before Her Majesty. One entry, quoted in Extracts
from the Accounts of the Revels at Court (Shaks. Soc. 1842, xxviii.) is sufficiently
curious to extract :—

"Paid upon a bill signed by the Lorde Chamberlayne To Willm. Hunys, M^r of the
Children of her M^{ts} Chappell, for xx^{tie} queares and a half of paper royall, at ij s. the
quere, xlj s. ; and for byndinge the same into xvij. books, whereof xiiij. at ij s. vj d. the
peece, and thre at xx d. the peece, xl s. ; and for writinge and prickinge ccx sheets in
the said xvij books, at xij d. the sheete, x li. x s. In all, by her Ma^{ts} especiall order
declared by the said bill, xv li. xj s. vj d."

Mr. Collier (Annals of the Stage, i. 235) says : "Hunnis was concerned in the enter-
tainment of the Queen at Kenilworth, and was the author of Interludes which were, no
doubt, acted by the boys under his government; he has hitherto been known only as the
author of various poems and translations of the Psalms, but that he wrote dramatic pieces is
evident from the following lines in his preface to Hunnis's Hive full of Honey, 1578,
by Thomas Newton :—

> ' In pryme of youth thy pleasaunt penne depaincted sonets sweete,
> Delyghtful to the greedy eare, for youthful humour meete,
> Therein appeerde thy pregnaunt wit, and store of fyled phrase,
> Enough t' astoune the doltish drone, and lumpish lout amaze.
> Thy Enterludes, thy gallant layes, thy roundletts and thy songes,
> Thy Nosegay and thy Widowe's Myte, with that therto belonges,
> With other fancies of thy forge,' &c."

Hunnis contributed a Devise and a copy of verses to the Princelie Pleasures of
Kenilworth, 1575; he has several poems in the Paradise of Dainty Devices, 1576,
and two in England's Helicon, 1600. Very little is known of his biography. In
1550 he calls himself "servant to the Ryght Honorable Sir William Harberd, Knight,"
and in 1568 a grant of arms was conferred upon him. (See Sir Egerton Brydges'
edition of Phillips' Theatrum Poetarum, 1800, p. 88.)

In the State Paper Office is preserved the "Petition of William Hunnys, Master to the
Children of the Queen's Chapel, to the Council," soliciting an increase of allowance for
maintenance of the children on account of many incidental expenses, the advance of
prices in all things since King Henry the Eighth's time, and the cessation of many

fees and emoluments. It is dated Nov. 1583. (See Calendar of S. P. Dom. Ser. 1581-90, p. 123.)

There was another William Hunnis living at the same time as the subject of our notice, who is frequently mentioned in the accounts of the Treasurers of the Chamber. He appears to have been " Supervizor and Keeper of the greate gardens and orchardes at Greenwich." It is hardly possible that the gardener and poet-musician were one and the same person ; but, as Mr. Cunningham remarks, "a Hive full of Honey and a Handfull of Honeysuckles seem to savour not a little of the gardens at Greenwich." (Revels at Court, 222.)

According to a later entry in the Cheque-Book (p. 5) Hunnis died June 6, 1597. On the back of the title-page to a copy of Sir Thomas More's Works, 1557, mentioned by Warton, are written in a contemporary hand (perhaps that of the Poet himself) the following lines :—

" My Last Will and Testament.

"To God my soule I do bequeathe, because it is his owne,
  My body to be layd in grave, where to my frends best known ;
  Executors I wyll none make, thereby great stryffe may grow,
  Because the goodes that I shall leave wyll not pay all I owe.

"W. Hunnys."

Ibid. *Hechins.*—William Huchins, Gentleman of the Chapel in the reigns of Edward VI. and Mary.

Ibid. *Mr. Alsworthe.*—Probably R. Ayleworth, Gentleman of the Chapel in the reigns of Edward VI. and Mary.

Ibid. *Subdean Grevesend.*—W. Gravesend, Gentleman of the Chapel in the reigns of Edward VI. and Mary.

Ibid. *Mr. Causton,* i.e. Thomas Causton.—Of this musician nothing personal has been discovered. He was a Gentleman of the Chapel in the reigns of Edward VI. and Mary. He contributed to the curious and rare set of part-books published by John Day, the eminent printer, in the sixteenth century. This collection, the first of its kind, is entitled Certain Notes, set forth in four and three parts, to be sung at the Morning, Communion, and Evening Prayer, 1560 ; in a later edition, Morning and Evening Prayer and Communion, set forth in four parts, &c., 1565. He was also one of the contributors to the collection of Psalm-tunes published by John Day in 1563, under the title of The whole Psalmes in foure partes, which may be sung to all musical instruments.

The writer of the present notice is in possession of a MS. set of part-books, which from internal evidence belonged to the Royal Chapel in the reign of Edward VI. This interesting set of books contains a number of Causton's compositions. They are remarkable for purity of part-writing and flowing melody, closely resembling the style of Orlando Gibbons, the great Church composer of a later period. Specimens of Causton's music, from Day's Service Book, were reprinted in 1859 by the Rev. Dr. Jebb, in the Ecclesiologist.

Ibid. *William Bird*, or *Byrd*.—Supposed to have been a son of the before-mentioned Thomas Byrd. He was educated in the Music School of St. Paul's Cathedral, and, according to Anthony Wood, his master was the celebrated Thomas Tallis. He was born about the year 1538. In 1554 he was senior chorister of St. Paul's, and consequently about fifteen or sixteen years old, when his name occurs at the head of the school in a petition for the restoration of certain obits and benefactions which had been seized under the Act for the Suppression of Colleges and Hospitals in the preceding reign. This petition, which is preserved among the records of the Exchequer (Michaelmas Term, 1 and 2 Philip and Mary), was granted and confirmed by letters patent, 14 Eliz. (see Dugdale's St. Paul's, edit. Ellis), and the payments are still received by the Almoner.

Byrd followed the example of his master, Tallis, by conforming to the Church Establishment in the reign of Elizabeth, and in 1563 was appointed organist of Lincoln Cathedral, where he continued till 1569, when, upon the accidental death of Robert Parsons (as we learn by the Cheque-Book), he succeeded to his place in the Chapel Royal. The chief part of Byrd's ecclesiastical compositions being composed to Latin words, he is supposed (notwithstanding the appointment he held) to have retained his predilection for the Romish Communion. In the Proceedings in the Court of the Archdeaconry of Essex, 11th May, 1605, we find the following entry :—

[Parish of] " STONDON MASSIE." [*Contra*] Willielmum Bird et Elenam ejus uxorem.

"Presentantur for Popyshe Recusants. He is a Gentleman of the King's Majesties Chapell and, as the Minister and Church Wardens doe heare, the said William Birde, with the assistance of one Gabriel Colford, who is now at Antwerp, hath byn the chiefe and principall seduceer of John Wright, sonne and heire of John Wright of Kelvedon, in Essex, Gent., and of Anne Wright, the daughter of the said John Wright the elder ; and the said Ellen Birde, as it is reported, and as her servants have confessed, have [*sic*] appointed business on the Saboth daye for her servants of purpose to kepe them from churche ; and hath also done her best endeavour to seduce Thoda Pigbone, her nowe mayde servant, to drawe her to Poperie, as the mayde hath confessed ; and, besides, hath drawn her mayde servants, from tyme to tyme these seven yeres, from comming to churche ; and the said Ellen refuseth conference ; and the minister and churchwardens have not as yet spoke with the said Wm. Birde, because he is from home," &c.

We also learn from the same " Proceedings " that " they," the Byrd family, " have byn excommunicated these seven yeares." What was the end of the affair does not appear, for the above extract is all that Archdeacon Hale has printed in his valuable Series of Precedents and Proceedings in Criminal Causes, extending from the year 1475 to 1640 ; extracted from Act-Books of Ecclesiastical Courts in the Diocese of London, 1847, 8vo.

The persecution of Nonconformists was very bitter in the reign of Elizabeth, but more so in that of her successor; and it seems more than probable that the flight of Dr. Bull and others to Antwerp was occasioned by threatened proceedings of a similar kind to the above. The tendencies of the old members of the Chapel Royal to the Romish religion are confirmed by a passage in Morley's Introduction to Practicall Musick (p. 151), where he says "Farefax, Taverner, Shepherde, Mundy, White, Parsons, M. Birde, and divers others, who never thought it greater sacriledge *to spurn against the image of a Saint*, than to take perfect cordes of one kinde together."

Byrd is thought to have derived very considerable pecuniary advantages from a patent granted to him and Tallis by Queen Elizabeth, for the exclusive privilege of printing music and vending music-paper. Upon the decease of Tallis, in 1585, the patent devolved wholly to Byrd, according to the conditions on which it had been granted. The following list of his works (printed under the patent) will show the important service he rendered to his art:—1. Cantiones quæ ab argumento sacræ vocantur. Authoribus Thoma Tallisio et Guilielmo Birde, 1575 ob. 4to. 2. Psalmes, Sonets, and Songs of Sadness and Piete, 1587, 4to. 3. Songs of Sundrie Natures; some of Gravitie and others of Myrth, 1589, 4to. 4. Liber Primus Sacrarum Cantionum, 1589, 4to. 5. Liber Secundus Sacrarum Cantionum, 1591, 4to. 6. Gradualia, ac Cantiones Sacræ, Lib. Primus, 1589, 4to. 7. Gradualia, ac Cantiones Sacræ, Lib. Secundus, 1610, 4to. 8. Psalmes, Songs, and Sonnets; some Solemne others Joyful, 1611, 4to.

Byrd was a contributor to many musical works of his time, besides being the author of three masses which were put forth without any name of printer. Of his compositions extant in MS. the greater number are for the Virginals. The so-called Virginal Book of Queen Elizabeth (in the Fitzwilliam Museum, Cambridge) alone contains no fewer than seventy pieces; and in Lady Neville's Virginal Book (in the possession of Lord Abergavenny) there are twenty-six different compositions. In a MS. collection of Motets, Madrigals, Fancies, &c., made in the year 1591 by John Baldwine, "singing-man of Windsor," are many of Byrd's Motets in score. The collections of Barnard, Boyce, and Tudway are rich in his Church compositions, and a very large number are preserved in the library of Christ Church, Oxford.

At one period Byrd was an inhabitant of the parish of St. Helen's, Bishopsgate, and resided opposite to Crosby Hall, and adjoining the garden of Sir Thomas Gresham. It was afterwards called Sun Yard, and a part of the site is now occupied by the pianoforte warehouse of Mr. George Peachey. In a list of places frequented by certain recusants in and about London, under date 1581, is the following entry: "Wyll'm Byred of the Chappele, at his house in p'rshe of Harlington, in com. Midds." In another entry he is set down as a friend and abettor of those beyond the sea, and is said to be residing "with Mr. Lister, over against St. Dunstan's, or at the Lord Padgette's house at Draighton."

We learn from the Cheque-Book (p. 10) that he died July 4, 1623. In the entry he is styled "A Father of Music," probably in allusion to his great age; for, if he was sixteen when his name appeared at the head of St. Paul's Choristers' School in 1554, he must have been eighty-five years old when he died: that he was considerably advanced in life there can be no doubt. Thomas Tomkins, one of his scholars, printed, in 1622, A Collection of Songs to 3, 4, 5, and 6 parts, one of which he dedicates to his " ancient and much reverenced Master, William Byrd."

The register of the parish of St. Helen's, Bishopsgate, contains the following entries, which probably relate to his family :—

Burials... { " Walter Byrd, the sonne of William Byrd, the xv daye of May, A.D. 1587."
{ " Alice Byrd, the daughter of William Byrd, the xv daye of Julye, A.D. 1587."

In another volume occurs an entry of Walter Bird's marriage in 1614, and of Robert Byrd's in April 1616. Byrd had a son named Thomas, who was educated in his own profession. He married Catherine, daughter of Thomas More, Esq., of Yorkshire, probably a descendant of the Lord Chancellor, some of whose family settled in that county.

In 1601 Thomas Byrd acted as substitute for Dr. John Bull, then travelling abroad for the recovery of his health, and in that capacity read the music lecture at Gresham College.

Page 3. *William Ednye or Edney.*—He died of the plague Nov. 13, 1581 (p. 4). In Davies's Scourge of Folly, 1611, 12mo., is an epigram " To my worthy friend and admired Mr in the art of Musicke, Mr. Peter Edney." This was probably a son of the person mentioned in the text.

Ibid. *Leonard Davies.*—This is the first entry relative to one who rose to occupy the post of Subdean of the Chapel. He died Nov. 9, 1623, and was buried in the church of Harmondsworth, co. Middlesex (p. 10). There is a stone to his memory on the floor of the chancel, which is inscribed " Leonard Davies, Subdeane, of Hereford, 1623." Lysons's Environs, Middlesex Parishes, 142. The entry on p. 58 shows us that the Children and Gentlemen of the Chapel attended his funeral, and that a sum of money was allowed for " coaches " and " boat hire " on the occasion.

Page 4. *Thomas Woodson or Woodeson.*—Several of the same surname occur in the course of the Cheque-Book. The Woodesons were a Berkshire family. (See Ashmole's Berkshire, iii. 69; and Dr. Bloxam's Register of Magdalen College, Oxford, 1, 93, 136.

Ibid. *Anthony Harrison.*—In the State Paper Office is preserved a letter to the Dean of Windsor to elect Anthony Harrison, Gentleman of the King's Chapel, to a Petty Canonry there, void by the death of William Barnes, dated Jan. 23, 1603-4. (Calend. Dom. Ser. 1603-10, p. 70.) He died Feb. 14, 1622-3 (p. 10).

Ibid. *William Maperley.*—Gentleman of the Chapel in the reigns of Edward VI. and Mary.

Ibid. *William Barnes.*—Petty Canon of Windsor. He died in 1603-4, when his place in the Chapel Royal was filled up by the appointment of Edmund Shergold (p. 6).

Ibid.   *William Randall or Randoll.*—In a MS. collection of the words of Anthems (Harl. MS. 6346) he is set down as the composer of two anthems, "If the Lord himself," and "O Father dear;" but his name does not occur in Clifford's book. Nothing is known of his biography but what appears in the Cheque-Book. He was educated in the choir of Exeter Cathedral, and on p. 33 he is styled "Organist" of the Chapel Royal. His name disappears from the Cheque-Book in March, 1603, when Edmund Hooper took his place (p. 6). We have no record of his death.

Ibid.   *Thomas Tallis.*—One of the greatest English musicians of the sixteenth century. He was born early in the reign of Henry VIII. and probably received his education in the music-school attached to St. Paul's Cathedral. If so, Thomas Mulliner, the predecessor of John Redford, was his master, and Heywood, Shelbye, Newman, Allwood, Blitheman, and others, his fellow-pupils. He seems to have been early admitted, even when "a singing-boy," into the Royal Chapel. The words at the end of the present entry, "child there," imply this, if they do not mean that he was wholly educated in that establishment. Before the death of Henry VIII. he was appointed a Gentleman of the Chapel, in which situation he continued during the reigns of Edward VI., Mary, and part of that of Elizabeth.

The studies of Tallis were early devoted to Church-music, and many of his youthful compositions for the organ, founded upon the ancient plain-song of the Romish church, are still preserved in the Booke for the Organ or Virginals kept by his master, Thomas Mulliner. In 1560, or probably a little earlier, he contributed the eight tunes which appear in The whole Psalter translated into English Meter, and "Imprinted at London by John Daye." This Psalter was the work of Dr. afterwards Archbishop Parker, and is conjectured to have been published about 1560. In the same year Day printed his Certain Notes set forth in foure and three partes, to be song at the Morning, Communion, and Evening Prayer. Tallis was a contributor to this magnificent work, which may justly be looked upon as the foundation of our present choral service.

In 1575, in conjunction with his celebrated pupil William Byrd, Tallis published a collection of motets with Latin words—Cantiones quæ ab argumento Sacræ vocantur. Appended to this work is a copy of a singular patent, granted by Queen Elizabeth to the author, for the term of twenty-one years, for the sole publication of vocal and instrumental music, and for the ruling and vending of music paper.

In 1641, John Barnard, a priest in orders, and one of the Minor Canons of St. Paul's, published his First Book of Selected Church Musick. Tallis's celebrated Full Service, so universally known, was *first printed* in this collection. It was subsequently reprinted in Boyce's Collection, &c. The library of Christ Church, Oxford, is rich in his MS. works, and specimens may be found in the British Museum, Fitzwilliam Museum, &c.

Tallis died, according to the present entry, Nov. 23, 1585, and was buried in the old parish church of Greenwich. Strype, in his edition of Stowe's Survey, 1720 (Circuit Walk, p. 90), says that he found in the chancel, upon a stone before the rails, a brass plate with the following inscription engraved thereon. But as the church was pulled

down soon after the year 1720, in order to be rebuilt, no memorial now remains either of
Tallis or of any other person buried there previous to that year :—

> " Enterred here doth ly a worthy wyght,
>> Who for long tyme in musick bore the bell :
>> His name to shew, was THOMAS TALLYS hyght,
>> In honest vertuous lyff he dyd excell.

> " He serv'd long tyme in chappel with grete prayse
>> Fower sovereygnes reygnes (a thing not often seen);
>> I meane Kyng Henry and Prynce Edward's dayes,
>> Quene Mary, and Elizabeth oure Quene.

> " He mary'd was, though children he had none,
>> And lyv'd in love full thre and thirty yeres
>> Wyth loyal spowse, whose name yclypt was JONE,
>> Who here entomb'd him company now beares.

> " As he dyd lyve, so also did he dy,
>> In myld and quyet sort (O happy man !)
>> To God ful oft for mercy did he cry,
>> Wherefore he lyves, let deth do what he can."

In 1726 Nicholas Haym issued proposals for the publication of a History of Music,
but not meeting with sufficient encouragement the undertaking was not proceeded with.
A number of engravings were prepared for the work, including portraits of Tallis and
Byrd in one plate. An impression of this plate, perhaps unique, is in the possession of the
editor. It was the kind gift of his ever ready friend Mr. William Chappell. Tallis's
autograph is preserved in the MS. of Waltham Holy-Cross (Lands. MS. 763).

Ibid. *John Bull.*—Born about 1563 in Somersetshire. He was educated under
William Blitheman of the Chapel Royal, a celebrated organist. On Dec. 24, 1582
(according to the Acts Book), he was elected organist of Hereford Cathedral, and afterwards master of the children. We learn from the present entry that in Jan. 1585 he
was admitted into the Royal Chapel, in Mr. Bodinghurst's place, and in 1591 upon the
death of his master he is said to have succeeded him as organist. But this is mere conjecture, as the Cheque-Book records that John Hewlett was Blitheman's successor in his
place of gentleman (p. 5) and the office of organist as a separate appointment did not
then exist. On July 9, 1586, he was admitted Mus. Bac. at Oxford, "having practised
in that faculty fourteen years," and on July 7, 1592, he was incorporated Mus. Doc. in
the same university, having previously taken the degree at Cambridge. (Wood's Fasti,
edit. Bliss, i. 235, 258.)

In 1596, upon the recommendation of Queen Elizabeth, Bull was the first appointed
Music Professor in Gresham College, and, although unable to compose and read his
lectures in Latin, according to the founder's original intention, such was his favour with
the Queen and the public, that the executors of Sir Thomas Gresham, by the ordinances

bearing date 1597, dispensed with his knowledge of the Latin language, and ordered "The solemn music-lecture twice every week, in manner following, viz. the theoretique part for one half-hour, or thereabouts, and the practique, by concert of voice or instruments, for the rest of the hour, whereof the first lecture *should* be in the Latin tongue, and the second in English ; but, because at this time Mr. Dr. Bull, who is recommended to the place by the Queen's Most Excellent Majesty, being not able to speak Latin, his lectures are permitted to be altogether in English, so long as he shall continue in the place of music-lecturer there." (Ward's Lives of the Gresham Professors, p. viii.)

In 1601 Dr. Bull went abroad for the recovery of his health, and, during his absence, was permitted to substitute as his deputy a son of William Byrd, named Thomas. He travelled incognito into France and Germany, and Wood tells a story of a feat performed by him at St. Omer's, where, to a composition originally in forty parts, he added forty more in a few hours.

After the death of Elizabeth, Bull still retained his post in the Chapel, and his fame as an organist was widely spread. On July 16, 1607, when James I. and Prince Henry dined at Merchant Taylors' Hall, the royal guests were entertained with music, both vocal and instrumental. And while His Majesty was at table, according to Stowe, "John Bull, Doctor of Musique, one of the Organists of His Majesties Chappell Royall, and free of the Merchant-taylors, beeing in a citizen's gowne, cappe, and hood, played most excellent melodie upon a small payre of Organes, placed there for that purpose onley." (Chronicles, edit. 1631, p. 891.) In December of the same year he resigned his professorship in Gresham College, but for what reason does not appear, as he continued in England several years afterwards. In 1611 he was in the service of Prince Henry, and his name stands first on the roll of the Prince's musicians, with a salary of 40*l*. per annum. (Birch's Life of Prince Henry, p. 486.)

In 1613 "John Bull, Doctor of Musicke, went beyond the seas without licence, and was admitted into the Archduke's service." (Cheque-Book, p. 7.) No valid reason can be assigned for his leaving the country, but it seems he had been preparing for this step some months previously. In the Add. MS. No. 6194 (Brit. Mus.) is preserved a letter from Dr. Bull to Sir M. Hicks, wishing his son's name to be inserted instead of his own in some patent, dated April 26, 1612. And the same MS. contains an extract from Mr. Trumbull's letter to James I. concerning the Archduke's receiving Dr. Bull, the King's Organist, into his chapel without permission, dated May 30, 1614.

The subsequent life of Dr. Bull has hitherto been simply conjecture, but the writer is fortunately enabled to clear up the latter portion of it from a letter written by the Chevalier Leon de Burbure, some few years back, in answer to certain inquiries. The Chevalier says, " I do not know that the Cathedral of Antwerp ever possessed any MSS. of Dr. John Bull, but at all events there have remained no traces for a long time. The only facts relative to John Bull that I have discovered are, that he became organist of Notre Dame at Antwerp in 1617, in the place of Rumold Waelrant, deceased ; that in 1620 he lived in the house adjoining the church, on the side of the Place Verte, in which the concierge of the Cathedral had lived ; that he died on the 12th or 13th of March, 1628, and was buried on the 15th of the same month in the Cathedral where he had been organist."

Specimens of Bull's compositions for voices may be found in Barnard and Boyce's Collections, and in Sir William Leighton's Teares or Lamentacions of a Sorrowfull Soule, 1614, fol. He joined Byrd and Gibbons in contributing to the Parthenia, a collection of pieces for the Virginal printed early in the seventeenth century, and a large number of his instrumental movements are extant in the volume in the Fitzwilliam Museum, known as Queen Elizabeth's Virginal-Book, and in other MSS. See a curious list in Ward's Lives of the Gresham Professors, pp. 203-8.

A portrait of Bull is preserved in the Music-School at Oxford. It is painted on a board, and represents him in the habit of a bachelor of music. On the left side of the head are the words " An. Ætatis svæ 26, 1589," and on the right side an hour-glass, upon which is placed a human skull, with a bone across the mouth. Round the four sides of the frame is written the following homely distich :—

> " The bull by force in field doth raigne :
> But Bull by skill good-will doth gayne."

Ibid. *George Waterhouse.*—Wood tells us, under the date 1592, that " George Waterhouse, of the Queen's Chappel, who had spent there several years in the practical and theoretical part of music, supplicated for the degree of batchelor, but was not, as I can find, admitted." (Fasti, ed. Bliss, i. 257.) Thomas Morley calls him " my friend and fellow," and says that in canon writing he " surpassed all who ever laboured in that kinde of studie." Introduction to Practicall Musicke, 1597, p. 115. A later entry (p. 6) records that he died Feb. 18, 1601-2.

Ibid. *Edward Pearce or Pears.*—In the year 1600 he resigned his place in the Chapel to become Master of the Children of " Poules " (p. 5), having succeeded Thomas Giles in the offices of Master and Almoner. He assisted Thomas Ravenscroft, who had been his scholar, by contributing some excellent part-songs to his Brief Discourse of the true but neglected use of charactering the degrees by their perfection, imperfection, and diminution in measurable music, 1614, 4to. He was succeeded in his appointments at St. Paul's by Martin Pierson, Mus. Bac., but the date of his death has not been ascertained.

Ibid. *Robert Allison.*—After serving in the royal establishment for twenty years he sold his place, Feb. 8, 1609-10, to Humphrie Bache (p. 7). Nothing is known of his biography. He was probably related to Richard Allison, who harmonized some of the psalm-tunes for Este's Collection in 1592, and published The Psalmes of David in Meter, 1599, folio. This work was sold by the author " at his house in the Duke's place, near Alde-gate."

Ibid. *Mr. Palfriman, i.e. Thomas Palfreyman.*—His name occurs in a list of the chapel establishment of Edward VI., in conjunction with those of Tallis, Farrant, Hunnis, &c. He was a writer of verse, after the fashion of the Hunnis-school, although his published writings are chiefly prose. They are as follows : 1. Tho. Palfreyman his

Paraphrase on the Romans, n. d.; 2. An Exhortation to Knowledge and Love of God, 1560; 3. Divine Meditations, dedicated to Mistress Isabell Harrington, one of the Gentlewomen of the Queen's Privy Chamber, 1573; 4. The Treatise of Heavenly Philosophie, dedicated to the Earl of Sussex, 1578. The latter work contains some short sentences in meter towards the end. He enlarged William Baldwin's Treatise of Morall Phylosophie, a popular little book of the sixteenth century, and the title-page of an edition, without place or printer's name, adds, "Nowe the fourthe time enlarged by Thomas Paulfreyman, one of the Gentlemen of the Queenes Majesties Chappell, 1579." (See Hazlitt's Hand-Book, p. 22.)

Page 5.   *William Blithman or Blitheman.*—This eminent musician is said by Tanner to have belonged to the choir of Christ Church, Oxford, and to have been Master of the Choristers in 1564. (Wood's Fasti, ed. Bliss, i. 235.) He had the honour of being musical instructor to the celebrated Dr. John Bull, and is called by Stowe "organist to the Queen's Chapel." He died on Whitsunday, 1591, and was buried in the parish church of St. Nicholas Cole-abbey. The following epitaph, engraven on a brass-plate, and fixed to the north wall of the chancel, has been preserved in Anthony Munday's edition of Stowe's Survey, 1618, p. 675 :—

> " Heere *Blitheman* lyes, a worthy wight,
>   Who feared God above ;
> A friend to all, a foe to none,
>   Whom rich and poore did love.
> Of Princes Chappell Gentleman,
>   Unto his dying day;
> Whom all tooke great delight to heare
>   Him on the organs play.
>
> " Whose passing skill in Musicks art,
>   A scholler left behind ;
> *John Bull* (by name) his masters vaine
>   Expressing in each kind.
> But nothing here continues long,
>   Nor resting place can have ;
> His soule departed hence to Heaven,
>   His body here in grave."

Ibid.   *Anthony Anderson.*—Was collated to the Vicarage of Stepney, Feb. 21, 1586-7, having previously held for a month the living of Dengie, co. Essex. He died Oct. 10, 1593, according to the Cheque-Book, having held office as Subdean of the Chapel Royal for little more than a year.

Ibid.   *Thomas Goolde.*—Brought up in the Royal Chapel. He died July 28, 1608. (p. 7.)

Ibid. *Thomas Morley.*—As a composer and writer this musician is eminently distinguished. We know little of his biography. He was probably educated in the choir of St. Paul's Cathedral, of which establishment he was certainly organist before 1591. When Queen Elizabeth was in progress at Elvetham in Hampshire, during that year, " A notable consort of six musicians so highly pleased her that she gave a new name unto one of those *pavans* made long since by Master Tho. Morley, then Organist of St. Paul's Church." Nichols's Progresses, &c. of Eliz. iii. 108. He took his degree as Mus. Bac. at Oxford, July 8, 1588 (See Wood's Fasti, edit. Bliss, i. 242); and from the present entry we learn that he was admitted into the Royal Chapel July 24, 1592; and on Nov. 18 of the same year, he was sworn into the place of Gospeller (p. 34). In 1597 he printed his Plaine and Easie Introduction to Practicall Musicke, which he dedicated " To the Most excellent Musician Maister William Birde, one of the Gentlemen of her Majesties Chappell." This most interesting work is divided into three parts : the first teaching to sing; the second treating of descant, or the method of composing or singing on a plain song; and the third is on composition in three and more parts. " Each of the three parts of this book is a several and distinct dialogue, wherein a master, his scholar, and a person competently skilled in music are the interlocutors ; and in the course of their conversation so many little particulars occur relating to the manners of the times as render the perusal of the book in a great degree entertaining to those who are acquainted with the subject of it." (Hawkins, iii. 334.)

Morley's printed works consist of : 1. Canzonets, or Little Short Songs to Three Voyces, 1593 ; 2. Madrigalls to Foure Voyces, 1594 ; 3. The first Booke of Ballets to Five Voyces, 1595 ; 4. The First Book of Canzonets to Two Voices, 1595 ; 5. Canzonets, or Little Short Songs to Foure Voyces, collected out of the best and approved Italian Authors, 1597 ; 6. Canzonets, or Little Short Aers to Five and Sixe Voices, 1597 ; 7. Madrigals to Five Voyces, selected out of the best approved Italian Authors, 1598 ; 8. The First Booke of Consort Lessons, made by divers exquisite Authors, 1599 ; 9. The Triumphs of Oriana, to Five and Six Voices, 1600 ; 10. The First Booke of Aires, or Little Short Songes to sing and play to the Lute with the Base-Viol, 1600. It does not appear that any of his Church music was printed in his lifetime. A service is printed in Barnard's Collection, and the words of several anthems are given in Clifford's book. His Burial Service is well-known, and said to be the first part-service set to the words of our liturgy. He was a contributor to the MS. volume known as Queen Elizabeth's Virginal-Book, but his talent did not shine in the composition of instrumental music.

After the expiration of the patent for the exclusive printing of music granted to Tallis and Byrd, Morley obtained of Queen Elizabeth one of the same tenour, but giving more extensive powers. It was granted to him 40 Eliz. A.D. 1598. Under this patent William Barley printed most of the music-books which were published during the time that it continued in force.

In 1602, Morley's place in the Royal Chapel was filled up by the appointment of George Woodeson, from the choir of Windsor (p. 6). The date of his death is unknown, but it is not improbable that the last-named entry records it.

Mr. Burgon in his Life of Sir Thomas Gresham (ii. 465), speaking of the celebrated inhabitants of the great merchant's locality, adds :—" To this brilliant catalogue must be added the interesting name of Thomas Morley, the celebrated musician and writer of madrigals; who, as the parish register informs us, resided with his family in St. Helen's: and often must Crosby Hall have re-echoed his sweet strains ! . . . What is remarkable, William Bird was also an inhabitant of the same parish ; and it is well known that Wilbye the composer lived hard by.   These facts harmonize well with Gresham's endowed lectureship for the promotion of the divine art, which Morley, Bird, and Wilbye cultivated with so much success."

Ibid.   *Nathaniel Giles.*—According to Wood this musician " was born in or near to the city of Worcester, and was noted as well for his religious life and conversation (a rarity in musicians) as for excellence in his faculty." (Fasti, ed. Bliss, i. 229).   He was educated as a chorister of Magdalen College, Oxford, and took his degree as Mus. Bac. June 26, 1585.   In 1595 he was nominated to a situation in St. George's Chapel, Windsor, the terms of which appointment are thus given in one of the Ashmolean MSS. (No. 1125-33):—" The Dean and Canons of St. George's Chapel, Windsor, by deed dated 1 Oct. 1595, nominate Nathaniel Gyles, B.M. to be Clerk in the Chapel, and one of the players on the organs there, and also to be master, instructor, tutor, and creansor, or governor, of the ten choristers, agreeing to give him an annuity of 81*l.* 6*s.* 8*d.* and a dwelling-house within the Castle, called the *Old Commons*, wherein John Mundie did lately inhabit, with all appertenances, as one Richard Farrante enjoyed the same.   The stipend to be paid monthly by the treasurer, over and besides all other gifts, rewards, or benevolence that may be given to the choristers for singing of ballads, plays, or the like: also such reasonable leave of absence as the statutes allow, except when Her Majesty shall be resident, or an installation or funeral of any noble person shall be solemnized : on condition that the said Nathaniel Gyles shall procure meet and apt choristers within the space of three months after avoidance (Her Majesty's Commission for the taking of children being allowed unto him), and that he shall instruct them in singing, pricksong, and descant, and bring up such as be apt to the instrument ; and that he shall find them sufficient meat and drink, apparel, bedding and lodging at his own costes within the *New Commons* lately appointed for them ; and that he shall find a sufficient deputy during the times of sickness and absence."   On the death of William Hunnis, June 6, 1597, he was appointed Gentleman Extraordinary and Master of the Children of the Chapel Royal ; and on the accession of Charles I. was nominated (according to Wood) organist of the same establishment.   In 1622 he took his degree as Mus. Doc. although Wood tells us, " In 1607 he supplicated the Ven. Congregation of Regents to be admitted Doctor: which desire of his was granted conditionally that he composed a Choral Hymn of eight parts to be publicly sung in the Act wherein he should proceed ; but for what reason he did not perform that obligation I cannot justly say.   Sure I am, that in the Act wherein he proceeded, were certain questions to be appointed to be discussed between him and Dr. Heather, which being *pro formâ* only, and not customarily to be done, were omitted. The questions were: 1. Whether discords may be allowed in music? Affirm.; 2. Whether any artificial instrument can so truly as the natural voice? Negat.; 3. Whether the practice be the more useful part of music or the theory ? Affirm."

The Children of the Chapel, under Dr. Giles, were frequently called upon to act before the Court. The following entry is one of many that might be adduced: " To Nathaniell Gyles, M^r of the Children of the Chappell, uppon the Councell's Warraunte dated at Whitehall, 4 May, 1601, for a play presented before her Matie on Shrove-sondaye at night x^{li}, and for a showe wth musycke and speciall songes prepared for ye purpose on Twelfth Day at night, c^s, in all xv^{li}."—Extracts from Accounts of the Revels at Court. (Shaks. Soc. xxxiii.)

Dr. Giles was an excellent musician, if we may judge from the few specimens of his talent that remain. A service is printed in Barnard's Selected Church Musick, 1641, and the words of several of his anthems are given in Clifford's Divine Services and Anthems, 1663 and 1664. In the Appendix to Hawkins's Hist. of Music is preserved " A Lesson of Descant of thirtie-eighte Proportions of Sundrie Kindes, made by Master Giles, Master of the Children at Windsor." He is generally stated to have died about the year 1635, but the correct date is Jan. 24, 1633-4. He was buried in one of the aisles adjoining to St. George's Chapel, Windsor, with the following inscription over his grave, preserved in Ashmole's Berkshire, iii. 183: " In memory of that worthy Doctor Nathaniel Giles, Doctor of Musique, who served Q. Elizabeth, K. James, and K. Charles. He was Master of the Children of this Free Chapell of St. George 49 years, Master of the Children of His Majesty's Chaple Royall 38 years. He married Anne, the eldest daughter of John Stayner, of the county of Worcester, Esq. with whom he lived 47 years and had issue by her four sons and five daughters, whereof two sons and three daughters are now living. He died the 24th day of January, 1633, when he had lived 75 years."

On another grave-stone near the former is this inscription :

" Pattern of Patience, Gravitie, Devotion,
Faithful to the end, now Heyre of Heavn's Promotion.

Pietatis ergo Nat. Gyles, Filius natu maximus, mœrens posuit 2 Feb. 1634.
Die cinerum versus est in cineres."

One of Dr. Giles's sons, Nathaniel, became a Canon of Windsor and Prebendary of Worcester. His daughter Margaret married Dr. Herbert Croft, Bishop of Hereford.

Ibid. *John Baldwin.*—He is called " a singing-man of Windsor," a statement confirmed by the present entry. He is remarkable for having transcribed into one volume a large collection of motetts, madrigals, fantasias, and other musical compositions by his contemporaries, both Foreign and English. The date at end of the MS. is 1591. Prefixed is a long poem eulogizing, in homely language, the various composers whose works grace the volume. He died Aug. 28, 1615 (p. 8).

Page 6. *Stephen Boughton.*—Dr. Bloxam (Register of St. Mary Magdalen College, Oxford, i. 22) gives us the following notice of this old worthy: " Boughton, Stephen, Matr. *pleb. fil.* Bucks. 2 July, 1584, æt. 13 ; res. 1591 ; Clerk, 1594 ; B.A. 13 May, 1594 ; Chaplain in St. George's Chapel, Windsor, 1604 ; Canon of Worcester Cathedral,

1628; Sub-dean of the Chapel Royal; Vicar of Great Marcle, co. Hereford. He died before the Restoration."

In Davies's Scourge of Folly, 1611, 12mo., is an Epigram, " To my loving friend, Stephen Boughton, one of the Gentlemen of his Majesties Chappell."

In the State Paper Office is preserved a petition of Stephen Boughton, Subdean of the Royal Chapel, to the Council. The petitioner states that, being only a lodger in Saint Martin's-in-the-Fields, during his attendance at Whitehall, is by the inhabitants taxed in the sum of 35s. for ship money, wherein he conceives himself hardly dealt with, in regard he pays in other places. 1636 ? (Calend. Dom. Ser. 1636-7, p. 289.)

Ibid. *William Lawes.*—Son of William Lawes of Steeple Langford: Thomas Lawes, Vicar-choral of the Cathedral of Salisbury, who died Nov. 7, 1640, was probably his uncle. The date of his birth is uncertain. He was educated under Giovanni Coperario (John Cooper) at the expense of the Earl of Hertford. He became a member of the choir of Chichester, and was called from thence in 1602 to the office of Gentleman of the Royal Chapel. On May 5, 1611, he resigned his place, but was re-admitted Oct. 1, in the same year (p. 45). He was also one of the musicians in ordinary to Charles I. Fuller says : " He was respected and beloved by all who cast any looks towards virtue and honour." His gratitude and loyalty to his royal master were such that he took up arms in his cause; and although, to exempt him from danger, Lord Gerrard made him a Commissary in the Royal Army, yet the activity of his spirit disdained this intended security, and at the seige of Chester, in 1645, he lost his life. The King is said to have been so much affected at his death that he wore particular mourning for him. His memory is celebrated by Herrick in his Hesperides ; by Tatham in his Ostella, 1650; and by Robert Heath in his Clarastella, 1650.

Lawes composed the music to many of the Court masques of his time, two volumes of which (autograph MSS.) are preserved in the music-school, Oxford. Many of his compositions for viols are extant in MS. Printed specimens of his vocal music may be found in Select Musicall Ayres and Dialogues, 1652 ; Catch that Catch Can, 1652; and other of Playford's publications. See also Choice Psalmes put into Musick for Three Voices ; Compos'd by Henry and William Lawes, Brothers, and Servants to His Majestie. Lond. 1648, 4to.

Ibid. *Anthony Kirby or Kirkby.*—Afterwards Chaplain. He was living April 20, 1641, when his name appears in a list of the Chapel establishment, exempting its members from the payment of subsidies. (See Collier's Annals of the Stage, ii. 103.)

Ibid. *John Woodeson or Woodson.*—Of the choir of Windsor before his admission into the Royal Chapel. He was living in 1641, but his name does not appear in the Chapel establishment at the Restoration of Charles II.

Ibid. *Edmund Hooper.*—Native of North Halberton, co. Devon, and probably educated in the choir of Exeter Cathedral. He succeeded Henry Leeve as organist of Westminster

Abbey in 1588, and was appointed Master of the Children of the same foundation by patent dated Dec. 3 in the same year. He was the first *regularly* appointed organist of the Abbey. His patent, dated May 9, 1606, was renewed for life in 1616. From the old books of the Abbey we learn that he was occasionally employed in " mending the organs," and in " pricking new song-books,"—in other words transcribing music for the choir. Two of his anthems are printed in Barnard's Selected Church Musick, and a large number are preserved in MS. He died July 14, 1621 (p. 10), and was buried in the cloisters of Westminster Abbey on the 16th of the same month. " Margaret Hooper, widow of Edmund Hooper," was also buried there, March 7, 1651-2.

Ibid. *Orlando Gibbons.*—Not only " one of the rarest musicians and organists of his time," as Wood calls him, but one of the finest musical geniuses that ever lived. He was born at Cambridge in 1583, and it seems probable that he was the son of William Gibbons, who, Nov. 3, 1567, was admitted one of the waytes of the town of Cambridge, with the annual fee of 40*s*.* Upon the death of Arthur Cock in 1604-5, he was appointed a Gentleman of the Royal Chapel, and in 1606 he took his degree as Mus. Bac. at Cambridge. In 1622 he was created Mus. Doc. at Oxford, that honour being conferred on him at the recommendation of Camden, who was his intimate friend. It has been asserted that, besides his own exercise, composed for this occasion, he wrote that which gained a similar degree for Dr. Heyther ; but it is easy to raise reports of this kind, and impossible to refute them after a lapse of years. He succeeded John Parsons in 1623 as Organist of Westminster Abbey. Wood says, " At length being commanded to Canterbury to attend the solemnity of the nuptials between K. Charles I. and Henrietta Maria, a daughter of the King of France (in order to which he had made vocal and instrumental compositions), died there of the small-pox, to the great reluctancy of the Court, on the Day of Pentecost, an. 1625." (Fasti, ed. Bliss, i. 406.) See also the entry in the Cheque-Book recording his death (p. 11). He was buried in Canterbury Cathedral, and

---

* In the Corporation Common Day Book, under the date of the 25th of November, 1567, is this entry:—"Memorandum, that at the Court holden the xxvth daie of November, in the tenthe yere of the reign of Soveraign Ladie Quene Elizabeth, Mr. Maior did delyver to William Gibons, musitian, fyve sylver collers, called the waites collers, ponderinge xxvij ounces di. And the said William Gibbons hathe found sureties for the delyverye of the same collers agayne when they be required, viz. William Barnes & Richard Gravenes." On the last day of July, 1573, William Gibbons of Cambridge, musician, in consideration of 30*l*., bargained and sold to John Hatcher of Cambridge, M.D., a messuage late in the occupation of William Bright, one of the aldermen of the town, in the parish of St. Edward, and at the Court of Pleas held on the 11th of August following, Mary, wife of William Gibbons, released to Dr. Hatcher her dower in the premises. The messuage mentioned in the foregoing bargain and sale abutted on the south on another tenement of William Gibbons, then late belonging to Corpus Christi College. (Cooper's Annals of the University and Town of Cambridge, iii. 176.)

his widow erected over his grave a monument with a bust (of which there is an engraving in Dart's Hist. of the Cathedral Church of Canterbury), the inscription upon which is as follows :—

" ORLANDO GIBBONIO Cantabrigiæ inter Musas et Musicæ nato, sacræ R. Capellæ Organistæ, Sphærarumq. Harmoniæ, digitorum pulsu, æmulo ; Cantionum complurium, quæque eum non canunt minus quam canuntur, conditori ; Viro integerrimo et cujus vita cum arte suavissimis moribus concordissimè certavit, ad nupt. C. R. cum M. B. Dorobern. accito, ictuque heu sanguinis crudo et crudeli fato extincto, choroque cœlesti transcripto die Pentecostes A.D.N. MDCXXV. Elizabetha conjux septemque ex eo liberorum parens, tanti vix doloris superstes merentiss° mœrentiss[a] P. Vixit A. [   ], M. [   ], D. [   ]. (The figures for his age left blank.) Over the monument are his bust and shield of arms—Argent, a lion rampant sable, depressed by a bend gules charged with three escallops or.

In the State Paper Office is preserved the copy of a grant, dated July 19, 1615, to Orlando Gibbons, of two bonds forfeited by Lawrence Brewster of Gloucester, and his sureties, for his non-appearance before the High Commission Court at Lambeth. In the same repository is the petition of Orlando Gibbons, Organist of the King's Chapel, to the Earl of Salisbury for a lease in reversion of forty marks per an. of Duchy lands, without fine, as promised him by the Queen. (Cal. Dom. Ser. 1611-1618, pp. 107, 295.)

Gibbons was concerned jointly with Dr. Bull and William Byrd in the composition of the collection of virginal pieces known as the Parthenia. In 1612 he published Madrigals of five parts for Voices and Viols. He also composed the tunes to Wither's Hymns and Songs of the Church, and a set of Fancies for Viols. These, with the exception of two short sacred vocal pieces in Sir William Leighton's Teares or Lamentacions of a Sorowfull Soule, 1614, constitute the whole of his works printed during his life-time. A large number of his secular compositions exist in MS. But Gibbons's greatest glory is his Church-music. Two services and a number of anthems have descended to our times. Dr. Tudway, speaking of them, says they are " the most perfect pieces of Church-music which have appeared since the time of Tallis and Byrd ; the air so solemn, the fugues and other embellishments so just and naturally taken, as must warm the heart of any one who is endued with a soul fitted for divine raptures." Undoubtedly the general characteristic of Gibbons' music is fine harmony, unaffected simplicity, and grandeur.

Orlando Gibbons married Elizabeth, daughter of John Patten of Westminster, gent. (Yeoman of the Vestry of the Royal Chapel), by whom he had the following children : James, bapt. June 2, 1607 (buried June 4 in the same year); Alice, bapt. Aug. 5, 1613; Christopher, bapt. Aug. 22, 1615 ; Anne, bapt. Oct. 6, 1618 ; Mary, bapt. April 9, 1621 ; Elizabeth, bapt. March 16, 1621-2 ; and Orlando, bapt. Aug. 29, 1623. These entries (kindly furnished by Col. Chester) are from the books of St. Margaret's Westminster, of which parish Gibbons was an inhabitant. He lived in the Long Wool-staple, which was situated on the site of the present Bridge Street, outside the north wall and gate of New Palace Yard : adjoining it, on the north side, was Canon Row. (See Overseer's Books, and Walcott's Westminster, p. 79.) Gibbons's widow did not long survive her husband. She died in 1626, and her will was proved July 30 in the same year.

Ibid. *Richard Cotton or Coton.*—He was living April 20, 1641, when his name appears among the Chaplains of the Royal Chapel, in a list exempting the members of that establishment from the payment of subsidies. (See Collier's Annals of the Stage, ii. 103.)

Page 7. *George Cooke.*—Engrafted into the Royal Chapel from the choir of St. George's Chapel, Windsor. He died in Aug. 1660 (p. 12).

Ibid. *George Sheffield.*—A member of the Durham choir before his admission into the Royal Chapel. He was living in 1641, as appears by the list of Gentlemen of the Chapel in that year. . (See Collier's Annals of the Stage, ii. 130.)

Ibid. *Thomas Pearce or Peirs.*—A member of the choir of Westminster Abbey before his admission into the Royal Chapel. He was probably related to Edmund Pearce, Master of the Choristers of St. Paul's. He contributed some catches to John Hilton's Catch that Catch can, 1652. He died Aug. 10, 1666 (p. 14).

Ibid. *John Frost.*—There were evidently two members of the Chapel of this name : the one here referred to, expressly said to be " of Westminster," that is, of the Abbey choir, and " John Frost, Clerk, a base from Salisbury," sworn April 26, 1621 (p. 10). The first-named was of Colebrook, co. Devon, and educated in the choir of St. Peter's, Exeter. He became " Chanter " of Westminster Abbey in 1623, died in 1642, and was buried May 10, 1642, in the north aisle of the Abbey. The second died in 1696 (p. 21), and was buried in the north cloister of the Abbey. The date of his death given in the Cheque-Book is June 1 : in the Registers of the Abbey, December, in the same year.

Ibid. *Ezechiel Waad or Wade*—Afterwards Chaplain. He was living April 20, 1641, when his name occurs in a list of the Chapel establishment, exempting its members from the payment of subsidies. (See Collier's Annals of the Stage, ii. 103.)

Ibid. *Robert Stone.*—The old chorister whose death is here recorded, at the great age of 97, had certainly been connected with the Royal Chapel for more than half a century. He was in all probability the " Stones " whose name appears in John Day's Morning and Evening Prayer, 1560. He was of Alphington, co. Devon, and was educated at Exeter, from which cathedral he was engrafted into the choir of the Chapel Royal. He was buried in the cloisters of Westminster Abbey, July 3, 1613.

Ibid. *Matthew White.*—His name occurs as a Gentleman of the Chapel in 1603 (p. 70). He resigned his place in 1614, probably for some preferment (p. 8). On July

2, 1619, in conjunction with Cuthbert Joyner, " Clerk of the Vestry," he received a grant of the surveyorship of lands, &c. belonging to rectories, vicarages, and rural prebends in England and Wales. A copy of the grant is preserved in the State Paper Office (Cal. Dom. Ser. 1619-23, p. 58). On July 18, 1629, he accumulated the degrees of bachelor and doctor of music at Oxford. (Wood's Fasti, ed. Bliss, i. 450.) The words of some of his anthems are given in Clifford's book, so frequently mentioned in these notes. He also contributed some catches to Catch that Catch can, or the Musical Companion, 1667.

Page 8. *William Crosse.*—His name occurs in the list of Gentlemen of the Chapel in 1641. See Collier's Annals of the Stage, ii. 130. He probably died before the Restoration of Charles II. as his name does not appear among the Gentlemen of the Royal Chapel who attended at the Coronation of that monarch.

Ibid. *William Heyther or Heather.*—Born at Harmondsworth, co. Middlesex, but the date is nowhere given. He was a chorister of Westminster, previous to his admisssion into the Royal Chapel. He was an intimate friend of Camden. In town they lived in the same house ; and when in 1609 a pestilent disease reached the locality, and Camden was seized with it, he retired to the house of his friend Heyther at Chislehurst to be cured.

Camden, a few years before his death, determined to found a history-lecture at Oxford, and on May 17, 1622, he sent his friend Heyther with the deed of endowment properly executed to the Vice-Chancellor Dr. Piers. Out of compliment to Camden, and probably at his suggestion, the University on the following day conferred the degree of Mus. Doc. upon Heyther and his friend Orlando Gibbons. (See Epistles to and from Camden, 1691, p. 329). Such was the regard of Camden for Dr. Heyther that he appointed him executor to his will ; and in the deed executed by Camden, March 17, 1621-2, containing the endowment of his history-lecture at Oxford, the grant thereby made of the manor of Bexley in Kent is subject to a proviso that the profits of the said manor, estimated at 400*l.* a year, should be enjoyed by Mr. William Heyther, his heirs and executors, for the term of ninety-nine years, to commence from the death of Mr. Camden, he and they paying to the history professor 140*l.* per annum, at the expiration of which term the estate was to vest in the university." (Biog. Brit. art. Camden.)

Taking example by his friend Camden, Dr. Heyther in 1626 founded a music-lecture in the same university. The deed of foundation bears date Feb. 20, 2 Chas. I. and under it Richard Nicholson, Mus. Bac. and organist of Magdalen Coll. became first professor.

Dr. Heyther died the latter end of July, 1627 (p. 12), and was buried, Aug. 1, in the broad or south aisle adjoining the choir of Westminster Abbey. He gave to the hospital in Tothill Fields, Westminster, 100*l.*, as appears by a list of benefactions to the parish of St. Margaret in that city, printed in Hatton's New View of London, i. 339.

The Music-school, Oxford, possesses a portrait of Dr. Heyther in his Doctor's gown and cap.

Ibid. *John Miners* or *Minors.*—He was one of the musicians in the establishment of Prince Henry in 1612, at a salary of 40*l.* per annum. (Birch's Life of Prince Henry,

p. 466.) His death is recorded to have taken place July 2, 1615. (See the same page of Cheque-Book.)

Ibid. *Thomas Day.*—One of the musicians in the establishment of Prince Henry in 1612. Upon the accession of Charles I. to the throne, he issued a grant in favour of the royal musicians, a copy of which is preserved in Rymer's Fœdera. (Tom. xviii. p. 278.) From this we learn that Thomas Day had 40*l.* yearly for his wages, and " for keeping a boy," 24*l.* extra. He was organist of Westminster Abbey and Master of the Choristers from 1625 to 1632. He was also Master of the Children of the Chapel Royal in 1637 (Calend. S. P. Dom. Ser. 1637-8, p. 22); and also Clerk of the Cheque. (See p. 48 of the present volume.) His death is said to have taken place in 1654, but it is not recorded in the pages of the Cheque-Book. " Daniel Day, son of John Day," was buried in the cloisters of Westminster Abbey, June 1, 1627.

Ibid. *Walter Porter.*—Son of Henry Porter, Mus. Bac. of Christ Church, Oxford, 1600. He was appointed Master of the Choristers of Westminster in 1639. He published Madrigales and Ayres of Two, Three, Foure, and Five Voyces, 1632, and Motetts of Two Voices for Treble or Tenor and Basse, 1657. The former work is dedicated to " John, Lord Digby of Sherburne, Earle of Bristow." The address, " To the Practitioner," has the following curious passage : " Before you censure, which I know you will, and they that understand least most sharply ; let me intreate you to play and sing them true, according to my meaning, or heare them done so ; not, instead of singing, to howle or bawle them, 'and scrape, instead of playing, and perform them falsly, and say they are nought." The copy of the latter work in the Music-school, Oxford, is a presentation-copy, and has a letter on the fly-leaf, in the handwriting of the author, commencing, " Dr. Wilson : Worthy Dr. and my loving Cos."

After being ejected from his appointments at the rebellion, he was patronized by Sir Edw. Spencer. It seems probable that he died before the Restoration.

Page 9. *Edmund Nelham or Nellam.*—In a warrant exempting the members of the Royal Chapel from the payment of subsidies, dated April 20, 1641, his name occurs among the Chaplains. He was also a Minor Canon of Westminster, and died in 1646. The Registers of the Abbey record his burial in the cloisters, Aug. 17 in that year. Some compositions of his are contained in John Hilton's Catch that Catch can, or a Choice Collection of Catches, Rounds, and Canons, 1652.

Ibid. *Roger Nightingale.*—One of the few members of the Chapel, admitted at this period, who survived to resume office at the Restoration. In June, 1660 (p. 48), we find he was appointed Confessor to the King's household. Hawkins tells us that he dwelt with Williams, Bishop of Lincoln, at Buckden in Huntingdonshire, the episcopal seat ; and, when that prelate was translated to York, he took Nightingale with him to Cawood

Castle, and, as a mark of his favour, settled upon him a lease worth 500*l.* He died Nov. 25, 1661 (p. 12), and was buried in the east cloister of Westminster Abbey on the 28th of the same month.

Page 10.   *Thomas Tomkins.*—"The Tomkins family," says Burney, "produced more able musicians during the sixteenth and seventeenth centuries than any other which England can boast." According to Wood, they descended from a family of the same name at Listwithyel in Cornwall. (Fasti, ed. Bliss, i. 320.) Burney speaks only of one musician of the sixteenth century—Thomas Tomkins, "chanter of the choir of Gloucester," and the father of the better known Thomas and John. He was a Minor Canon of Gloucester, and the author of an account of the Bishops of that See, a MS. referred to by Dr. Bliss. In the Chapter Books of Worcester, under the date 1590, is an entry that the Dean, the Rev. Francis Willis, " at the motion of Mr. John Tomkins, organist," gave the sum of 4*l.* for the old organ of St. Mary's Church, Shrewsbury. This musician has hitherto escaped notice, unless he was the brother of Thomas; but it is more probable that he was an uncle, the brother of the Minor Canon of Gloucester. Wood mentions several members of the Tomkins family, but confesses his inability to range them "according to seniority." This the writer is also unable to do, but some little help is afforded by the dedications to Thomas Tomkins's Songs of 3, 4, 5, and 6 Parts, printed for Matthew Lownes, 1622. (This was the work of the musician alluded to in our text.) The first song is inscribed, "To my deare father, Mr. *Thomas* Tomkins;" the fourth, "To my brother, Mr. *Nicholas* Tomkins" (afterwards Gentleman of the Privy Chamber to Charles I.); the tenth, "To my brother, *Peregrine* Tomkins;" the twelfth, "To my brother, *Giles* Tomkins" (afterwards Organist of Salisbury Cathedral); the twenty-sixth, "To my brother, Mr. *John* Tomkins" (afterwards Organist of St. Paul's Cathedral); and the twenty-eighth, "To my sonne, *Nathaniel* Tomkins" (afterwards Prebendary of Worcester).

Thomas Tomkins, the author of the above-named work, was educated at Magdalen College, Oxford. He was student 1604-6; usher 1606-10; and Mus Bac. July 11, 1607. He studied music under the celebrated William Byrd, and early in life occupied the post of organist of Worcester Cathedral, a situation which he retained till his death. Burney says he contributed a madrigal to the well-known collection, The Triumphs of Oriana, 1600; but, from the above dates, this is simply impossible. The madrigal in question must have been the production of his father. Thomas Tomkins the younger was the composer of a noble collection of church-music entitled Musica Deo Sacra et Ecclesiæ Anglicanæ. The greater part of these services and anthems were written for the Royal Chapel in the time of Charles I. The work was published in 1664, after the author's death, and is advertised in 1666, "to be had at the chaunter's house, Westminster." Wood speaks also of his MS. collection of church-music, bequeathed to the library of Magdalen College by James Clifford, the author of the Divine Services and Anthems, and "still preserved in the archives thereof." The MS. collection is not now to be found in the library. Thomas Tomkins joined the Royal Chapel in 1621, and in the record entered in the Cheque-Book (at the above page) he is called "Organist of

Worcester." He died in 1656. In the parish register of Martin-Hussingtree, co. Worcester, is the following entry: "1656. Buried Mr. Thomas Tomkins, Organist of the King's Chapel and of the Cathedral, Worcester, June 9." In Abingdon's Antiquities of Worcester Cathedral, 1723, p. 77, is preserved an epitaph on "Alicia or Ales, the wife of Thomas Tomkins, one of the Gentlemen of his Majesties Chappell Royall, a woman full of faith and good works. She dyed the 20th of Jan. 1641." The Rev. J. Toy, of Worcester, preached her funeral sermon, which was published in 4to. in the following year.

Ibid. *Ralph Amner.*—Son of John Amner, Mus. Bac., Organist, and Master of the Choristers of Ely Cathedral from 1610 to 1641. It appears from the Ely Register that Ralph was elected a lay clerk in 1604, and was succeeded by Michael Este in 1609. Amner was then probably admitted into holy orders, as he is styled "Vicar," viz. Minor Canon. Some of his anthems are preserved in the books of Ely Cathedral. See the Rev. W. E. Dickson's Catalogue of Ancient Choral Services and Anthems in the Cathedral Church of Ely, 1861, 8vo. He died at Windsor, March 3, 1663-4 (p. 13). In Catch that Catch can, or the Musical Companion, 1667, (p. 7) is "a Catch in stead of an Epitaph upon Mr. Ralph Amner of Windsor (commonly called the Bull-Speaker) who dyed 1664," the music composed by Dr. William Child.

Page 11. *Thomas Warwick.*—Was by birth a gentleman, descended from the Warwicks or Warthwykes of Warwicke, co. Cumberland, and bearing the same arms : Vert, three lions rampant argent. In Sir Edward Bysshe's Visitation of Kent, his father Thomas Warwick is styled "of Hereford," where probably the son was born. Davies of Hereford in his Scourge of Folly, 1611, has a short poem "To my deere friend, countryman, and expert Master in the liberall science of Musicke, Mr. Thomas Warrock." He was one of the Royal musicians for the lute in 1625, and Wood says he was Organist of Westminster Abbey (MS. Ashmole, 8568, 106), but his name does not occur in the roll of organists of that establishment. The same authority tells us that he composed a song of forty parts, which was performed before Charles I. about 1635, by the members of the Royal band and their friends. In March 1630 he received a reprimand from the Dean and Chapter of the Royal Chapel for insufficiency in his organ-playing (p. 78). But it must be borne in mind that he succeeded Orlando Gibbons. It required more genius than Warwick possessed to worthily occupy a post once filled by so great a man.

Thomas Warwick held office as a commissioner for granting dispensations for converting arable-land into pasture, and was evidently a man of some position in society. He married Elizabeth, daughter and co-heir of John Somerville of Somerville, Aston-le-Warwick. Sir Philip Warwick, the well-known statesman, author of the Memoirs of the reign of Charles I. (born at Warwick House, Westminster, Dec. 24, 1609), was his son. The time of his death is uncertain. The last notice of his name occurs in a list of the Royal Band in 1641, a document exempting the King's musicians from the payment of subsidies. (See Collier's Annals of the Stage, ii. 103.)

Ibid. *Henry Lawes.*—Son of William Lawes of Steeple Langford, and born at Dinton, co. Wilts. in 1596. He is erroneously said to have been the son of Thomas Lawes, vicar-choral of Salisbury Cathedral. He received his musical education under Giovanni Cope-rario, and at the expense of the Earl of Hertford. He entered the Royal Chapel in 1625, and passed through the grades of "Pistler" or Epistler, Gentleman, and Clerk of the Cheque. He was also a member of the Royal Band of Charles I. In 1634 Milton's Masque of Comus, one of the brightest gems of English poetry, was written for the Earl of Bridgewater, at whose mansion it was first performed. Henry Lawes composed the music, and performed the part of the attendant spirit. He taught music in the family of Lord Bridgewater, and Lady Alice Egerton was his pupil. Lawes was highly praised by Milton and Waller. Fenton says that "the best poets of Lawes' time were ambitious of having their verses set to music by this admirable artist." He published three books of Ayres and Dialogues, with the respective dates 1653, 1655, and 1658. In these collections are songs written by Thomas, Earl of Winchelsea; William, Earl of Pembroke; John, Earl of Bristol; Lord Broghill ; Thomas Carey, son of the Earl of Monmouth; Henry Noel, son of Lord Campden; Sir Charles Lucas ; and Carew Raleigh, son of Sir Walter Raleigh. Many of the songs of these amateur poets possess great merit; and Lawes's three books contain a body of elegant and spirited lyric poetry which deserves to be better known. He set to music the songs in the masque Cœlum Britannicum by that sweet poet Thomas Carew, and all the lyrics of Waller. He composed the airs and songs in the plays and poems of William Cartwright, and the Christmas Odes in Herrick's Hesperides. He further composed tunes for Sandys's Paraphrase of the Psalms, published in 1638. He and his brother William also composed a volume of Choice Psalmes, which was not published till 1648; though Milton's sonnet, prefixed to it and addressed "To Mr. H. Lawes on the *publishing* of his Airs," is dated February 9, 1645-6.

The usurpation of Cromwell put an end to masques, and music of all kinds, and Lawes was dispossessed of all his appointments. The prefaces to his published works contain many sensible reflections upon the state of the art. In one of them he speaks of the Italians as being great masters of music; but, at the same time, his own nation had produced as many able musicians as any in Europe. He censures the partiality of the age for songs sung in a foreign language, and in ridicule of it speaks of a song of his own composition, which was nothing more than an index of the initial words of some old set of Italian madrigals. He says that this index, which he had set to a varied air and which read together was a strange medley of nonsense, passed with a great part of the world as an Italian song! In another preface he says: "As for myself, although I have lost my fortunes with my Master (of blessed memory), I am not so low to bow for a sub-sistence to the follies of the age, and to humour such as will seem to understand our art better than we that have spent our lives in it." At the Restoration Lawes was restored to his places in the Royal Chapel, and he composed the Coronation Anthems for Charles II. He died Oct. 21, 1662, and was buried in the cloisters of Westminster Abbey on the 25th of the same month.

Ibid. *Richard Boughton.*—A Member of the Choir of St. George's Chapel, Windsor, before his admission into the Royal Chapel. He was living in 1641, when his name appears in the list of Gentlemen of the Chapel, dated April 20, in that year. (See Collier's Annals of the Stage, ii. 130.)

Ibid. *John Tomkins.*—Educated at King's College, Cambridge. The brother of Thomas Tomkins, before mentioned. He was probably a chorister of Gloucester Cathedral (where his father was minor-canon), and, upon losing his voice, grafted into the University of Cambridge for the completion of his education, according to the Cathedral statutes. From the roll of organists of King's College, Cambridge, it is certain that John Tomkins was appointed to that office in 1606, and that he held it till 1622, when he came to London to fill the same important post in the Metropolitan Cathedral. He was succeeded at Cambridge by his brother Giles.

The period of John Tomkins's marriage is not known; but he had a son, Thomas, born in Aldersgate Street, who was educated at Oxford, and rose to be D.D., Chancellor of the Cathedral of Exeter, and Rector of Lambeth. He was the author of some commendatory verses prefixed to Edmund Elys's Divina Poemata, 1665, and was probably the editor of his uncle's work, Musica Deo Sacra, in the previous year. He died August 20, 1675, and was buried at Martin-Hussingtree, co. Worcester. He had another son, Robert, who was one of the Royal Musicians in 1641.

The date of John Tomkins's death is variously given. Wood (Fasti, i. 320) says Sept. 27, 1626; Fisher (Monuments of St. Paul's, p. 79) says 1636; Dugdale (Hist. of St. Paul's, ed. 1818, p. 58) says Sept. 27, 1638; and Carew (Survey of Cornwall, ed. 1811, p. 165) says 1646. Dugdale's date is the correct one, as is proved by the entry in the Cheque-Book, p. 12. He was buried in St. Paul's Cathedral.

William Lawes, the unfortunate brother of "tuneful Harry," wrote the following "Elegie on the death of his very worthy friend and fellow-servant, Mr. John Tomkins, Organist of his Majesties Chapell Royall." It is extracted from the Choice Psalmes put into Musick for Three Voices, by the brothers Lawes, published in 1648:—

> " Musick, the master of thy art is dead,
>   And with him all thy ravisht sweets are fled :
>   Then bear a part in thine own tragedy,
>   Let's celebrate strange griefe with harmony :
>   Instead of teares shed on his mournfull herse,
>   Let's howle sad notes stol'n from his own pure verse."

Ibid. *Thomas Rayment.*—Of the choir of Salisbury in the early part of the seventeenth century. He was living in 1641, when his name appears among the members of the Royal Chapel. (See Collier's Annals of the Stage, ii. 130.)

Page 12. *Richard Sandy.*—A member of the choir of St. Paul's before his admission into the Royal Chapel. On March 29, 1630, he was admonished by the Dean and Chapter of the Chapel Royal, and recommended to be more " industrious and studious '' for the future (p. 78). His name occurs in the list of Gentlemen of the Chapel in 1641. He probably died before the restoration of Charles II.

Page 12. *Nathaniel Pownall.*—He was admonished by the Dean and Chapter of the Royal Chapel on March 29, 1630, at the same time with Richard Sandy (p. 78). He was living in 1641, but his name does not appear at the restoration of Charles II.

Ibid. *Thomas Holmes.*—Son of John Holmes, who, according to a note in a MS. organ-book, was "Organist of Winchester and afterwards of Salisberrie" in the time of Queen Elizabeth. This John Holmes was the musical instructor of Adrian Batten, as we learn from another MS. note in the book above referred to : "All these songs of Mr. John Holmes were prickt from his own pricking in the year 1635 by Adrian Batten, one of the vickers of St. Paul's in London, who some time was his scholler." A few of Thomas Holmes' catches are contained in Hilton's Catch that Catch can, 1652. According to some MS. Collections for a History of Musicians, by Tho. Ford, Chaplain of Christ Church, Oxon., he died at Salisbury, March 25, 1638, a date confirmed by the Cheque-Book.

Ibid. *John Hardinge.*—One of the "Musicians for the Violins" in the royal band of Charles I. Dec. 20, 1625. He died Nov. 7, 1684 (p. 18), and was buried on the 10th of the same month in the cloisters of Westminster Abbey.

Ibid. *John Cobb.*—A catch and four canons of his composition are contained in Hilton's Catch that Catch can, 1652, and an excellent glee, "Smiths are good fellows," may be found in Playford's Musical Companion, 1667. He wrote an "Elegie on the death of his friend and fellow-servant, Mr. William Lawes," which is printed in the Choice Psalmes, by the brothers Lawes, 1648. No particulars of his life are known.

Ibid. *Richard Portman.*—This is the only entry in the Cheque-Book relative to this musician. He was a pupil of Orlando Gibbons, and succeeded Thomas Day as organist of Westminster Abbey in 1633. He is said to have resided sometime in France with Dr. Williams, Dean of Westminster, who was a great patron of music and musicians. Many of his anthems are extant in the old books of the cathedrals, and the words of some may be found in Clifford's Divine Services and Anthems, 1663, and in Harl. MS. 6346. The date of his death is not recorded.

Ibid. *Edward Braddock.*—He was chosen Clerk of the Cheque in 1688 (p. 18). He was also a lay-clerk of Westminster Abbey, Master of the Choristers in 1670, and copyist in 1690. His only daughter, Elizabeth, married Dr. John Blow. He died June 12, 1708 (p. 25), and was buried in the north cloister of the Abbey on the 17th of the same month.

Page 13. *Roger Hill.*—John Hill, "one of the waites of the citie of Westminster," in

1663 (Harl. MS. 1911), was perhaps a relative. Roger died March 2, 1673-4, and was buried in the little cloister of Westminster Abbey, on the 4th of the same month.

Ibid. *George Lowe.*—Probably a brother of Edward Lowe (p. 17). Both were natives of Salisbury, He died at Westminster May 16, 1664, and was buried in the little cloister of the Abbey on the following day.

Ibid. *John Wilson.*—Born at Faversham, co. Kent, in 1594. Until the year 1626, a period of thirty-two years, we are entirely ignorant of any particulars concerning his life. It is during this period that he is supposed to have been the "Jack Wilson" of Shakespeare's stage. (See Who was Jack Wilson the Singer of Shakespeare's stage? an attempt to prove the identity of this person with John Wilson, Doctor of Musick in the University of Oxford, A.D. 1644, 8vo. 1846.) Wood says, "being naturally inclin'd in his youth to vocal and instrumental music [he] became at man's estate so famous for it, that he was first made a gent. of his Maj. Chappel, and afterwards his servant in ordinary in that faculty." His name does not occur in the Cheque-Book as a member of the Chapel in the reign of Charles I., but the imperfect manner in which this book was kept may easily account for the omission. He was a celebrated performer on the lute, and a great favourite with Charles I., with whom he was in "constant attendance." In a copy of verses prefixed to Wilson's Cheerfull Ayres or Ballads, 1660, the writer, "J. H. O. C.," speaking of some of the songs having been performed before the King, concludes in this strain:—

> "I do not wonder that the King did call,
> 'Wilson! there's more words, let's heare them all:'
> Such was your skill, that what the rest o' the Court
> Perhaps thought long, judicious ears thought short.
> Excellent artist! whose sweet strains devour
> Time, swift as they, and make days seem an hour.
> But what need more, since 'tis enough to tell
> But this, King Charles hath heard and lik'd them well."

He was created Mus. Doc. at Oxford in 1644, at which time he appears to have taken up his residence in the University, for Wood says, "after the surrender of the garrison at Oxon, an. 1646, he spent some years in the family of Sir William Walter, at Sarsden, in the parish of Churchill in Oxfordshire, who with his lady were great lovers of music." (Fasti, ii. 71.) In 1656, at the request of Mr. Thomas Barlow made to Dr. Owen, Vice-Chancellor of the University, who had been his pupil, he was constituted Music-Professor and had lodgings assigned him in Balliol College, where, being assisted by some of the Royalists, he lived very comfortably, exciting in the University, according to Wood, "such a love of music, as in a great measure accounts for that flourishing state in which it has long subsisted there," and for those numerous private music-meetings of which this writer in his own life has given such an amusing relation. At the Restoration Wilson was reinstated in his various appointments. He accordingly quitted the University and took up his residence in London. He married the widow of Matthew Peniall, Jan. 31, 1670-1, an died at his house near the Horse-ferry, Westminster, at nearly 79 years of age. He was buried in the little cloister of Westminster Abbey, Feb. 27, 1673-4.

Page 13. *Thomas Blagrave.*—Of an ancient Berkshire family. Eldest son of Richard Blagrave, member of the royal band of Charles I. (eldest son of John Blagrave of Bulmarsh, Reading, co. Berks. by his third wife, Anne, daughter of Tho. Mason of Northwood, Isle of Wight, Gent.) Appointed a Gentleman of the Chapel Royal at the restoration of Charles II. Hawkins tells us that "upon the revival of choral service, in the Royal Chapel especially, they were necessitated, for want of treble voices, to make use of cornets, and on particular occasions sackbut sand other instruments were also employed." Blagrave, he says, was a performer on the cornet (Hist. of Music, 767, edit. 1853). Some of his songs are printed in Select Ayres and Dialogues, 1669, and in other of Playford's numerous publications. His portrait is in the Music-School, Oxford. He died Nov. 21, 1688 (p. 18), and was buried in the north cloister of Westminster Abbey on the 24th of the same month. His wife, Margaret, was buried in the same grave. Hatton notices these burials, but says the dates are illegible on the monument. (New View of London, ii. 533.)

Ibid. *John Cave.*—The circumstance here recorded is also mentioned in Pepys' Diary under the date Feb. 1, 1663-4 : "I hear how two men last night, jostling for the wall about the New Exchange, did kill one another, each thrusting the other through; one of them of the King's Chapel, one Cave, and the other a retayner of my Lord Generall Middleton's." Cave was buried in the cloisters of Westminster Abbey, Feb. 18, 1663-4.

Ibid. *William Jackson.*—Matriculated at Oxford (servitor Ch. Ch.) April 1, 1656; B.A. Nov. 1, 1659; M.A. July 15, 1662. He was buried in the west cloister of Westminster Abbey, Feb. 29, 1663-4.

Ibid. *Henry Purcell.*—The father of the celebrated Henry. He seems to have entered the Royal Chapel at the restoration of Charles II. (at least there is no trace of him before), and his name occurs among the Gentlemen of that establishment serving at the Coronation (p. 128). In 1663 he was appointed a member of the royal band, as appears by the following document (copy) in the writer's possession : "These are to certify, That Mr. Henry Purcell, who succeeded Segnor Angello in his place of the private musicke; That the said Mr. Henry Purcell tooke possession of his place in the year 1663, upon St. Thomas' Day ; deceased the 11th August, 1664 :—

"These are to certifye the death of Mr. Henry Purcell.
{
Henry Cooke.
Tho. Purcell.
Alfonso Marsh
Gregory Thorndale.
Edward Colman."
}

He was buried in the east cloister of Westminster Abbey on the 13th of the same month. His widow, Elizabeth, was buried at St. Margaret's Westminster, Aug. 26, 1699.

Page 14. *William Hopwood.*—A member of the choir of Exeter Cathedral, where, in all probability, he was educated. Afterwards a Petty Canon of Westminster. He died July 13, 1683, and was buried in the east cloister of the Abbey on the 17th of the same month.

Ibid. *Matthew Peniall* or *Pennell.*—One of the Gentlemen of the Chapel at the Coronation of Charles I. (p. 128). He was buried in the little cloister of Westminster Abbey Jan. 13, 1666-7.

Ibid. *Thomas Hazard.*—His name appears for the first time in the Cheque Book among the Gentlemen of the Chapel who attended the Coronation of Charles I. He was a " singing man " of Westminster, and was buried in the cloisters Jan. 25, 1666-7.

Ibid. *Pelham Humphrey* or *Humphries.*—Received his education as a chorister of the Chapel under Captain Cooke. Upon the death of his master in July 1672, he succeeded him in his office as Master of the Children (p. 15). " By the direction and at the charge of Charles II., Pelham Humphreys was sent to Paris to study under Lulli, and, like his master, therefore *he* formed his style, though at second-hand, on that of Carissimi, and on his return home was the means of making his artistic brethren acquainted with a number of effects, many of them beautiful and all new, and a system of composition differing in plan and detail from that of the great English masters of the second period as widely as the Lyrical Ballads of Wordsworth differ from the Pastorals of Pope." Hullah's Lectures on the Third or Transition Period of Musical History, 1865, p. 201.

A MS. in the writer's possession purporting to be an account of Secret Service Monies (temp. Car. II.) kept by Sir John Shaw, contains the following items :—

" 1664. To Pelham Humphreys to defray the charge of his journey into France and Italy, 200*l.*"

" 1665. To Pelham Humphreys, bounty, 100*l.*"

" 1666. To Pelham Humphreys, bounty, 150*l.*"

His return to England is noticed by Pepys in the following passages of his characteristic Diary :—

" Nov. 1, 1667. To Chapel, it being All Hallows Day, and heard a fine anthem, made by Pelham, who is come over."

" Nov. 15, 1667. Home, and there find, as I expected, Mr. Cæsar and little Pelham Humphreys, lately returned from France, and is an absolute Monsieur, as full of form and confidence and vanity, and disparages everything, and everybody's skill but his own. But to hear how he laughs at all the King's musick here, as Blagrave and others, that they cannot keep time or tune, nor understand anything ; and at Grebus [Louis Grabut], the Frenchman, the King's Master of the Musick, how he understands nothing, nor can play on any instrument, and so cannot compose; and that he will give him a lift out of his place; and that he and the King are mighty great."

On Aug. 8, 1672, he was appointed "Composer in Ordinary for the Violins to his Majesty." (Sign Manual Warrant.) His career however was a short one, as he died July 14, 1674, aged 27, and was buried in the cloisters of Westminster Abbey " near the east door " on the 17th of the same month. In the third book of Playford's Choice Ayres and Songs, 1681, there is " A Pastoral song set by Mr. William Gregory in memory of his deceased friend Mr. Pelham Humphrys, &c."

Humphrey married about 1672. His wife was remarkable for her beauty, if we may trust to Richard Veel, who wrote " An Hymeneal to his dear friend Mr. P[elham] H[umphrey]," printed in his New Court Songs and Poems, 1672, 8vo.

Page 14.   *Edward Coleman.*—The son of Dr. Charles Coleman, one of the royal band temp. Charles I., who died in 1664. He took part in the performance of The Siege of Rhodes in 1656, and was the husband of Mrs. Coleman who performed Ianthe in the same play, one of the first English female actresses on our stage. See Notes and Queries, 2nd Series, iii. 471.

Ibid.   *William Turner.*—Educated in the chapel at the same time as the celebrated Henry Purcell. He was a Vicar Choral of St. Paul's, and a Lay Vicar of Westminster Abbey. In 1696 he took his degree of Mus. Doc. at Cambridge. An anthem is in existence, "I will alway give thanks," called the Club Anthem, as having been composed by Humphrey, Blow, and Turner in conjunction, and intended by them as a memorial of the strict friendship that subsisted between them. Dr. Turner died Jan. 13, 1740, aged 88, and was buried in the cloisters of Westminster Abbey.

Page 15.   *James Hart.*—Gentleman of Westminster Abbey. He was one of the singers in the "Ode to St. Cecilia," 1687. Many of his songs are printed in Choice Ayres, Songs, and Dialogues, 1676-84; The Theatre of Musick, 1685-7; The Banquet of Musick, 1688-92; and other musical works of the latter part of the seventeenth century. He was the father of Philip Hart, organist of St. Andrew-Undershaft and St. Michael's Cornhill, and subsequently of St. Dionis Backchurch. There were two other members of the chapel of the same name, *i. e.* Richard Hart, admitted April 26, 1671, and George Hart, admitted Sept. 10, 1694, probably of the same family.

James Hart died May 8, 1718, aged 71, and was buried in the west cloister of the Abbey, on the 15th of the same month.

Ibid.   *Dr. Walter Jones.*—Eldest son of John Jones of Worcester, Gent. by Anne Dews of Powick, co. Worcester. He was of Christ Church, Oxford, and took his M.A. degree Oct. 24, 1634, at the age of seventeen. He married Philippa, daughter of Dr. Fell, Dean of Christ Church, Dec. 17, 1643; he had previously taken his B. A. degree. On Oct. 19, 1660, he became D.D. He died July 15, 1672, and was buried in Westminster Abbey.

The Rev. James Clifford dedicated his interesting work The Divine Services and Anthems usually sung in Cathedrals and Collegiate Choirs in the Church of England, 1663, to "The Reverend Walter Jones, Doctor in Divinity and Sub-Dean of His Majesties Chappel Royal, &c." In a high style of laudation, Clifford asks the Sub-Dean " to be pleased, therefore, to intermit awhile those Seraphical Raptures, in the excellency whereof, and your thereto tuned piety, you are so famously happy, and vouchsafe an eare to the mean addresse of these rudiments (as it were) of Church musick, which, like other perfections, hath suffer'd meerly through the people's ignorance." Then, after declaring that if the book is favourably received by him to whom it is inscribed, the compiler expresses his opinion that if the worthy Sub-Dean will " descend and deign a favourable approbation thereunto, it cannot but command reception from others ; " since," he adds, " my knowledge at Oxford (improved further at London) of your eminency this way, cannot so far disoblige the world as not to believe you have the Supreme Mastery in religious music." Making due allowance for the amount of flattery which we are accustomed to in addresses of this kind, it proves that Dr. Jones was a lover of the divine art, and a fitting man for the post he occupied in the royal establishment.

Ibid. *Durant Hunt.*—His name occurs in the list of Gentlemen of the Chapel at the Coronation of Charles II. (p. 128). He was buried in the nave of Salisbury Cathedral, where a small tablet of grey marble records that " Durantius Hunt died 23rd April 1671." Harris's Copies of the Epitaphs in Salisbury Cathedral, &c. 1825, p. 92.

Ibid. *Captain Henry Cooke.*—Brought up in the Chapel in the reign of Charles I. which he quitted at the commencement of the rebellion to join the King's Army. Here he is said to have so distinguished himself that he obtained a captain's commission in 1642. His skill in music, as well as his loyalty, recommended him to the favour of Charles II. and he was appointed Master of the Children of the Chapel at the Restoration. Pepys gives some characteristic notices of him, from which we extract the following :—

> " May 18, 1662. (Whitsunday.) By water to White Hall, and there to chapel in my pew . . We had an excellent anthem, sung by Captain Cooke and another, and brave musique . . After dinner to chapel again; and there had another good anthem of Captain Cooke's."

> "Sept. 14, 1662. (Lord's Day.) To White Hall Chapel, where sermon almost done, and I heard Captain Cooke's new musique. This the first day of having vialls and other instruments to play a symphony between every verse of the anthems ; but the musique more full than it was the last Sunday, and very fine it is. But yet I could discern Captain Cooke to overdo his part at singing, which I never did before."

> " Feb. 13, 1666-7. Discoursed most about plays and the Opera, where, among other vanities, Captain Cooke had the arrogance to say that he was fain to direct Sir W. Davenant in the breaking of his verses into such and such lengths, according as would be fit for musick, and how he used to swear at Davenant and com-

mand him that way, when W. Davenant would be angry, and find fault with this or that note. A vain coxcomb he is, though he sings and composes so well."

In 1663 Cooke solicited and obtained from the King a grant for himself and his successors in office to receive 30*l.* per annum, for dieting, lodging, washing, and teaching each of the Children of the Chapel; and in July 1664 he was appointed to the office of "Composer of the King's Private Musick for Voices," at a salary of 40*l.* per annum.

On May 28, 1666, in conjunction with Thomas Purcell and other Gentlemen of Chapel, he petitioned, "on behalf of themselves, the pages of the Chapel, and boys whose voices have changed, for payment, there being no money assigned to the Treasurer of the Chamber for that purpose."

Ashmole in his Order of the Garter, speaking of the Festival of St. George at Windsor April 17, 1661 (pp. 563-576), adds: "To complete the pomp of this great ceremony, we may (in the last place) fitly remember the musick as a part thereof; it being particularly taken notice of in most places of the register where the grand procession is recorded. The choirs, both of the Sovereign's Chapel at Whitehall and this at Windsor, being here (as before is noted) united, all singing the sacred hymn together, while the grand procession devoutly passeth on. This hymn was composed and set with verse and chorus by Captain Cook, Master of the Children of the Sovereign's Chapel, by whose direction some instrumental loud musick was at that time introduced, namely, two double sackbuts and two double courtals, and placed at convenient distance among the classes of the Gentlemen of both choirs, to the end that all might distinctly hear, and consequently keep together in both time and tune: for one sackbut and courtal was placed before the four petty canons who begun the hymn, and the other two immediately before the prebends of the College."

Wood observes (MS. Ashmole 8568) that "Captain Cook was the best musician of his time till Mr. Pelham Humphrey, one of the children of the Chapel educated by himself, began to rival him, after which he died with great discontent." He was buried in the east cloister of Westminster Abbey July 17, 1672.

Page 15. *Dr. Richard Colebrand.*—Rector and Dean of Bocking, co. Essex, 1660; afterwards Rector of Topsfield. "1664, 1 Dec. Ric. Colebrand clericus S. T. P. admiss. ad rect. de Toppesfield [in com. Essex] per promot. Edwardi Wolley S. T. P. ad ep. Clonfort. *Reg. Lond.*" (Wood's Fasti, ed. Bliss, ii. 53.) He died Aug. 28, 1674. (p. 16.)

Ibid. *Philip Tynchare or Tinker.*—Matriculated at Oxford Nov. 2, 1621. He was installed Chanter of Westminster Abbey Feb. 11, 1660-1; and in 1662 he was made "Confessor to his Majesties Household." (p. 49.) He died May 9, 1673, and was buried "near the door of Lord Norris's monument" on the 12th of the same month. (Stanley's Mem. of Westm. Abbey, p. 198.) He was the compiler of the first part of the earliest existing Burial Register of the Abbey, contained in one volume, folio, 1606 to 1706. This is one of those volumes which has occupied the undivided attention for some years of that learned and laborious antiquary Colonel Chester, a gentleman to whom the writer is under so many obligations for material to illustrate the present volume.

Page 15. *Stephen Crespion.*—Son of Jeremiah Crespion of London by Camilla, eldest daughter of Stephen and Camilla Nau. Matriculated from Christ Church, Oxford, July 13, 1666, aged 17; B.A. May 17, 1670 ; M.A. March 22, 1672-3 ; Confessor to the Royal Household Nov. 1, 1673 ; Sacrist of Westminster Abbey July 25, 1683 ; Prebendary of Bristol Aug. 3, 1683 ; Chanter of Westminster 1683-4. The Cheque-Book records his death Nov. 25, 1711 (p. 26). He was buried in the south cloister of Westminster Abbey.

Ibid. *John Blow.*—Born at North Collingham co. Notts. in 1648. He was brought up in the Chapel Royal, and distinguished as a youthful composer. (See Clifford's Divine Services and Anthems, 1664.) In 1669, at the age of 21, he was appointed Organist of Westminster Abbey, which situation he resigned in 1680 in favour of the celebrated Henry Purcell. In July 1674, upon the death of Pelham Humphrey, he succeeded to the post of Master of the Children of the Chapel (p. 16). In 1685 he was appointed a member of the Royal Band, and "Composer in Ordinary to His Majesty," a title which Matthew Locke had enjoyed before him, but which appears to have been at that time merely honorary. He was also Almoner and Master of the Choristers of St. Paul's Cathedral, being appointed to these offices upon the death of Michael Wise in 1687. These latter situations he resigned in 1693 in favour of his pupil Jeremiah Clark. Blow was not a graduate of any university ; but Archbishop Sancroft, in virtue of his authority in that respect, conferred on him the degree of Mus. Doc. On the death of Henry Purcell, in 1695, he was again elected Organist of Westminster Abbey; and in 1699 he was appointed "Composer to the Chapel Royal" (p. 23) at a salary of 40*l.* per annum, procured through the influence of Dr. Tillotson. He died Oct. 1, 1708, and was buried in the north aisle of Westminster Abbey.

As a writer of church-music Dr. Blow holds a high rank, and an exhaustive collection of his services and anthems has been transcribed in score by the learned and diligent librarian of the Sacred Harmonic Society, Mr. W. H. Husk. His printed works are as follows: 1. Ode for St. Cecilia's Day, 1684 ; 2. Elegy on Queen Mary, 1695; 3. Ode on the death of Henry Purcell, 1696 ; 4. Lessons for the Harpsichord ; 5. Psalms for the Organ ; 6. Amphion Anglicanus, 1700. A number of his vocal pieces may be found in Playford's latter publications.

Dr. Blow married Elizabeth, the only daughter of Edward Braddock, one of the Gentlemen and Clerk of the Cheque of the Chapel Royal. By her he had one son and three daughters, most of whom died in early life. Blow's wife died Oct. 28, 1683, at the age of 30, and was buried in the north ambulatory of Westminster Abbey.

Page 16. *Dr. William Holder.*—Born in Nottinghamshire about the year 1614; educated at Pembroke Hall, Cambridge, and, in 1642, became Rector of Blechingdon, Oxfordshire. In 1660 he proceeded D.D., was afterwards Canon of Ely, Canon of St. Paul's, Subdean of the Chapel Royal, and Sub-almoner to the King. Amongst other works, noticed in Chalmers's Biog. Dict., he was the author of A Treatise on the Natural Grounds and Principles of Harmony, 1694, 8vo. He first treats of sound in general, how it is produced and propagated; then on the vibrations of sonorous bodies; on the nature of concord, as consisting in the coincidence of the vibrations of two chords; and on the three kinds of proportion, arithmetical, geometrical, and harmonical.   The work is written with great perspicuity.   It is said, in the introduction, to have been drawn up chiefly for the sake and service of the Gentlemen of the Chapel.   Dr. Holder was a great disciplinarian.   Michael Wise, who perhaps had fallen under his lash, used to call him Mr. *Snub*-dean.   He died at his official residence in Amen Corner, Jan. 24, 1696-7, aged 82, and was buried in the vault under the choir of St. Paul's Cathedral.

Page 16.   *Raphael Courteville.*—One of the old members of the Chapel who survived the restoration of Charles II.   His name appears in the list of Gentlemen at the Coronation of the King (p. 128).   John Courteville (probably a brother) has several songs in The Theatre of Musick, 1685-7.   Raphael's son and grandson were successively organists of St. James's Church, Piccadilly (1691-1771).   The latter was a political writer of some celebrity.   He was supposed to be in the pay of the state, for the purpose of writing up the government of Sir Robert Walpole, and was consequently stigmatized by the appellation of " Court-evil."

Ibid.   *Michael Wise.*—Born in Wiltshire, and educated in the Chapel Royal under Captain Cooke.   On April 6, 1668, on the death of Giles Tomkins, he was elected Organist and Master of the Choristers of Salisbury Cathedral.   On Jan. 27, 1686-7, he was appointed Almoner and Master of the Choristers of St. Paul's Cathedral.   Hawkins states (Hist. of Music, iv. 430), that Wise was much favoured by Charles II., but the assertion is not borne out by any known facts.   Certain it is that upon the death of that monarch he was under a suspension from his duties at the Chapel, and at the Coronation of James II. Edward Morton officiated in his place (p. 129).   He was, unfortunately, killed at Salisbury, in a midnight brawl with the watch, in Aug. 1687.   The place of his burial has not been ascertained.   A Latin inscription on a gravestone, formerly in the churchyard of Salisbury Cathedral, records " The remains of Jane, wife of Michael Wise, gent., and daughter of Robert Harwood, a magistrate of this city, rest here in peace.   She died July 10, 1682, aged 30 years."

Dr. Aldrich composed his anthem "Thy beauty, O Israel" on the death of this excellent church musician.

Ibid.   *William Howes.*—"Born near Worcester, where he was bred up with the waits.   He became petty canon of Windsor till the Rebellion, then he followed the King to Oxon, and was singing-man of Ch. Ch.   He returned after the wars to Windsor, and had a soldier's pay allowed him to subsist on till the Restoration settled him in his places. Afterwards he was a cornet [player] in the King's Chapel.   He died at Windsor, and was buried in St. George's Chapel-yard."   Wood's Lives of English Musicians (Ashm. MS. No. 8568.)

Ibid.   *Alphonso Marsh, jun.*—Some of his songs are contained in The Theatre of

Musick, 1685-7; The Banquet of Musick, 1688-92; and in other of Playford's publications. According to an entry on a subsequent page (p. 19), he died April 5, 1692. He was buried in the west cloister of Westminster Abbey, on the 9th of the same month.

Ibid. *Christopher Gibbons.*—Son of the celebrated Orlando Gibbons. Born in Westminster, and baptized at St. Margaret's Church, Aug. 22, 1615. He was educated under his uncle Ellis Gibbons, Organist of Bristol Cathedral. Before the Civil War he held the appointment of Organist of Winchester Cathedral, and when the dean and prebends fled, he accompanied them and served in one of the garrisons. At the Restoration he was appointed principal Organist of the Chapel Royal (p. 128), private Organist to the King, and Organist of Westminster Abbey. He was admitted to the degree of Mus. Doc. at Oxford, through the personal recommendation of Charles II., in July, 1664. He died, as the present entry shows, Oct. 20, 1676, and was buried in the cloisters of the Abbey on the 24th of the same month.

Dr. Christopher Gibbons married Sept. 23, 1646, Mary, daughter of Dr. Robert Kercher, Prebendary of Winchester. She died in April 1662, and was buried in the north cloister of the Abbey on the 15th of the same month. He married again, and his wife Elizabeth survived him. In his will, proved Nov. 6, 1676, he leaves her all his estates.

Ibid. *John Chrisostom Dusharoll* or *Sharole.* " M.A., Chaplain of the Regiment of Horse commanded by the Right Hon. James, Earl of Arran," also Petty Canon of Westminster. He died Aug. 5, 1687 (p. 18), and was buried in the cloisters of Westminster on the 8th of the same month. He signs his name " John Chrisostom *Sharole* " in his will.

Ibid. *Thomas Heywood.*—The following is an extract from the Audit Office Enrolments, 1660-1673 (p. 707) :—

" These are to pray and require you to pay or cause to be paid unto Pelham Humphryes, Master of the Children of His Majesties Chapel Royal, the sum of thirty pounds by the year, during His Majesties pleasure, for keeping of Thomas Heywood, late a child of the Chapel, whose voice is changed, and is gone from the Chapel, &c. To commence from the 25th of December last year, 1672. And this shall be your warrant. Given under my hand this 12th day of April, 1673, &c.

" St. Alban.

" To Mr. Edward Griffin, knt., Treas^r of His M^{ts} Chamber."

Mr. Cunningham, who quotes the above in his Introduction to Extracts from Accounts of the Revels at Court (Shaks. Soc. p. xxi.), says, " The Heywoods for a century and a half were connected with the stage. This is the last remembered of the name, and I see little to discountenance the supposition that he was a scion of the stock of Thomas Heywood, the most prolific writer of his age, and one of the best and most successful." Heywood returned to the Chapel after his voice became settled, as appears by the present entry. He resigned his place at Michaelmas, 1688 ? (p. 18). His after career is not known.

Page 16. *John Gostling.*—The Rev. John Gostling, M.A., Minor Canon of Canterbury, priest of the Chapel Royal, and Subdean of St. Paul's Cathedral. He was celebrated for his fine deep base voice, and Purcell took advantage of it in the composition of several of his anthems, particularly " They that go down to the sea in ships." There are several anecdotes communicated by his son (the Rev. W. Gostling, M.A., well known by his Walks in and about Canterbury) in Sir J. Hawkins's History of Music. To which may be added what Charles II. is reported to have said of him, " You may talk as much as you please of your nightingales, but I have a *gosling* who excells them all." Another time the same merry monarch presented him with a silver egg filled with guineas, saying that he had heard " eggs were good for the voice." Nichols's Collection of Poems, vii. 227.

On Nov. 22, 1727, he was re-admitted into the Chapel Royal " as newly confirm'd by George II." but was then too old to take a journey from Canterbury to London to be sworn in (p. 50).

Ibid. *William Tucker.*—Junior priest in the Chapel at the time of the Coronation of Charles II., and also a Minor Canon of Westminster Abbey. He was an excellent musician, and the composer of several anthems, the words of which are given in the Divine Harmony, 1712. The present entry records his death. He was buried in the Abbey March 1, 1678-9. In Moneys received and paid for Secret Services of Charles II., &c. (Cam. Soc. p. 98) is the following entry: " To Eliz. Tucker, widº, relict of Wm Tucker, for her husband's writing in 15 books the Anthems with Symphonies for King Charles the 2nds use in his Chappell Royal, 15*l.*"

Page 17. *John Abell.*—Celebrated for his fine alto voice and skill on the lute. He was greatly patronized by royalty, and between the years 1679 and 1688 received " bounty money," amounting to no less a sum than 740*l.* See Moneys received and paid for Secret Services of Charles II. and James II. (Cam. Soc.) Charles II. sent him to Italy to study, and, after his return home, Evelyn thus describes meeting him:—" Jan. 24, 1682-3. After supper came in the famous treble, Mr. Abel, newly returned from Italy. I never heard a more excellent voice, and would have sworn it had been a woman's, it was so high, and so well and skilfully managed, being accompanied by Signor Francesco on the harpsichord." He remained in the service of the Chapel until the Revolution of 1688, when he was dismissed in consequence of his supposed leaning to the Romish religion. After this he travelled abroad, visiting France, Germany, Holland, and Poland, leading a vagrant sort of life, and depending for support upon his voice and lute. A number of marvellous tales are told of his adventures during his wanderings. About the latter end of the reign of Queen Anne, Abell returned to England, and occupied a prominent position on the stage. Congreve, in a letter dated Lond. Decem. 10th, 1700, says, " Abell is here: has a cold at present, and is always whimsical, so that when he will sing or not upon the stage are things very disputable, but he certainly sings beyond all creatures upon earth, and I have heard him very often both abroad and since he came over."—Literary Relics, 1792, p. 322.

In 1701 Abell published A Collection of Songs in Several Languages, which he dedicated to William III., expressing a grateful sense of his Majesty's favours abroad, and more especially of his great clemency in permitting his return to his native country. In the same year he published A Collection of Songs in English. Prefixed to this latter work is a very curious poem, of some length, addressed " To all Lovers of Musick." We have only space to quote the opening lines:—

> " After a twelve years' industry and toil,
> Abell, at last, has reach'd his native soil,
> And hopes so long an absence may prepare
> This audience to be kind as it is fair.
> Not that he vainly boasts of bringing home
> The spoils of France, of Italy, and Rome,
> Or thinks to please the judges of the town,
> From any other climate than his own ;
> But humbly begs, since foreigners could raise
> Your admiration, and receive your praise,
> Since soft *Fideli* could your passions move,
> And fortunate *Clemente* gain your love,
> That he with some advantage may appear,
> And, being English, please an English ear."

His death is not recorded, but it was after 1716, when he gave a concert at Stationers' Hall.

Ibid. *Morgan Harris.*—Composed some secular music, which may be seen in Playford's various publications. He died Nov. 2, 1697 (p. 22), and was buried in the south cloister of Westminster Abbey, on the 5th of the same month.

Ibid. *Alphonso Marsh, sen.*—Son of Robert Marsh, one of the Musicians in Ordinary to Charles I. He was baptized at St. Margaret's Westminster, Jan. 28, 1626-7. He officiated as one of the Gentlemen of the Chapel at the Coronation of Charles II. Many of his compositions may be seen in Choice Songs and Dialogues, 1676, and in other of Playford's publications. The date of his death here recorded is not noticed by Hawkins or Burney.

Ibid. *Edward Lowe.*—Born at Salisbury ; he received his musical education from John Holmes, Organist of the Cathedral. In 1630 he succeeded Dr. Stonard as Organist of Christ Church Cathedral, Oxford. For some years he was Deputy Professor of Music in the University, and upon Dr. Wilson retiring from that office he was appointed Professor in his place. Wood says that, though not a graduate, he was esteemed a very judicious man in his profession. Shortly after the Restoration he was appointed Organist of the Chapel Royal. His death is recorded in the present entry. He was buried at the upper end of the Divinity Chapel, on the north side of the Cathedral of Christ Church, Oxford.

Edward Lowe was the author of Some Short Directions for the Performance of Cathedral Service, Oxford, 1661, 12mo. This valuable work was reprinted in 1664, " with many useful additions." The latter edition is dedicated " To the Reverend, his much honoured friend, Dr. Walter Jones, Subdeane of his Majesties Chappell Royall, Prebend of Westminster, &c."

Page 17. *Henry Purcell.*—Born in the year 1658, probably at Westminster. His father Henry and his uncle Thomas were both musicians and singers, established in the metropolis, and attached to the Court in various capacities. The young Henry lost his father when but six years of age, about which time he appears to have entered as one of the Children of the Chapel, under Captain Cooke, then Master, to whom therefore it is more than probable he was indebted, not only for his initiation in the principles of music, but for much of his knowledge of its practice. In Clifford's Divine Services and Anthems, 1664, the names of Blow, Humphrey, and Robert Smith, " *Children* of his Majesty's Chapel," are included among those of other ecclesiastical composers mentioned in the book. " That children," it has been remarked, " should be found exercising the duties of cathedral composers is a curious record of the time, and Purcell, though the particulars of his boyish achievements are less accurately preserved than might be wished, seems to have shone as a composer even at an earlier age than either Humphrey or Blow." It is stated in all the biographies of Purcell that " in 1676, being eighteen years of age, he succeeded Dr. Christopher Gibbons as Organist of Westminster Abbey." This statement, however, is wrong, as we find from the roll of organists of that establishment that he succeeded Dr. John Blow in 1680, when he was twenty-two years old. Two years later, in 1682, he became (as we learn by the present entry) one of the organists of the Chapel Royal, and there, as well as at the Abbey, produced his numerous Services and Anthems, a complete collection of which has been given to the public by the late Mr. V. Novello. In the same year that he became Organist of the Chapel he was also appointed " Composer in Ordinary to his Majesty," and it was for the service of the Court that he wrote many of his magnificent odes, welcome-songs, &c., the greater part of which still remain in MS. He died Nov. 21, 1695, at the early age of 37, and was buried in Westminster Abbey, underneath where the organ formerly stood. A flat stone covers his grave, with its Latin inscription totally effaced by the footsteps of passengers. On a pillar near the spot is a tablet, placed there by the Lady Elizabeth Howard, with an inscription commonly attributed to Dryden.

Purcell's works for the theatre are quite as numerous as those for the church. The versatility of his talent, and the division of his labours, led the facetious Tom Brown, in his Letters from the Dead to the Living, to say that musical men " hang between the church and the play-house as Mahomet's tomb does between the two loadstones, and must equally incline to both, because by both are equally supported." His works, printed during his lifetime, including those put forth by his widow, are as follows: 1. Sonnatas of Three Parts, 1683 ; 2. Ode for St. Cecilia's Day, 1683, 1684 ; 3. The Vocal and Instrumental Musick in Dioclesian, 1691 ; 4. The Songs in the Fairy Queen, 1692 ; 5. The Songs in Don Quixote, 1694; 6. The Songs in the Indian Queen, 1695; 7. Elegies on Queen Mary, 1695; 8. Lessons for the Harpsichord, 1696 ; 9. Ayres for the Theatre, 1697 ; 10. Te Deum and Jubilate, 1697 ; 11. A Second Set of Sonatas, 1697 ; 12. Orpheus Britannicus, two vols., 1698-1702.

Purcell was born in a house, of which some vestiges still remain, in Old Pye Street, Westminster, and lived, as organist of the Abbey, in a house on the site of that now occupied by the Precentor, in Dean's Yard. Whilst sitting on the steps of that house (as the story goes) he caught that cold which ended fatally. In his will, which is dated Nov. 1, 1695, he states that at the time of making it he was " very ill in constitution," but of sound mind. He makes no particular mention of his estate or effects, or of his children, but nominates his "loving wife Frances his sole executor." This will was proved by her in the Prerogative Court of Canterbury, Dec. 7, 1695. He had two brothers: one named Edward, whose history is contained in a monumental inscription on a grave-stone in the chancel of the church at Wightham, near Oxford ; the other the composer and well-known punster, Daniel Purcell.

Of Purcell's children, with the exception of Edward, nothing has hitherto been known but (by the kind assistance of Col. Chester), the writer is enabled to enumerate them as follows :—John Baptist, bap. Aug. 9, 1682, and buried in the cloisters of Westminster Abbey Oct. 7, in the same year ; Thomas, buried in the east cloister Aug. 3, 1686 ; Henry, bap. at St. Margaret's, Westminster, June 9, 1687, and buried in the east cloister Sept. 3, in the same year ; Frances, bap. May 30, 1688; Edward, bap. Sept. 6, 1689 ; Mary Peters, bap. Dec. 10, 1693. With one exception these baptisms took place in Westminster Abbey.

Purcell's only surviving son, Edward, was educated as a musician. He was elected Organist of St. Margaret's, Westminster, in July, 1726, and was also Organist of St. Clement's, Eastcheap. He died in 1740, and was succeeded in the latter place by his son Henry, who was Organist of St. Edmund the King, and afterwards of St. John's, Hackney.

A fine portrait of Henry Purcell, painted by Closterman, is preserved in the meeting-room of the Royal Society of Musicians. It has been beautifully engraved in mezzotinto by Mr. George Zobell.

Ibid. *Thomas Purcell.*—This entry records the death of the celebrated Henry Purcell's uncle. He probably entered the Chapel at the Restoration, as we find his name included in the list of Gentlemen at the Coronation of Charles II. (p. 128.) He was a Gentleman of Westminster Abbey, and "copyist" in 1661. On Nov. 29, 1662, he was appointed " to serve in the place of one of our musicians in ordinary for the lute and voice, in the room of Henry Lawes deceased." (Royal Sign-Manual Warrant in Audit Office.) In 1672, in conjunction with Pelham Humphries, he was at the head of the Royal Band, at a salary of 100*l.* per annum.   On May 15, 1681, a power of attorney was granted by Thomas Purcell of St. Martin's parish, authorizing his son, Matthew Purcell, to receive his salary as Gentleman of the Chapel Royal.   He died shortly after, as is shown by the above entry, and was buried in the cloisters of Westminster Abbey Aug. 2. 1682.

Page 17.   *Josiah Boucher* or *Bouchier.*—An entry on p. 21 records his death Dec. 16, 1695.   There was a singer at the theatres of the same name.   The following curious paragraph is extracted from The Flying Post, Aug. 16-18, 1696 : " Mr. Boucher, a player, having formerly won 36,000 pistoles from the Elector of Bavaria, who promised to pay him at a convenient time, his Highness hath now sent for him to come and take his money, and we hear he goes accordingly with this convoy."   See W. H. Husk's Musical Celebrations of St. Cecilia's Day, 1857, p. 23.

Ibid.   *Samuel Bentham.*—Appointed " Confessor to the Royal Household " Nov. 9, 1716.   (p. 28.)   He was a Minor Canon of Westminster, of St. Paul's, and of Ely.   He died in March, 1729-30, and was buried in the cloisters of Westminster Abbey on the 5th of the same month.   Dr. Edward Bentham, Regius Professor of Divinity at Oxford, and the Rev. James Bentham, the historian of Ely, were his grandsons.

Page 18.   *John Lenton.*—He was one of the Royal Band in 1694 (See Chamberlaine's Angliæ Notitia), and an eminent performer on the flute and violin.   He published, in conjunction with Thomas Tollet, a work entitled A Consort of Musick in Three Parts ; also, The Gentleman's Diversion, or the Violin explained.   Many of his catches are preserved in the various editions of The Pleasant Musical Companion.

According to the Cheque-Book, a John Lenton was sworn Groom of the Vestry in 1708 (p. 147.)   And another entry (p. 134), records his death in May, 1719.   These various entries may relate to one and the same person.

Ibid.   *Moses Snow.*—He was sworn Gentleman in Ordinary of the Chapel, April 8, 1692 (p. 19), and "Epistler," Feb. 24, 1693 (p. 20).   He died Dec. 20, 1702 (p. 24), and was buried in the north cloister of Westminster Abbey on the 24th of the same month.   He contributed songs to many of the publications of his day, including The Theatre of Music, 1685-7 ; Vinculum Societatis, 1687-91 ; Comes Amoris, 1687-93 ; The Banquet of Musick, 1688-92, &c.

Ibid.   *Thomas Linacre.*—He was promoted to be " Gospeller," Oct. 1, 1694 (p. 20); and to a " full place " in 1699 (p. 23).   He was in holy orders and a Minor Canon of Westminster.   He died in Aug. 1719, and was buried in the west cloister of Westminster Abbey on Aug. 28, aged 79.   In his will he signs his name *Linaker.*

Page 19.   *Dr. Ralph Battle.*—He was born April 11, 1649, and educated at Peter-

House, Cambridge. In 1662 he succeeded Humphry Talbot as Rector of All Saints, with the vicarage of St. John annexed, in the town of Hertford ; and, in 1680 (on the decease of Joseph Glanvill,) was made a Prebendary of Worcester. In 1689 (as we learn by the present entry) he became Sub-dean of the Chapel Royal, upon the resignation of Dr. Holder. He was a staunch lover and advocate of music, and is said to have been a skilful performer on the organ. He died March 20, 1712-13, and was buried in the cemetery of All Saints in Hertford.

Nathaniel Battle, " son of the Sub-dean," was buried at St. Margaret's Westminster, July 21, 1715.

Page 19. *Alexander Damascene.*—A well-known composer of songs. He died July 14, 1719 (p. 20). Some of his compositions are contained in Choice Ayres and Songs, 1676-84 ; Vinculum Societatis, 1687-91; The Theatre of Musick, 1685-7; The Banquet of Musick, 1688-92; Comes Amoris, 1687-93, &c. In the Choice Ayres he is called " *Sen.* Damasene."

Ibid. *John Howell.*—He was advanced to be " Pisteler " Oct. 1, 1694 (p. 20), and Gentleman " in full place," Dec. 10, 1695 (p. 21). He died July 15, 1708 (p. 25). He was a celebrated counter-tenor singer, and frequently in request at concerts and other musical performances. He took part in the performance of Purcell's Ode to St. Cecilia in 1692.

Ibid. *Daniel Williams.*—Chosen Clerk of the Cheque June 12, 1708 (p. 25). He was also a member of the choir of Westminster Abbey. He died March 12, 1719-20, aged 52, and was buried in the south cloister of the Abbey on the 15th of the same month.

Page 20. *Mr. Barnes, i. e. Charles Barnes.*—A counter-tenor singer of great excellence, frequently in request at musical performances. He died Jan. 2, 1710-11 (p. 26).

Page 21. *Francis Piggot.*—Appointed Organist of the Temple Church, May 25, 1688 ; Mus. Bac. Cantab. 1698. He succeeded Henry Purcell (as the present entry shows) as Organist of the Chapel Royal. He died May 15, 1704 (p. 25). His son succeeded him as Organist of the Temple, and afterwards held the same office at St. George's Chapel, Windsor. Upon the decease of a relative, Dr. Pelling, Rector of St. Anne's Westminster, he came into a large fortune. He died in 1726.

Ibid. *John Church.*—Born at Windsor in 1675, and educated as a chorister at St. John's College, Oxford. On January 31, 1696-7, he appears to have been received into the Chapel Royal as a gentleman extraordinary, and upon the death of James Cobb was elected Aug. 1, 1697, a gentleman in his place. The Cheque-Book tells us that he died Jan. 6, 1741. He was the author of An Introduction to Psalmody, containing some Instructions for Young Beginners, explain'd in a familiar and easie manner by way of Dialogue, &c. Engraved by T. Cross for R. Meares, Musick Printer, at the Golden Viol in St. Paul's Church Yard, 1723. 8vo. This rare little volume, written after the manner of old Thomas Morley, contains some excellent precepts, and a number of psalm-tunes and easy anthems by various masters. To him also may be assigned a little work entitled Divine Harmony, or a New Collection of Select Anthems us'd at Her Majesty's Chappels Royal, Westminster Abbey, St. Paul's, Windsor, both Universities, Eaton, and most Cathedrals in her Majesty's Dominions, &c. Printed and sold by S. Keble, &c., 1712. 8vo. This collection of the words of anthems (the first of its kind since Clifford's) was " Publish'd with the approbation of the Subdean of Her Majesty's Chappel Royal, and of several of the greatest Masters," and contains an interesting preface, giving a short account of church music from the reign of Henry VIII. In a MS. written by Thomas Ford, Chaplain of Christ Church, Oxford, in the middle of the eighteenth century, entitled Collections for a History of Musicians, and an Account of their Works, is this notice : " Church (John), Chorister of St. John's Oxon. Gent. of the Chappell to Q. Ann. Collected the Words of the Anthems sung in Chap. Royal, &c. 8vo. London, 17—." The collection here referred to can be no other than the Divine Harmony, a supposition borne out by a copy of the work now before the writer, which has on the fly-leaf " Anne Weldon, yᵉ gift of John Church." It is but right to say that Hawkins attributes this anthem-book to Dr. Croft, although internal evidence would seem to show that he could not have been its compiler.

Page 21. *William Child.*—Born at Bristol in 1604 and educated in the choir of the Cathedral under Elway Bevin. In 1631, being then of Christ Church, Oxford, he took his degree of Mus. Bac.; and in 1636 was appointed one of the organists of St. George's Chapel, Windsor. After the Restoration he was appointed " Chanter of the King's Chapel at Whitehall," and one of the organists. He took his degree as Mus. Doc. July 13, 1663. (Wood's Fasti, ed. Bliss, ii. 265.) He published Psalms of Three Voices, &c. with a continual bass, either for the Organ or Theorbo, Composed after the Italian way. Lond. 1630. Some of his church-music is printed in Boyce and Arnold's Collections, and many pieces exist in MS. He was buried in St. George's Chapel, Windsor, with the following inscription on his grave-stone: " Here lies the body of William Child, Doctor in Musick, and one of the organists of the Chapel Royal at Whitehall, and of his Majesty's Free Chapel at Windsor, 65 years. He was born in Bristol, and died here the 23rd of March, 1696-7, in the 91st year of his age. He paved the body of the choir.

> " Go, happy soul, and in the seats above
> Sing endless hymns of thy great Maker's love.
> How fit in heavenly songs to bear thy part,
> Before well-practic'd in the sacred art ;
> Whilst hearing us, sometimes the choire divine
> Will sure descend, and in our consort join ;
> So much the music thou to us hast given
> Has made our earth to represent their heaven."

He gave 20*l.* towards building the Town Hall, Windsor, and 50*l.* to the Corporation, to be disposed of in charitable uses at their discretion.

Page 22. *James Cobb.*—Entered the Chapel at the Restoration. He was probably a brother of John Cobb, before mentioned.

Page 23. *John Radcliffe.*—Minor Canon of Westminster, and "Confessor to the Royal Household." He died Oct. 29, 1716 (p. 28), and was buried in the east cloister of the Abbey on the 31st of the same month.

Ibid. *Jeremiah Clark.*—Educated in the Chapel under Dr. Blow, and for some time Organist of Winchester College. He was appointed Blow's successor as Almoner and Master of the Children of St. Paul's Cathedral in 1693, and in 1695, in addition to these offices, to that of Organist. On May 25, 1704, he was elected one of the organists of the Chapel Royal (p. 25). He died by his own hand in 1707, but the true date is not ascertained. Burney (iii. 597) says that Clark shot himself in July 1707, and Hawkins (v. 58) tells us that the event occurred Nov. 5 in the same year. The last-named date is probably the correct one. (See the entry of his successor in the Chapel on p. 25.)

Ibid. *William Croft.*—Born at Nether Eatington, co. Warwick, in 1677, and educated in the Chapel under Dr. Blow. He originally wrote his name Crofts. His first appointment was that of Organist of St. Anne's, Westminster. The present entry shows that he was appointed a Gentleman of the Chapel in 1700. On May 25, 1704, he and his fellow pupil Jeremiah Clark were made joint organists of the same establishment; and on the death of Clark, in 1707, he became sole organist (p. 25). On the death of Dr. Blow he was appointed Organist of Westminster Abbey and Master of the Children and Composer to the Chapel Royal (p. 26). In 1715 an addition was made to the old establishment of the Chapel, viz. four gentlemen, a second composer, a lutanist, and a violist; at the same time an allowance of 80l. per annum was made to Dr. William Croft, as Master of the Children, "for teaching the children to write, and accompts, and for teaching them to play on the organ, and to compose musick" (p. 28). Croft took his degree of Mus. Doc. at Oxford in 1713. The chief of his anthems composed for the use of the Chapel Royal are contained in a magnificent work published in two folio volumes, 1724, under the title of Musica Sacra, or Select Anthems in Score, consisting of 2, 3, 4, 5, 6, 7, and 8 parts. To which is added the Burial Service as it is now occasionally perform'd in Westminster Abbey, &c.

Dr. Croft's biographers say that his death was caused "by a disease brought on by his attendance at the Coronation of George II." This, however, could not have been the case ; George II. was crowned on October 11, 1727, and Croft died on Aug. 14 preceding. He was buried in Westminster Abbey on the north side of the choir.

Ibid. *John Freeman.*—He was promoted to a "full place" Dec. 23, 1702 (p. 24). He was also a member of the choirs of Westminster and St. Paul's ; and, possessing a fine tenor voice, he was often in request at concerts and music meetings. Some of his compositions may be seen in Playford's Deliciæ Musicæ, 1695-6. He died in December 1736,

(p. 52), and was buried in the west cloister of Westminster Abbey on the 14th of the same month, aged 70.

Page 23. *John Weldon.*—Born at Chichester, and received his first instructions in music from John Walter, Organist of Eton College. He afterwards studied under Henry Purcell, and was for some time Organist of New College, Oxford. On the decease of Dr. Blow, in 1708, he succeeded him as one of the organists of the Chapel Royal (p. 26); and, on the establishment of a second composer's place (Aug. 8, 1715) in that establishment, he succeeded to it (p. 28). He was also Organist of St. Bride's, Fleet Street, and of St. Martin's in the Fields. He published Divine Harmony : six select Anthems for a Voice alone, with a Thorow-Bass for the Organ, &c. n. d. folio. These anthems were composed for the celebrated singer Richard Elford. He died May 7, 1736 (p. 51), and was buried in the churchyard of St. Paul's, Covent Garden.

Page 24. *Richard Elford.*—He was educated in the choir of Lincoln Cathedral, and afterwards became a member of the Durham Choir. He came to London and made his appearance on the stage, but, his figure being ungainly and his actions clumsy, he was not successful. He then joined the Chapel Royal, and was appointed a lay vicar of St. Paul's and Westminster Abbey. His voice was a fine counter-tenor. Hawkins says, " As gentleman of the chapel he had an addition of a hundred pounds a year to his salary ; " but the fact is not borne out by the Cheque-Book. Weldon composed many anthems to show his extraordinary voice, some of which are printed in that author's Divine Harmony. He died Oct. 29, 1714 (p. 27).

Page 25. *John Goodgroome.*—He was educated in the choir of Windsor, and appointed a Gentleman of the Chapel at the restoration of Charles II. On Nov. 28, 1664, he had a grant of the office of " Musician in Ordinary for the Lute and Voice, in place of Henry Purcell deceased." Some of his songs are printed in the Treasury of Musick, 1669. Hawkins, writing in 1776, says, " One of the same name, probably his son, was about fifty years ago organist of the church of St. Peter in Cornhill, London." Hist. of Music, p. 768, edit. 1853. Theodore Goodgroome, probably a brother of the subject of our notice, is frequently mentioned in Pepys's Diary.

Ibid. *Bernard Gates.*—In Chamberlaine's Angliæ Notitia, 1702, his name appears among the " Children of the Chapel." He was appointed gentleman in 1708 (p. 26). He is said to have been afterwards " Master of the Children," but this does not appear by the Cheque-Book. In 1758 he retired to North Aston, co. Oxford, where he died at the age of 88, Nov. 5, 1773. He was buried in the north cloister of Westminster Abbey on the 23rd of the same month. A tablet to his memory was placed in the church of North Aston, erected at the expense of his pupil Dr. T. S. Dupuis.

Page 26. *Francis Hughes.*—A singer of some reputation, who took part in Camilla, Arsinoe, Rosamund, and other operatic performances of the early part of the eighteenth century. He died in April 1744 (p. 55).

Page 26. *Edward Aspinwall.*—On March 20, 1717-18, he was sworn Subdean of the Chapel Royal (p. 29), at which time he was M.A.; and in the same year Chaplain to the Earl of Radnor. He took his D.D. degree in 1728 at Cambridge (see the curious entry on p. 90). He died August 3, 1732, and was buried in Westminster Abbey (of which collegiate church he was a Prebendary) on the 8th of the same month. He was the editor of A Collection of Anthems, as the same are now performed in His Majesty's Chapels Royal, 1724, a book of the words published at intervals under the direction of the then Subdean.

Page 27. *George Laye.*—He died in Sept. 1765. (MS. Chapel Royal.)

Ibid. *Samuel Weely.*—A celebrated bass-singer, educated in the choir of St. Paul's Cathedral. He died in Nov. 1743 (p. 54).

Ibid. *William Morley.*—He took his degree as Mus. Bac. at Oxford in 1715. In conjunction with John Isum, he published about 1720 A Collection of New Songs set to Musick. He died Oct. 29, 1721 (p. 30).

Ibid. *George Carleton.*—A member of St. John's College, Cambridge. He took his B.A. degree in 1704, and his A.M. degree in 1708. He was appointed Chanter of Westminster Abbey Sept. 4, 1728. On Aug. 16, 1732, he was sworn Sub-dean of the Chapel Royal, in the room of Dr. Aspinwall, deceased (p. 30.) He edited the Collection of Anthems (words only), for the use of the Chapel Royal, published in 1736. He died December 15, 1746.

Ibid. *Thomas Baker.*—Minor Canon of Westminster Abbey, Canon of St. Paul's, and Rector of Nailstone, co. Leicester. He died May 10, 1745, aged 59, and was buried in the north cloister of the Abbey on the 13th of the same month.

Ibid. *Andrew Trebeck.*—" A bass singer from Worcester," as recorded in his admission (p. 15), and afterwards in holy orders.

Ibid. *Luke Flintoft.*—In the entry of his admission he is described as coming from Worcester. Sworn " Reader in the Chapel, Whitehall, July 9, 1719 " (p. 29). He was also a Minor Canon of Westminster. A celebrated chant in G minor, one of the earliest chants in double form, is attributed to him. He died Nov. 3, 1727, and was buried in the south cloister of the Abbey on the 6th of the same month.

Page 28. *Peter Randall.*—He probably died in 1746, as Thomas Barrow succeeded to his place in the Chapel March 31 in that year. (MS. Chapel Royal.)

Ibid. *John Shore.*—Son of Matthias Shore, Serjeant-Trumpeter, and the most celebrated performer of his time on the trumpet. Upon the death of his uncle William, who had succeeded Matthias in his office, John Shore became Serjeant-Trumpeter ; and, at the public entry of George I. in 1714, he rode in that capacity in cavalcade, bearing his mace. He was the inventor of the tuning-fork. He died Nov. 20, 1752.

Page 28. *Francis Goodsens.*—He died in Jan. 1741-2 (p. 53).

Page 29. *James Chelsum.*—He died in Nov. 1743 (p. 54).

Ibid. *Dr. Mangey.*—Thomas Mangy, son of Arthur Mangy of Leeds. He was of St. John's Coll. Cambridge. Admitted subsizar June 28, 1704, in his 16th year; A.B. 1707; A.M. 1711; Fellow of his College 1715 ; LL.D. 1719 ; S.T.P. 1725.

Ibid. *Talbot Young.*—Son of John Young, a maker of violins and other musical instruments in St. Paul's Church-yard. He was brought up in the choir of St. Paul's under Dr. Greene. He held weekly meetings at his father's house for the practice of music. Being well attended, they were removed to the Queen's Head in Paternoster-Row, and in 1724 to the Castle in the same locality. These meetings grew to be of some importance in the spreading of musical taste at the beginning of the 18th century. He died in March 1758. (MS. Chapel Royal.) His portrait was painted by Woolaston.

Ibid. *Rev. Thomas Blennerhaysett.*—One of the ministers in the French Chapel, St. James's Palace, which office he resigned May 8, 1725. (MS. Chapel Royal.)

Ibid. *Rev. John Henry Winckelhausen.*—He died Oct. 21, 1721 (p. 30).

Ibid. *The Dutch Chapel, St. James's.*—Founded by William III. on his accession to the English throne, and was continued up to the year 1839, when, in consequence of a fire in the Palace, the service was altogether discontinued.

Page 30. *Sebastian Vandereyken.*—He died April 26, 1749. (MS. Chapel Royal.)

Page 31. *Rev. Henry Alard Butjealer.*—He was minister of " His Majesty's German Chapel " from 1732 to 1771, when he died.

Ibid. *The German Chapel, St. James's.*—" The German Lutheran Royal Chapel, St. James's, was founded by Queen Anne and her consort, Prince George of Denmark, about the year 1700, when the chaplains, a reader, and the necessary officers were appointed to it. * * * The German Chapel was originally situated in the interior of the Palace of St. James's. In 1781 it was exchanged for the present chapel, which up to that time, and since it had ceased to be a Catholic Chapel, had been the Dutch and French Protestant Chapel. * * * The Chapel itself was built by Inigo Jones, and is considered a very fine specimen of architecture.'' (Burn's Foreign Refugees, p. 235.)

Page 33. *Robert Greene.*—He was admitted into the Chapel from " Poules," Jan. 31, 1566-7 (p. 2), and sworn Subdean Feb. 14, 1584-5 (p. 4).

Page 37. *Arthur Cocke.*—He took his degree of Mus. Bac. at Oxford, Feb. 25, 1593-4, at which time he was organist of Exeter Cathedral. Some of his compositions are preserved in the Music School, Oxford. He died Jan 26, 1604-5 (p. 6.)

Page 39. *Dr. Montague.*—Elected Bishop of Bath and Wells March 29, 1608 ;

translated to Winchester Oct. 4, 1616. This entry of his appointment as Dean of the Chapel Royal should have been inserted among the notices of the Deans at p. 126.

Page 42. *Elway Bevin.*—An eminent theoretical and practical musician. He was of Welsh extraction, and had been educated under Tallis. According to Wood (MS. Ashmole, 8568, 106), he was Organist of Bristol Cathedral in 1589. Hawkins says it was upon Tallis's recommendation that he was admitted a gentleman extraordinary of the Chapel, June 3, 1589. But this is an error: he was not admitted until June 3, 1605, at which period Tallis had been dead just upon twenty years! In 1637, it being discovered that Bevin was of the Romish persuasion, he was expelled the Chapel. He also forfeited his situation at Bristol at the same time. Wood, who states this, refers to the Chapter-books of Bristol as his authority. He composed a service, printed in Barnard's Selected Church Musick, 1641, and in Boyce's Cathedral Music, and several anthems of his are extant in MS. But the work by which he is best known is his Briefe and Short Instruction of the Art of Musicke, to teach how to make Discant of all proportions that are in use : very necessary for all such as are desirous to attaine to knowledge in the art, and may, by practice, if they can sing, soone be able to compose three, four, and five parts, and also to compose all sorts of canons that are usuall, by these directions, of two or three parts in one upon the Plain Song. London: Printed by R. Young, at the signe of the Starre on Bread-street Hill, 1631. 4to. This valuable and instructive treatise is dedicated to Dr. Goodman, Bishop of Gloucester, to whom the author says he is " bound for many favours." The work is ushered in by a copy of verses from one Thomas Palmer of Bristol.

Page 43. *John Shepperd.*—Perhaps a son of old John Shepperd, one of the great band of Church musicians who flourished at or shortly after the Reformation. See Dr. Bloxam's Register of Magdalen College, Oxford, ii. 187, *et seq.*

Page 49. *William Wake.*—Organist of Exeter Cathedral, and the master of Matthew Locke. Locke's Little Consort of Three Parts for Viols, 1651, was " composed at the request of William Wake, for his scholars." No particulars of him are known.

Page 50. *John Dolben.*—Grandson of the Archbishop of York. He was born at Bishopthorpe, co. York, Feb. 12, 1683-4, and became a student of Christ Church, Oxford, in 1702. He took his degrees in the following order : B.A. Jan. 22, 1704-5 : M.A. July 8, 1707 ; B.D. and D.D. July 6, 1717. He was chosen Prebendary of Durham April 2, 1718, and succeeded his father as second Baronet Oct. 22, 1722. He died Nov. 20, 1756.

Page 51. *William Boyce.*—He was born in 1710, but of his early career nothing is known with certainty. In 1734 he was appointed Organist of Oxford Chapel, Vere Street; and two years afterwards, on the death of Kelway, he was elected to a similar post at St. Michael's, Cornhill. On June 21, 1736 (as we learn by the present entry), he was appointed Composer to the Chapel Royal ; and in 1749 he took his degree as Mus. Doc.

at Cambridge. He also held the post of Master of the Royal Band. In addition to Dr. Boyce's own admirable productions, the musical world is indebted to him for the finest collection of Cathedral music, by the great English masters, that has ever been published. He died Feb. 16, 1779, and was buried in the vault under the brass grate in the centre of the dome of St. Paul's Cathedral.

Page 51. *Jonathan Martin.*—Organist of St. George's, Hanover Square, at the time of his admission to the Chapel. He held his appointment for less than a year, dying in May, 1737 (p. 52).

Page 52. *John Higgate.*—David Walter Morgan was sworn into his place in the Chapel Sept. 17, 1761. (MS. Chapel Royal.)

Ibid. *John Travers.*—He received his musical education in St. George's Chapel, Windsor, and having gained the good will of Dr. Godolphin, Dean of St. Paul's and Provost of Eton College, was by him put apprentice to Dr. Greene. About the year 1725 he succeeded Kelway as Organist of St. Paul's, Covent Garden, and subsequently became Organist of Fulham. He relinquished the latter situation upon being appointed to the Chapel Royal. Some of his compositions for the Church have been printed in Arnold's Collection. He died in 1758.

Ibid. *Rev. James Serces.*—Jacques Serces, " et Vicaire d'Apleby," &c. See Burn's Foreign Refugees, p. 157. He died April 10, 1762. (MS. Chapel Royal.)

Page 53. *Philip Menard.*—Philippe Ménard, Minister of the French Chapel, St. James's Palace, from 1700 to 1737, the year of his death.

Ibid. *Rev. Francis Flahault.*—He died in Dec. 1744 (p. 55).

Ibid. *Mr. Declaris.*—The Rev. Peter de Claris. He was appointed Reader in the French Chapel, St. James's Palace, Dec. 28, 1724. (MS. Chapel Royal.)

Ibid. *Prince Gregory.*—Probably a descendant of William Gregory, the composer of several anthems and songs; whose portrait is preserved in the Oxford Music School. On July 24, 1663, a warrant was issued to the Master of the Great Wardrobe, authorising him to pay 59*l.* 13*s.* 4*d.* to William Gregory and three others, " for apparilling and breeding up two boys to the wind instruments."

Prince Gregory probably died at the end of 1755, as we find by a MS. in the Chapel Royal that William Coster succeeded to his place on Dec. 24 of that year.

Ibid. *Anselm Bayly.*—Son of Anselm Bayly, of Haresfield, co. Gloucester. He was a student of Oxford, matriculated (Exeter Coll.) Nov. 4, 1740, aged 21, and entered the Chapel Royal in the following year. On March 13, 1743-4, he was admitted a Priest in Ordinary of the same establishment ; at the same time he resigned his place as Gentleman (p. 54). He took his degree of B.C.L. (Ch. Ch.) June 12, 1749 ; that of D.C.L. July 10,

1764. He became a Minor Canon of St. Paul's and of Westminster Abbey, and also Sub-dean of the Chapel Royal. He died in 1794. His works are :—1. The Antiquity, Evidence, and Certainty of Christianity Canvassed, 8vo.; 2. A Plain and Complete Grammar of the English Language, 8vo.; 3. A Grammar of the Hebrew Language, 8vo.; 4. The Old Testament English and Hebrew, with remarks, 4 vols, 8vo.; 5. The Com-mandments of God in the Jewish and Christian Churches, 8vo.; 6. A Practical Treatise on Singing and Playing, 8vo.; 7. The Alliance of Musick, Poetry, and Oratory, 8vo. He also edited a Collection of Anthems used in His Majesty's Chapel Royal, &c. 1769, a work remarkable for its learned and interesting Preface on Church Music.

Page 53. *Peter Gillier.*—He was the author of A Collection of New Songs, with a thorow-bass to each song, for the Harpsichord, Theorbo Lute, or Spinet. Printed by J. Heptinstall for Henry Playford, &c. 1698, folio. It is dedicated to Captain Wortley.

Page 54. *Rev. Bernard Diemel.*—He died in Aug. 1770. MS. Chapel Royal.

Ibid. *William Richardson.*—He died June 15, 1747, and was buried on the 20th of the same month in the south cloister of Westminster Abbey, aged 32. Another chorister of the same name, " William Richardson, Organist of Deptford," published in 1729 a book entitled The Pious Recreation, containing a new set of Psalm-tunes, in three parts. He says in the dedication to James Jennings, Esq. of Hayes, co. Middlesex, " I have always delighted in Church musick, being brought up in the Chapel Royal, and educated under the late worthy and famous Dr. John Blow."

Ibid. *Thomas Vandernan.*—Appointed Copyist to Westminster Abbey in 1763. He made a selection of the chants commonly used in our Cathedrals, which was published under the title of Divine Harmony, or a Collection of Single and Double Chants in Score, small 4to. 1770. He died about 1778.

Page 55. *Robert Wass.*—He died in May 1764. MS. Chapel Royal.

Ibid. *William Savage.*—He succeeded Charles King as Almoner and Master of the Choristers of St. Paul's in 1748. He died in 1774.

Ibid. *Rev. Michael Nollet.*—The Rev. Michel Eloy Nollet, Minister of the French Chapel, Marylebone. He died Oct. 8, 1755. Burn's Foreign Refugees, p. 157.

Page 59. *Records of suits for additional pay.*—Although it is certain that Queen Eliza-beth had a great love for music, and an affection for the choral service, she does not appear to have responded to the call of the Gentlemen of her Chapel for a " yearly increase of their livings." It seems that the suit instituted in 1595 fell to the ground, or at least remained in abeyance for a period of nine years. By this time the Queen had died, and the application backed by some of the Lords of the Council was renewed to the new sovereign with more success. The document on pp. 60 and 61 is a record of what was done by James I. in his " Kinglie bountie " for the furtherance of the views of the various members of his Royal Chapel. Byrd alludes to this augmentation in the dedication to Henry Howard, Earl of Northampton (one of the promoters of the suit) prefixed to his Gradualia, and in Howes' edition of Stowe's Annales, 1631, is the following notice of " King James his Bounty " (p. 1037) :—" The King at his first comming made *James Montague*, Doctor of Divinity, Deane of his Highnesse Chappell, which deanry stood voyd full eight yeares. The King enlarged the yearely fee of the Gentlemen of his said Chappell, being thirty-three in number, from thirty pound a yeare, unto forty pound a year unto every of them. And in the same manner hee enlarged the yearely fees of the Sergeantes of the Vestrie, and added 4 pence a day unto the two Yeomen and Groomes of the Vestrye. The King also enlarged the aunciente allowance of six pence a day for every childe, unto the Master of the Children of the Chappell, unto ten pence a day for every of them, being twelve in number."

Page 62. *John Patten.*—His will was proved Sept. 17, 1623. He leaves to the " children of Orlando Gibbons and my daughter his wife 200*l.*" Orlando Gibbons was executor and residuary legatee.

Page 73. *When the Kinges Majestie is from a standinge house.*—That is when the King is away from any of his ordinary palaces. " The beere that is used at noble men's tables in their fixed and *standing houses*, &c." (Harrison's England, 167, quoted in Halliwell's Archaic Dict. 797.)

Ibid. *Cuthbert Joyner.*—He entered the Chapel June 26, 1608, when " Serjeant Fletcher made over his place to him " (p. 131). Among the State Papers is preserved a " Warrant for delivery of stuff, books, &c. to Cuthbert Joyner, Serjeant of the Vestry, for the King's Chapel," dated April 11, 1610. On July 2, 1619, in conjunction with Matthew White of London, he received a grant of the surveyorship of lands, &c. belonging to rectories, vicarages, and rural prebends in England. (See Cal. of State Papers, Dom. Ser. 1619-23, p. 58.) He died Jan. 5, 1625, " and was buried in the Savoy churche the daye followinge."

Page 74. *An admonition with a prick was sett upon his head.*—This means that a mark equivalent to a *bad* mark was set against his name. (See also p. 104.) A musical note was called a prick (hence prick-song), and a dot, following a note, was called a prick of addition. Prick is a Saxon word signifying a small mark or point.

Page 76. *Standards and other such necessary utensills.*—A standard was a large chest generally used for holding plate, jewels, and articles of value, but sometimes for linen. " Item, the said Anne shall have two standard-chestes delivered unto her for the keeping of the said diaper, the one to keep the cleane stuff, and th'other to keep the stuff that hath been occupied." (Ordinances and Regulations, 215 ; Halliwell's Archaic Dict. 797.) Also used for holding the service-books. (See pp. 84, 93.)

Page 77. *Boudge of Court.*—"*Bouge of Court*, a corruption of *bouche*, French. An allowance of meat and drink for the tables of the inferior officers, and others who were occasionally called to serve and entertain the court. Skelton has a kind of little drama, called *Bouge of Court*, from the name of the *ship* in which the dialogue takes place. It is a very severe satire, full of strong painting, and excellent poetry. The courtiers of Harry must have winced at it." Gifford's note, Ben Jonson's Works, vii. 428. See Hormanni Vulgaria, sig. S. iii. ed., 1530 ; Cotgrave's Dict.; Stowe's Survey, B. vi. 49, ed. 1720, &c.

Page 91. *Thomas Miller or Mellor.*—He entered the Chapel April 21, 1606, (p. 109) and was "Serjeant of the Vestry" when he died June 25, 1636 (p. 132). He was buried at St. Margaret's, Westminster, on the 28th of the same month.

Page 93. *Silke points for the coapes.*—Copes were commonly used at this period. Pepys, speaking of the Coronation of Charles II. says, March 23, 1661, " A great pleasure it was to see the Abbey raised in the middle, all covered with red, and a throne (that is a chair) and footstool on the top of it, and all the officers of all kinds, so much as the very fiddlers, in red vests. At last comes in the Deans and Prebends of Westminster, with the Bishops (many of them in cloth of gold copes), and after them the nobility, all in their parliament robes, which was a most magnificent sight." See Hierurgia Anglicana, 138, *et seq.* for numerous notices of the use of ecclesiastical vestments in the seventeenth century.

Ibid. *Three Black-jacks, three gispins,* &c.—Black-jacks were large cans made of leather, formerly in great use for small beer. See Ordinances and Regulations, p. 392. A gispen, or gispin, was a small pot or cup made of leather. They were used in Winchester School. See Kennett, MS. Lansd. 1033.

Ibid. *One perfuming pan of iron.*—This was for the incense which was used in the Chapel Royal upon all special occasions. Evelyn, in his Diary, March 30, 1684, says, " Easter Day. The Bishop of Rochester [Dr. Turner] preached before the King, after which his Majesty, accompanied with three of his natural sons, the Dukes of Northumberland, Richmond, and St. Alban's (sons of Portsmouth, Cleveland, and Nelly), went up to the altar, the three boys entering before the King, within the rails, at the right hand, and three Bishops on the left, viz. London (who officiated), Durham, and Rochester, with the Sub-dean, Dr. Holder. The King kneeling before the altar, making his offering, the Bishops first received, and then his Majesty, after which he retired to a canopied seat on the right hand. Note : there was perfume burnt before the office began." In the Coronation procession of George III. appeared the King's Groom of the Vestry, " in a scarlet dress, holding a *perfuming pan*, burning perfumes, as at previous coronations." Thomson's Coronation of George III., quoted in The Book of Fragments, p. 206.

Page 94. *George Whicher or Whitcher.*—Sworn " youngest Yeoman of the Vestry " in Nov. 1660 (p. 132). He died " Eldest Yeoman," Feb. 4, 1680-1 (p. 133), and was buried in the cloisters of Westminster Abbey on the 12th of the same month. His will was proved March 7, 1680-1, by Sir Richard Lloyd, knt. and Hugh Squire, Esq. He is remembered at the present day by the following act of charity : " Mr. George Whitcher his 6 Alms-Houses in *Tuttle Side*, founded *Anno* 1683, for 6 poor people, who have each 5*l. per ann.* and a gown. Here is a chapel for their use, and they that read prayers to the rest have 20*s.* more *per ann.*"—Hatton's New View of London, ii. 782. Hatton notices Whitcher's burial in the cloisters, but calls him "George *Whitaker.*" (ii. 531).

Page 102. *Richard Patten.*—Son of John Patten (before mentioned) and brother to the wife of Orlando Gibbons. He purchased his place as " Groom of the Vestry " Sept. 30, 1615 (p. 131), and on March 20, 1620-1, he was " raised to a yeoman's place." (p. 131.)

Page 113. *The Lord Bishop of London.*—Richard Fletcher, first Bishop of Bristol ; translated to Worcester 1592, and to London Dec. 30, 1594.

Ibid. *The Lord Bishop of Chichester.*—Anthony Watson. Nominated June 1, 1596 ; died Sept. 10, 1605.

Page 115. *The Lord Bishop of London.*—Humphrey Henchman. Elected Bishop of Salisbury Oct. 4, 1660; translated to London 1663.

Page 120. *Doctor Nease* [Neyle].—Richard Neyle. Translated from Durham to Winchester Dec. 10, 1627 ; translated to York Oct. 1632.

Page 122. *The Chapel Feast.*—The custom of giving a buck at certain periods to the Gentlemen of the Royal Chapel, with a gratuity to pay for the feast or wine, appears to have been an established practice of early times. In the Household Expenses of Henry VII. July 25, 1504, we have " It'm to the gentylmen of the Kinges Chapell to drinke with a bucke, xl s." In the Privy Purse Expenses of Elizabeth of York are the following entries:—(1502) " It'm the same day to my Lady Bray for money by hir delivered to the Ministers of the Kinges Chapelle to drinke at a taverne with a buk, xx s." (1530) " It'm the vj daye paied to the Dean of the Chapell for the chapell feaste, xl s." (1532) " It'm the xj daye paied to Maister Dean of the Kinges Chapell the olde ordinary reward for the Chapell feaste, xl s." Several copies of warrants for payments towards the " Chapel Feast " are preserved in the State Paper Office. See the various Calendars.

Page 126. *The Salsary, i.e. the Saucery.* The " Salsery " of the royal household is mentioned in the Privy Purse Expenses of the Princess Mary, 103, 141. " The Saucery was, it seems, the department of the King's household which provided the sauces. In the 33rd of Henry VI. the officers of the saucery consisted of a serjeant, clerk, yeoman and groom for the King's mouth, and of a yeoman and three grooms for the hall. Regulations of the Royal Household, 4to. 1790, p. *22. In the 17th Henry VIII. in the Statutes of Eltham, the duties of the clerk and yeomen of ' the pastry and sausery ' are defined; the principal of which were to see all their baked meats well seasoned and served, according to the appointment of the clerk of the kitchen, ' without embesselling or giveing away any of the same, and also that there be no wasteful expenses made of flower nor sauce within the said office.' " Privy Purse Expenses of Elizabeth of York, (Note of the Editor,) 220.

Ibid. *Cheat fine and coarse.*—The second sort of wheaten bread, ranking next to manchet. There were two kinds of cheat bread, the best or fine cheat, mentioned in Ord. and Reg. p. 301, and the coarse cheat, ravelled bread, ib. 307. See Halliwell's Archaic Dict. i. 243.

Page 129. *Marmaduke Alford.*—Son of Robert and Anne Alford, *alias* Oldford. He was baptized in the parish church of Curry Ryvell, co. Somerset, May 10, 1647. At p. 134 we learn that he died, " Serjeant of the Vestry," May 10, 1715. He was buried at St. Margaret's, Westminster, on the 14th of the same month.

Page 134. *Matthew Fairless.*—Sworn Groom of the Chapel, April 14, 1697 (p. 147). His death is here recorded on July 14, 1708. He was buried at St. Margaret's Westminster, on the 19th of the same month. In the entry of burials he is called " *Francis* Fairless, Usher of the Queen's Chapel." This is undoubtedly the same person.

Page 145. *Thomas Dunkley.*—" Thomas Dunkley, Closet Keeper to His Majesty, obitt Feb. 5, 1688," was buried in the cloisters of Westminster Abbey. See Hatton's New View of London, ii. 533. He was buried Feb. 8, 1688-9. He married a niece of Sir Stephen Fox.

Page 150. *Her Majestes Travers.*—A " traverse " was a kind of screen with curtains, used in chapels, halls, and other large rooms:—" We will that oure sonne in his chambre and for all night lyverye to be sette, the *traverse* drawn anon upon eight of the clocke ; and all persons from thence to be avoided." Reg. for Royal Household of Edward Prince of Wales, 13th Edward IV.

Pages 153, 155. The word " half-pace " here is a popular corruption of *haut pas*, the raised temporary platform erected for the ceremony. (J. G. N.)

Page. 154. *The Funeral of King James I.*—The Heralds' account of the ceremonial of King James's funeral is printed in Nichols's Progresses, &c. of King James I. vol. iv. pp. 1036-1048, from the Lansdowne MS. 885. (J. G. N.)

Page 154. *Denmark House.*—"Shrove-Tuesday, the fourth of March, this year 1616, Queen [Anne of Denmark] feasted the King at her Pallace in the Strand, formerly called Somerset-house, and then the King commanded it should no more be so called, but that it should from henceforth bee called Denmarke-house, which said Denmarke house the Queene had many wayes repaired, beautified, new builded, and enlarged, and brought to it a pipe of conduit water from Hyde-park." Howes' edit. of Stowe's Chronicle, 1631, p. 1026.

Page 157. *The Coronation of Charles I.*—This was the second coronation performed in the English language, and according to the reformed rites. The account here given is very interesting.

Page 160. *The Marriage of the Marquis of Northampton.*—This nobleman, the brother of Queen Katherine Parr, was created Baron Parr of Kendal, and afterwards Earl of Essex, by Henry VIII.; and in the first of Edward VI. was advanced to the title of Marquis of Northampton. He must have been an aged man at the period of his marriage (his third) here recorded. He died Oct. 28, 1571—a few months after his marriage, supposing the date to be correct ; and in the *Inquisitio post mortem* March 14, 1572, it is noted that "The said William Parr before his death took to his wife a certain Helena now Marchioness of Northampton, and they say that she is still living." " Mrs. Frohelin " must have been the designation, rather than the name, by which this Swedish "young lady " (*fraulein*) was known at Court. She is styled on their monument in Salisbury Cathedral " Hellene Suachenberg." See Sir R. C. Hoare's Modern Wiltshire, where there are two folio plates of this magnificent monument. She remarried with Sir Francis Gorges, and died April 1, 1635, at the great age of 86.

Ibid. *The Marriage of the Earl of Warwick.*—The marriage of the Earl of Warwick to the Lady Anne Russell is misdated. It really took place on the 11th Nov. 1565; see in Stowe's Chronicle, and in Nichols's Progresses, &c. of Queen Elizabeth, vol. i. p. 199, an account of the military exercises with which it was celebrated. (J. G. N.)

Ibid. *The Marriage of Sir Thomas Leighton.*—Sir Thomas Leighton, of Feckenham, co. Worc. Governor of Guernsey, Constable of the Tower of London, and " of the Council to Queen Elizabeth; " younger brother to Sir Edward Leighton, of Wattlesborough, co. Salop. His wife was Anne, daughter of Sir Francis Knollys, K. G. a maid of honour to Queen Elizabeth and her Majesty's cousin, through her mother Katharine (Cary) niece of Queen Anne Boleyne. See pedigree of Cary in the Herald and Genealogist, iii. 39, and pedigree of Leighton in Stemmata Botevilliana, 4to. 1858, p. 184. (J. G. N.)

Ibid. *The Marriage of Sir William Drury.*—Sir William Drury, of Hawsted, Suffolk, son of Robert (who died v. p.) by a daughter of Lord Chancellor Rich. See Cullum's History of Hawsted. He was killed in France in 1589, in a duel with Sir John

Burroughs about precedency; and his widow, who was daughter to Sir William Stafford of Grafton, was remarried to Sir John Scott. Sir William Drury's granddaughter was the Mistress Elizabeth Drury, celebrated by Dr. Donne both in English verse and in a Latin epitaph ; of whom there is a whole-length picture, as lying on a couch, engraved by James Basire, inserted in the History of Hawsted, and in Nichols's Leicestershire, vol. ii. plate cxxxi. p. 817. (J. G. N.)

Page 160. *The Marriage of the Earl of Pembroke.*—The Earl of Pembroke's marriage with Mary Sidney is said to have taken place " about 1576." Ballard's Memoirs of Brit. Ladies, ed. 1775, p. 183. The entry in the Cheque-Book is in all probability misdated.

Ibid. *The Marriage of Sir Philip Herbert.*—Sir Philip Herbert was the younger son of the marriage last recorded. He was created Earl of Montgomery in 1605, and succeeded his elder brother William as Earl of Pembroke in 1630; died 1650. See a description of his marriage written by Sir Dudley Carleton in Winwood's Memorials, ii. 43, or Nichols's Progresses, &c. of King James I. i. 470. (J. G. N.)

Page 161. *The Marriage of the Earl of Essex.*—This marriage was celebrated at Court by a masque composed by Ben Jonson, printed in his Works, and in the Progresses of King James I. (J. G. N.)

Ibid. *The Marriage of Lord Hay.*—This marriage was celebrated at Court by a masque written by Dr. Thomas Campion, published at the time, and reprinted in the Progresses, &c. of King James I. vol. ii. pp. 105, *et seq.* (J. G. N.)

Ibid. *The Marriage of Lord Haddington.*—For Lord Haddington's marriage a masque was composed by Ben Jonson which may be seen *ut supra.* Mr. Chamberlain's account of the festivities will be found in Progresses, &c. of King James I. vol. ii. p. 189, and in the Court and Times of King James I. (J. G. N.)

Ibid. *Publication of the banns of marriage between Frederick Count Palatine and the Princess Elizabeth.*—Frederick was affianced to his future bride, December 27, 1612, in the banqueting house at Whitehall, and in the presence of the King, seated in state, and of the assembled Court. The Palsgrave was first led in, attended by Prince Charles and several of the nobility, and clad in a black velvet cloak adorned with gold lace. Then followed the Princess in a black velvet gown, "semé of crosslets, or quarterfoiles, silver; and a small white feather in her head, attended with ladies." Shortly after entered the King, who being seated under the canopy of state, the Palsgrave and the Princess stepped forward, and stood together on a rich Turkey carpet which had been prepared for the purpose. Sir Thomas Lake then read formally in French, from the Book of Common Prayer :—" I, Frederick, take thee Elizabeth to my wedded wife," &c. which was repeated *verbatim* by the Palsgrave. The same form having been gone through by the Princess, the Archbishop of Canterbury pronounced the benediction :—" The God of Abraham, the God of Isaac, the God of Jacob, bless these espousals, and thy servants," &c. (Harl. MS.

5176.) It is a remarkable circumstance that this marriage was asked by the publication of banns in the Chapel Royal.

Page 163. *The Marriage of the Princess Elizabeth to Frederick Count Palatine of the Rhine.*—Another and fuller relation of the ceremonial of this marriage will be seen in King James's Progresses, vol. ii. p. 541, *et seq.*

Page 166. *The Marriage of the Earl of Somerset.*—The talents of both Ben Jonson and Doctor Campion were retained for the entertainments provided at the Earl of Somerset's marriage. See their compositions, and full details of the festivities, in King James's Progresses, &c. (J. G. N.)

Page 167. *The Marriage of Sir John Villiers.*—See further particulars of this marriage in King James's Progresses, &c. iii. 439, 440, and of its preliminary arrangements, about which there was much difficulty, ibid. pp. 225, 231, 371. (J. G. N.)

Ibid. *The Baptism of the Princess Mary.*—Another full description of this ceremony is given in Howes' continuation of Stowe's Chronicle, and reprinted in Nichols's Progresses, &c. of King James I. vol. i. p. 512. Regarding an extraordinary error in the inscription upon the monument of this Princess in Henry the Seventh's Chapel, assigning her death to December 16, instead of September 16, 1607, see a memoir by Colonel Joseph Lemuel Chester, read to Historical Society of Great Britain, and printed in 1871, 8vo. noticed in abstract in the Herald and Genealogist, vii. 186. (J. G. N.)

Page 169. *The Queen's Churching.*—Another account of this ceremonial will be found in Howes' continuation of Stowe's Chronicle, and in Nichols's Progresses, &c. of King James I. i. 514. (J. G. N.)

Page 170. The birth and funeral of the Lady Sophia are noticed in Stowe's Chronicle, as continued by Howes, and in the Progresses, &c. of James I. ii. 52. The agreement for making her tomb in Westminster Abbey at the cost of 140*l.* by Maximilian Poutrain *alias* Coult, is printed in Lodge's Illustrations of British History. It represents an infant in her cradle, " wherewith (says Fuller in his *Worthies,*) vulgar eyes, especially of the weaker sex, are more affected (as level to their cognizance, more capable of what is *pretty* than what is *pompous,*) than with all the magnificent monuments in Westminster." (J. G. N.)

Page 172. *Confirmation of Prince Charles.*—A short account of this is also given in Howes' continuation of Stowe, p. 1007, edit. 1631. (J. G. N.)

Page 173. *James, son of the Earl of Southampton.*—See a letter in Winwood's Memorials, ii. 54, and in Nichols's Progresses, &c. of King James I. i. 500. (J. G. N.)

Page 174. *Lord Matravers.*—Respecting this christening see letters in Hunter's Hallamshire, p. 96. (J. G. N.)

Page 174. *James, son of the Lord Aubigny.*—Afterwards the fourth Duke of Lennox. Malcolm (Londinum Redivivum, iv. 275) in his notices of "Baptisms at Whitehall" says, "the officers of the vestry had to their fees 40*l.*"

Pages 175, 177, 178. *Prayers for the Order of the Garter.*—We cannot trace these prayers in Ashmole's Order of the Garter, nor in any other work. They appear to have been changed from time to time to suit successive sovereigns.

Page 175. *The birth of the Princess Mary.*—See the account of the baptism of this Princess, p. 167, *ante.*

Pages 178, 179. *Prayers for the Maundy.*—These prayers have long been disused. Other forms occur in a MS. Cheque-Book of later date, preserved in the Chapel Royal.

Errata et Corrigenda.

Page 10. The third date in margin, "1621," (so in MS.) should probably be "1622."

Page 19. The first date in margin should be "1689," not "1688."

Page 20. The fourth date in margin should be "1694," not "1695."

Page 21. Josiah Boucher is here said to have died Dec. 16, 1695; and the following entry records his successor as being appointed Dec. 10 in the same year. The first date is wrong, as the Registers of Westminster Abbey fix the date of his burial in the east cloister, Dec. 11.

Page 49. For "Tho. Raynes" read "Tho. *H*aynes."

Page 68. Insert the name of "Thomas Sampson" before that of "Richarde Granwall."

Page 87. For "S. Dolben" read "*J.* Dolben."

Page 128. For "William Tinker," in the list of Ministers at the Coronation of Charles II. read "William *Tucker.*"

Page 132. Eighth line from bottom of page, for "Whitell" (so in MS.) read "*Whitcher.*"

INDEX OF NAMES.

INDEX OF SUBJECTS AND PLACES.

T